The Shallow Graves of Rwanda

The Shallow Graves
of Rwanda

Shaharyar M. Khan

Foreword by
Mary Robinson

I.B.Tauris *Publishers*

Published in 2000 by I.B.Tauris & Co Ltd
Victoria House, Bloomsbury Square, London WC1B 4DZ
175 Fifth Avenue, New York NY 10010
Website: http://www.ibtauris.com

In the United States and Canada distributed by St. Martin's Press
175 Fifth Avenue, New York NY 10010

ISBN 1-86064-616-6

A full CIP record for this book is available from the British Library
A full CIP record for this book is available from the Library of Congress

Library of Congress catalog card: available

Typeset in Bookman Old Style by A. & D. Worthington, Newmarket
Printed and bound in Great Britain by MPG Books Ltd, Bodmin, Cornwall

Contents

Illustrations

Foreword

The last decade of the twentieth century witnessed one of the worst crimes in human history: the genocide in Rwanda. The brutal mass killings, carried out in a planned fashion, evoked horror and condemnation. They also raised fundamental questions: Could they have been prevented? What lessons can the United Nations and the international community learn? And, perhaps most importantly, how can we stop such horrors from recurring? There are no easy or comfortable answers – the issues raised by the Rwandan genocide will continue to trouble us for years to come.

In presenting this account of his experience as Special Representative of the Secretary-General in Rwanda, Ambassador Khan brings to bear his first-hand witness of the events immediately following the mass killings. This makes his book a particularly useful addition to the growing literature on the Rwandan genocide. When I met him in Rwanda in 1994 I had the sense of someone who was appalled by what he encountered, but who was determined to give of his best, whatever the circumstances.

The international community let down the people of Rwanda. The least we can do to honour the memory of the victims and to do justice to the survivors and their families is to redouble our resolve that such horrors will never be allowed to happen again.

Mary Robinson
United Nations High Commissioner for Human Rights

Preface

I began writing a diary in Kigali initially to inform friends of the unbelievable human tragedy that Rwanda's gentle people had lived through in this virtually unknown and beautiful land. Later, I felt I had a message for everyone. I had intended publishing my diary immediately after I left Rwanda in April 1996, before the horrifying images began to fade from public memory. On reflection, I felt I was too near the events to make a balanced judgement, especially on the role of UN peace-keeping.

The Shallow Graves of Rwanda is therefore a diary – a chronicle – of the events I witnessed at first hand as the UN Secretary-General's Special Representative in the cauldron of Rwanda's tragedy. In the last two chapters I have tried to analyse the reasons for the UN's failures – and its successes – and have attempted to glean some lessons for peace-keeping in the future. I have not published this chronicle as a political scientist, diplomat or social historian, but mainly to share the experience of an insider who was privy to mankind at its most savage. The message is clear. People racked by poverty, illiteracy, deprivation and the denial of basic freedoms are liable to descend towards barbarism. Religion alone cannot save them. Enlightenment cannot be taken for granted simply by the march of time.

I closed the diary and the lessons learnt from it towards the end of 1999. Since then, I have given a copy of this manuscript as my testimony to the UN Secretary-General's Special Commission for Rwanda, which interviewed me. Their report takes account of my impressions as contained in this book. As I write, fresh UN peace-keeping operations are being conducted in the Democratic Republic of Congo and in Sierra Leone. The wheel keeps turning.

In writing this book, I have been encouraged by my family, especially my son Ali who served his own baptism of fire with UNI-CEF in Somalia, his wife Mariyam who briefly kept house for me in Kigali, and also my daughter Faiza who visited me twice in Rwanda. I made them all witness the shallow graves of Nyarbuye and Kibuye so that these horrifying images could be part of their learning experience, as it was mine.

The book could not have been completed without the compassion of my immediate family, the assistance of my capable and ever smiling Chef de Cabinet, Isel Rivero, my saintly secretaries, Betty Kivu and Amsale Ritta in Kigali and later Zahirul Haq, Abdur Rahman and Rashed Malik in Pakistan, my enthusiastic publishers I.B.Tauris, the wisdom of Dr Lester Crook and the amazing perfectionism of Alison Worthington, to all of whom I owe a debt of gratitude. I am especially honoured that Mary Robinson, former President of Ireland and now UN High Commissioner for Human Rights, has written the foreword.

I dedicate this book to the people of Rwanda, the victims and survivors of genocide.

Acronyms

ASEAN	Association of South-East Asian Nations
BBGNU	Broad-Based Government of National Unity – formed in Rwanda on 19 July 1994 after the military success of the RPF
CAO	Chief Administrative Officer – in SRSG's Office
CDR	Coalition pour la Défense de la République
CIS	Commonwealth of Independent States (of former Soviet Union)
Civpol	Civilian police
DHA	Department of Humanitarian Affairs at UN HQ
DPA	Department of Political Affairs at UN HQ
DPKO	Department of Peace-Keeping Operations at UN HQ
ECOWAS	Economic Co-operation Organization of West African States
FALD	Field Administration Logistics Division at UN HQ
HPZ	Humanitarian Protection Zone – in south-west Rwanda
HRC	Human Rights Commission
HRFOR	Human Rights Field Operation Representation
ICAO	International Civil Aviation Organization
ICI	International Commission of Inquiry (into militarization in refugee camps)
ICRC	International Committee of the Red Cross
ICTR	International Criminal Tribunal for Rwanda
IDP	Internally Displaced Person – i.e. refugee in native country
IOM	International Organization for Migration
JEEAR	Joint Evaluation of Emergency Assistance to Rwanda
MDR	Mouvement Démocratique Républicain
Milob	Military Observer
MRND	Mouvement Révolutionnaire National pour le Développement
MSF	Médécins Sans Frontières (French doctors' group)
NGO	Non-Governmental Organization

OAS	Organization of American States
OAU	Organization of African Unity
OIC	Organization of Islamic Countries
RECAMP	Renforcement des Capacités Africaines de Maintient de la Paix
RENP	Rwanda Emergency Normalization Plan
RGF	Rwanda Government Force
RPA	Rwanda Patriotic Army
RPF	Rwanda Patriotic Front
SOMA	Standard Operations Mission Agreement
SRSG	Special Representative of the UN Secretary-General
TCN	Troop-Contributing Nation
UNAMIR	United Nations Assistance Mission in Rwanda
UNDP	United Nations Development Programme
UNGA	United Nations General Assembly
UNHCR	United Nations High Commission for Refugees
UNICEF	United Nations International Children's Emergency Fund
UNOR	United Nations Office in Rwanda – a scaled-down successor to UNAMIR
UNREO	United Nations Rwanda Emergency Office
UNSG	United Nations Secretary-General
WFP	World Food Programme
WHO	World Health Organization

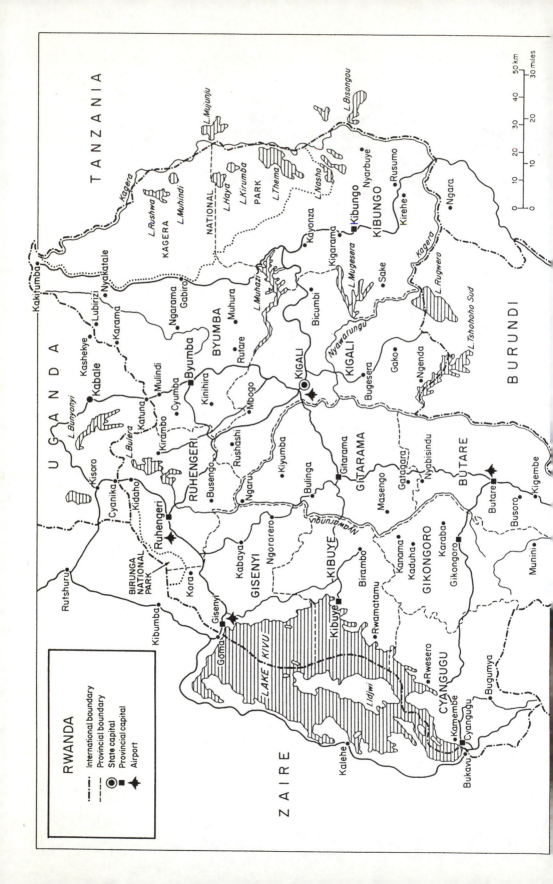

Introduction

The origins of Rwanda's tragedy are recent, dating back to the 1930s. Before that, Hutus and Tutsis had, for centuries, worked out a modus vivendi. Of course, there had been wars, even massacres, but water had found its level until the later colonialists sought to impose Western norms and values on an African milieu. The complete reversal of the established order saw the latent hostility between the two ethnic forces emerge into the open. Rwanda was no pre-partitioned India or even a Cyprus, in which hostile opponents could be separated into independent geographic units. Here, the rising tension saw frequent bloodshed and massacres, and eventually genocide that was unleashed from 6 April 1994. It is one of the most horrifying events in the history of mankind, made all the more poignant because the onset of genocide was misread by the world as yet another tribal war in Africa. Preventive action came much too late, by which time nearly a million[1] innocent people had been massacred.

This book seeks to assess accusations of tardiness levelled against the United Nations and against the international community. It also analyses the failures and successes of the United Nations peace-keeping operation in Rwanda and seeks to draw lessons from the Rwanda experience. But first and foremost it is a chronicle of the important events that I witnessed from the day I arrived in Rwanda as the UN Secretary-General's Special Representative, on 4 July 1994, to the end of my mission nearly two years later, on 19 April 1996. They mark a momentous period in Rwanda's history. For me, the abiding vision of this period is of shallow graves, around the church of Nyarbuye, in the refugee camps of Goma, beside the stadium at Kibuye, on the hilltops of Kibeho.

At the outset, two basic truths relating to Rwanda's tragedy need to be recognized. The first is that, between April and July 1994, two separate, blood-stained streams – one civil war, the other genocide – merged to form a river of horror in Rwanda. The fact that the Secu-

---

[1] I consider the figure of between 800,000 and 850,000 deaths during the civil war and genocide to be the most reliable.

rity Council and international community did not diagnose that genocide was being perpetrated in Rwanda until it was too late and confused the situation with a civil war, explains their failure to apply sharp focus and address the situation in time. The former Rwandan government (the Rwandan Government Force or RGF) will not accept this thesis of two separate phenomena. They still argue that there was no genocide and that only a civil war took place. However, the verdict of the International Commission of Experts, of the Special Rapporteur on Human Rights in Rwanda, René Degni-Segui, and of the UN Secretary-General himself is the opposite. They have unequivocally concluded that extremist elements of the former Hutu government committed genocide which amounted to the brutal killing of almost a million Rwandan Tutsis and moderate Hutus.

The Joint Evaluation of Emergency Assistance for Rwanda (JEEAR), prepared by the Danish government in co-operation with a number of other governments, international agencies and NGOs (Non-Governmental Organizations), emphatically supports this conclusion, as follows:

> The planned, deliberate effort to eliminate the Tutsi population of Rwanda that culminated in the massive slaughter of April – July 1994 fully meets the definition of genocide articulated in the 'Convention on the Prevention and Punishment of the Crime of Genocide', adopted by the UN General Assembly in 1948.

The second defining factor is the moral issue of the international agencies' and donor community's generous treatment of the refugees when contrasted with the nit-picking parsimony shown to the victims of genocide. The issue is not, of course, that refugees should be denied the care and succour that they surely deserve, but rather that their needs should be balanced with equal concern for the survivors. While the donor community gave US$2 million a day in humanitarian aid to the refugees, the total amount of aid actually disbursed in a whole year to assist the people who had been devastated by genocide amounted to only US$68 million. The JEEAR refers to this anomaly as follows:

> The failure of the international community as a whole to provide adequate support for the government of Rwanda has also undermined future stability and development efforts. In particular, insufficient attention and resources have been given to the survivors of genocide and the war inside Rwanda.

Moreover, the survivors were the victims of the genocide and had been saved by the military victors of the civil war. The refugees that poured into Tanzania and Zaire were under the tight, hypnotic hold of the leaders who had encouraged, if not actually perpetrated, genocide. It was this leadership that, having been defeated in the civil war, exercised control over the refugees and dispensed the vast amount of humanitarian aid that was cascaded into the refugee camps. Predictably, a part of these funds was converted into the military training, re-arming and cross-border sabotage that has led to further tension and conflagration in the region.

The moral dilemma that the international community must face is to ask itself whether the aid to Rwanda was even-handed and fair? Donor-country tax-payers must ask whether funds committed to the region helped to heal and diffuse tension or whether they exacerbated and fuelled another round of conflict.

A bird's eye view of Rwanda's history indicates that the Hutus and Tutsis have inhabited the region for centuries. The Hutus form 84 per cent of the population, the Tutsis 15 per cent and the Twa 1 per cent. Incidentally, approximately the same proportion is true of Burundi. Unlike most other ethnic divisions within a country, the Hutu and Tutsi share the same religion, language, customs, food, dress, culture and names. There has also been a fair amount of intermarriage. The only difference is of ethnicity or physical appearance. The Tutsis are tall and slim with sharp features, while the Hutus are generally short and thick-set. There is no anthropological proof that the Tutsis are outsiders, but Hutu extremists have propagated the line that the Tutsis were foreign invaders of Nilotic origin. Even an outsider can distinguish a Tutsi from a Hutu and would be right in seven cases out of ten. For the remainder, because of intermarriage and because some Tutsis are short and some Hutus are tall, it is difficult to tell. In such cases, only the identity card introduced by the Belgian colonialists before independence provided proof of ethnic origin. Thousands of Tutsis were murdered because they were betrayed by their identity cards when fleeing the country.

Over several centuries prior to independence Rwanda and Burundi formed one country, Ruanda-Urundi, whose hierarchical order saw the Tutsi minority dominate the Hutu majority. An economic, political and social system evolved in which the stock-breeding and cattle-owning Tutsi hierarchy established itself over the artisan and farmer community of Hutus. A Tutsi aristocracy emerged, headed by a Tutsi Mwami or king, in which the Tutsis not only enjoyed dominance but perpetuated their leadership through better education and access to resources and to levers of power. Over the years, some Hutus succeeded in gaining upward movement and became 'honorary Tutsis' while impoverished Tutsis came to be regarded as Hutus. The differences were therefore not entirely ethnic, but were occasionally economic. Gerard Prunier, in his excellent, succinct analysis of Rwanda's history,[1] states that most civil wars were fought between rival Tutsi power bases and were not ethnic wars. Even the early colonialists, the Germans in the first two decades of the twentieth

---

[1] Gerard Prunier, *Crisis in Rwanda. History of a Genocide* (Kampala, Uganda: Fountain Press, 1994).

century and the Belgians after the First World War, ruled through the established, Tutsi-dominated social and political order.

It was not until the 1940s and 1950s that the colonial powers, the Belgians and later the French, saw the apparent inequity of the minority dominating the majority. A deliberate wind of change began to blow across the established order of Ruanda-Urundi. Prunier ascribes this change to the influence of the Belgian Catholic Church which had played a key role in Central Africa and which was itself being increasingly dominated by Flemish priests, as distinct from the earlier Wolloons. These church leaders, imbued with modern concepts of democracy and fundamental human rights, sought to redress the imbalance by promoting education, jobs and access to power for the subjugated Hutu.

This restructuring of the political, social and ethnic order coincided with the sweeping changes across Africa that brought independence and self-rule to the former colonies. By this time, a Hutu resurgence had taken place and several ethnic massacres had occurred, leaving a deep ethnic divide in Rwanda. On 1 July 1961, the Trusteeship Agreement for Ruanda-Urundi was terminated by the Trusteeship Council and Rwanda and Burundi became two sovereign, independent states. In 1962, the Tutsi Mwami was deposed and several political parties seeking Hutu dominance took their place at the helm of Rwanda's political hierarchy.

In the period leading up to independence 120,000 people, primarily Tutsis, took refuge in neighbouring states to escape the violence which accompanied the gradual coming to power of the Hutu community. A new cycle of ethnic conflict and violence began after independence. Tutsi refugees in Burundi, Uganda, Tanzania and Zaire, seeking to regain their former position in Rwanda, began organizing into armed groups and staging military attacks against Hutu targets and the Hutu government. About ten such attacks occurred between 1962 and 1967, each leading to retaliatory killings of large numbers of Tutsi civilians in Rwanda and, in turn, creating new waves of refugees. Within two years of independence, the number of Rwandan refugees in neighbouring countries had increased to 150,000.

In 1973, Major-General Juvenal Habyarimana seized power in a military coup. He established a government dominated by a single party, the Mouvement Révolutionnaire National pour le Développement (MRND), which institutionalized ethnic discrimination through a policy known as 'establishing ethnic and regional balance', whereby a substantial part of the country's political and social life became subject to quotas established according to 'ethnic proportions'. The quotas were used to determine the jobs and resources to be allocated to the country's various ethnic groups. The Tutsi minority was allotted 10 per cent.

Such were the policies and practices of the government notwithstanding the fact that Rwanda's economic situation improved considerably in the late 1970s and early 1980s. While some neighbouring countries experienced sharp declines in gross national product (GNP), Rwanda's GNP grew steadily. Bilateral donors came to view Rwanda as a relative economic success story and international support to Rwanda grew rapidly. Roads were built, clean water was made available and a well-organized civil service was established. Nevertheless, Rwanda remained one of the world's poorest nations. The fall in the price of coffee, the country's main export, in 1987 saw Rwanda's economic situation begin to deteriorate rapidly. Population growth and a severe drought contributed to this decline.

Compounding the instability of this period was the on-going question of the return and resettlement of Tutsi refugees from neighbouring countries. By the end of the 1980s, some 480,000 Rwandans – approximately 7 per cent of the total population – had become refugees, primarily in Burundi (280,000), Uganda (80,000), Zaire (80,000) and Tanzania (30,000). Throughout this period, Tutsi refugees continued to call for the fulfilment of their international legal right to return to Rwanda. However, President Habyarimana took the position that population pressures in Rwanda were already too great and economic opportunities too few to accommodate large numbers of Tutsi refugees.

In 1988, the Rwanda Patriotic Front (RPF) was founded in Kampala, Uganda, as a political and military movement with the stated aim of securing the repatriation of Rwandans in exile and the reform of the government in Rwanda. The RPF was composed mainly of Tutsi exiles in Uganda, many of whom had served in President Yoweri Museveni's National Resistance Army, which had overthrown the previous Ugandan government in 1986. While the ranks of the RPF did include some Hutus, the majority, particularly those in leadership positions, were Tutsi refugees.

By this time, France had assumed a primal position with Rwanda which, because of its model role as a developing country, had become something of a 'jewel in the French crown'. Earlier, both China and Russia had sought to establish linkages, but with the end of the Cold War, France's influence became supreme in Rwanda which was, of course, a committed member of the francophone commonwealth. Pressures towards greater liberalization and multi-partyism began to build up, obliging President Habyarimana to seek a dialogue with opposition parties, including the RPF.

On 1 October 1990 the process of political liberalization was disrupted when the RPF launched a major attack on Rwanda from Uganda with a force of some 7000 fighters. Within three weeks, the Rwandese government army, assisted by French and Zairean forces, repulsed the attack, pushing the RPF back towards Uganda. However, in subsequent months the RPF continued its attacks from territory it held inside Rwanda along the Ugandan border.

The fighting displaced hundreds of thousands of people from farmland in the north and cut the main transport route out of the country, causing considerable damage to the economy. The RPF attack also prompted the government to undertake a significant build-up of its military forces. Before October 1990, the army had numbered 5000. Within a year it grew to 24,000, and during 1992 it expanded to 30,000. By 1994 it was over 40,000. In addition, the fighting led to the formation of local militia with alliances with the ruling MRND party and with the newly established Coalition pour la Défense de la République (CDR), an extremist offshoot of the MRND. The CDR opposed the government's decision to maintain a dialogue with the RPF.

In late October 1990, as a result of the RPF attacks and pressure from neighbouring states, from the Organization of African Unity (OAU) and from the international community, the government of Rwanda began fresh talks with the RPF on settling the refugee question. With the start of these talks, which from July 1992 became known as the Arusha Process, the stage was set for the United Nations to play a greater role in the efforts to bring a negotiated peace to the region. After bruising negotiations between the government and the RPF, seven detailed agreements, known as the Arusha Accords, were signed on 4 August 1993. President Mwini of Tanzania, President Mobutu of Zaire and the OAU Secretary-General, Dr Salim A. Salim, had played important roles in brokering them.

In the months after the signing of the Arusha Accords, the situation in Rwanda began to deteriorate. Several agreed deadlines were not respected and there were clear signs of militarization and ethnic tension. There were a number of incidents, even massacres, that led to panic and a renewed movement of refugees out of Rwanda. As a result of the growing instability, the UN Security Council, in its Resolution no. 893 of 6 January 1994, authorized the increase in military personnel by a battalion.

Between January and April 1994, tension continued to mount with several attempts to install a transitional government failing at the eleventh hour. President Habyarimana was under severe pressure from two opposite sides. The international community, the Security Council, the OAU and Rwanda's neighbours were insisting on his government honouring the Arusha Accords. Conversely, his own High Command, particularly his wife's family, insisted that too much had been given away at Arusha and that the power-sharing deal should not be implemented. Torn by these opposing pressures and seeing his country slide into instability and chaos, President Habyarimana went to Tanzania for a regional summit where he eventually committed himself to implementing the power-sharing accord signed at Arusha. Having crossed the Rubicon, he boarded the Presidential plane on 6 April and headed home for Kigali. The plane was hit by a rocket at 6.30 pm while coming in to land at Kigali Airport. By 7 pm the carefully planned massacres had begun.

In the succeeding three months, the militia and Interahamwe (militant Hutus), urged on by Hutu extremists, engaged in brutal massacres in which nearly a million Rwandans were murdered. Revenge killings by Tutsis also took place. Simultaneously, the Rwandan army (RGF) fought a civil war with the RPF in which it suffered a humiliating military defeat. The genocide took place behind the shield of the national army, but while it was sympathetic to its ethnic roots, on the whole it was not itself involved. The exceptions were the Presidential Guard and some maverick units who joined the Interahamwe and the militia in the indiscriminate slaughter of the innocent. In these three months, UNAMIR (the United Nations Assistance Mission in Rwanda) entered the second phase of its role. Previously it had been the referee between two sides who played by agreed rules of the game; now it was given the task of keeping the peace and protecting civilians at risk. Paradoxically, UNAMIR's strength was reduced by the Security Council from its approved level of 2658 to 270 after ten Belgian soldiers were murdered by the Presidential Guard. On 24 April, UNAMIR had 444 troops in Rwanda, comprising mainly the Ghanaian contingent and a Canadian headquarters unit to implement its onerous mandate. UNAMIR's failure to prevent the massacres or to mediate in the civil war was not through lack of effort or courage. It simply did not have the mandate, the personnel or the logistic back-up to fulfil its task. In fact, UNAMIR's performance in attempting to save as many lives as it could and creating safe havens in stadiums, churches, schools and hotels around Kigali was nothing less than heroic.

As genocide spread across the country and the international community failed to distinguish between the moral responsibility of stopping a deliberate crime and staying neutral in a civil war, there were international pressures for the UN to pull out of Rwanda altogether. The recent experience in Somalia almost certainly helped to fuel these pressures.[1] However, the Secretary-General continued to press for an increase rather than a reduction in UN forces in Rwanda. Eventually, the Security Council heeded his advice and on 21 April passed Resolution no. 912 authorizing a build-up of UNAMIR troops to 5500. By then, however, the government forces were in retreat and by mid-July had been defeated altogether. They retreated in disarray, along with the Interahamwe and militia, to the refugee camps of Zaire and Tanzania, taking with them vast numbers of simple Hutu folk into the camps of Eastern Zaire.

---

[1] In Somalia the killing of American and Pakistani UN peace-keepers by rebel leaders had led to the humiliating withdrawal of the peace-keeping force.

The third phase of UNAMIR's role in Rwanda was the period of recovery and consolidation after the devastating effect of the genocide and civil war. This is the period described in the book. UNAMIR did not reach full strength in terms of either equipment or of troops until December 1994, almost six months after the Security Council had passed its resolution. By this time, the situation on the ground had seen a qualitative transformation, so that while the troop strength was now adequate, perhaps more than adequate, UNAMIR's peace-keeping mandate was no longer relevant. The UN no longer required peace-keepers because peace and stability had been ensured by the RPF with the UN providing, at best, a helping hand. The need of the hour was for the UN to assume a peace-building and not a peace-keeping role. The book covers the period between 4 July 1994 and the closure of UNAMIR on 19 April 1996, and the lessons learnt from the UN's peace-keeping experience in Rwanda.

1. June – July 1994

Arrival at the scene of genocide

Preparations

I arrived in Rwanda on 4 July 1994, the day Kigali fell to the Tutsi-dominated Rwanda Patriotic Front (RPF).[1] In the 90 days since 6 April, when President Habyarimana's plane was shot down, nearly a million Rwandans had been killed in the most appalling massacres in living memory. On 19 April 1996, 21 months later, I completed my tenure as the UN Secretary-General's Special Representative in Rwanda. In the chronicle that follows, I have recorded and analysed the major events of Rwanda's tragedy as I saw them – the genocide trauma, the grim aftermath of war, Goma, overcrowded prisons, Kibeho, justice. I have also analysed the failures of peace-keeping in Rwanda and drawn lessons from them. But let us start at the beginning.

I retired from the Pakistan Foreign Service on 29 March 1994 after 37 years as a career diplomat, during the last four of which I served as Foreign Secretary. During these four years, I served under six prime ministers. On retirement, I decided to visit my eldest son Faiz in London, play a lot of cricket, go to the theatre and hole up at the India Office Library researching material for my book on my ancestors, *The Begums of Bhopal*.

For a good three weeks I had the time of my life, until one afternoon the telephone rang and my old friend, Jean-Claude Aimé, who was Chef de Cabinet to the UN Secretary-General, asked me if I could go to Geneva and meet Mr Boutros-Ghali. 'He has a proposition to make,' said Aimé. The next day, I was in Geneva where the Secretary-General asked me if I would take on the 'onerous responsibility' of seeking a peaceful settlement in Rwanda as his Special Representative. Mentally, I had steeled myself for such an offer as, at the time,

---

[1] The Rwandan Patriotic Front (RPF) and the Rwandan Patriotic Army (RPA) are treated synonymously in this book.

the proposition could only have concerned Yemen or Rwanda. And if
the UN Secretary-General makes a personal request, a professional
diplomat of 37 years does not decline. No terms or status were
mentioned and the deal was struck within a few minutes. My real
sorrow was that my idyllic holiday, with numerous cricket fixtures
scheduled, was now at an end.

When I broke the news to my family, I was surprised and delighted at their support. In Karachi, my wife was elated. She saw the
assignment as international recognition after a long career in the
Pakistan Foreign Service. She noted that I had neither sought the
post nor had the Pakistan government proposed my name. My son
Faiz was also genuinely pleased and remarked that 'for the first time
in your life, you might get a reasonable financial reward for your
efforts'. Of course, the horrific massacres in Rwanda that were
appearing prominently on television and on the front pages of every
newspaper were a source of concern which my family were too
diplomatic to mention. I knew my mother would feel excessively
anxious for my well-being and I tried, unsuccessfully, to reassure her
that I was not in danger. The truth was that Rwanda was a hazard.

I stayed in New York for two weeks being briefed, administered,
medically checked and generally oriented towards Rwanda. I stayed
with Ambassador Jamsheed and Arnaz Marker who are the finest
hosts in the world, thoroughly enjoying their company interspersed
with Brahms, the finest restaurants in New York, the morning jog
around Central Park and the best Cuban cigars. My mentors in New
York were Kofi Annan, Iqbal Riza, Hedi Annabi, Shaukat Fareed and
Benon Sevan. Among other senior officers who helped my orientation
towards Rwanda were Marrack Goulding, head of the Department of
Political Affairs (DPA), Peter Hansen, head of the Department of
Humanitarian Affairs (DHA), Ismat Kittani, whose long experience of
the UN and wise counsel led to him being the Secretary-General's
Political Adviser, and Chinmai Gharekhan, who acted as a bridge
between the Secretary-General and the Security Council. As a long-
serving diplomat and confirmed bilateralist, I had tended from the
outside to regard the UN mafia as somewhat glib and effete, but,
once inside, the feeling of an international camaraderie, of extraordinary commitment and of common cause for humanity had an
elevating effect on me. I now consider myself a convert to multilateral
diplomacy.

My briefings in New York were conducted mainly by the Depart-
ment of Peace-Keeping Operations (DPKO), but were also spread
across other related departments, notably Humanitarian Affairs,
Political Affairs, the UNDP (United Nations Development Programme)
and just about any department that had a finger in the Rwandan pie.
In New York I met the man named Prime Minister-designate in the
Arusha Accords, Faustin Twagiramungu, and also the Rwandan
Ambassador representing, of course, the Habyarimana government.

By coincidence, Rwanda found itself on the Security Council. I also travelled to Washington and was briefed at the State Department by the wise and experienced Under-Secretary, George Moose.

The main thrust of my mandate,[1] was to bring the civil war to a quick end through a ceasefire, to seek a return to the Arusha Accords signed on 4 August 1993, to avoid confrontation between the RPA and the French-dominated Operation Turquoise[2] and to urge national reconciliation. I was informed that because entire battalions had been withdrawn after the brutal killings of Belgian soldiers, fewer than 500 troops were available on the ground and that the remaining complement of 5500 sanctioned by the Security Council would not arrive before mid-August, as the financing, budgeting and movement of additional troops could not be achieved 'overnight'. Moreover, the logistic support promised to the mainly African contingents by Western governments would take time to reach Rwanda. My brief was therefore to hold on as best we could with our threadbare military resources on the ground and wait for reinforcements. This was not going to be an easy task as, already, the media had orchestrated a crescendo of criticism against the UN for its inability to recognize genocide and stop the killings in Rwanda. In all my briefings, from the Secretary-General downwards, I could sense the burden of Somalia, which seemingly influenced UN peace-keeping operations in the direction of excessive caution and restraint.

On 2 July, my preparations completed, I headed for Nairobi. My short stay there was enlivened by the hospitality of Pakistan's High Commissioner, Amir Mohammad Khan, who carried a wealth of experience of Kenya and in fact of peace-keeping operations because of Pakistan's commitment to the UN peace-keeping force in Somalia which used Nairobi as a transit point. Nairobi has a delightful climate and is obviously a modern, prosperous city with fine restaurants, excellent schools, safari outings and good living. The only blot is the security conditions which are appalling. Armed gangsters and muggers regularly invade houses, often overpowering security guards, and make off with cars, cash, TVs, etc. Amir himself was relieved of his official car, and in another incident the Zimbabwe High Commissioner and his wife walked home in their underwear because the thieves insisted on their undressing before driving off.

---

[1] UNAMIR II mandate, Security Council Resolution no. 918, dated 17 May 1994. The UNAMIR I mandate was intended to provide the glue for the Arusha Accords. Both mandates operated under Chapter VI of the UN Charter.

[2] Operation Turquoise was a single-country operation undertaken by France and sanctioned by the Security Council. The operation was mounted in July 1994 at a time when the UN and Security Council members were being severely criticized for lack of action in the face of genocide. France undertook the operation with the objective of controlling the massacres and providing security, but the RPF saw France's intervention as an attempt to bolster the RGF's sagging morale. Operation Turquoise eventually operated in the south-western triangle of Rwanda, which was still under the RGF's control – a region that was designated the Humanitarian Protection Zone (HPZ). Operation Turquoise concluded its mission on 22 August 1994.

On 4 July, having done my laps in the hotel swimming pool and having declined Amir's offer of eating crocodile and zebra kebabs in a local restaurant, I set off for Entebbe with my new colleagues, Abdul Hamid Kabia of Sierra Leone, my Executive Director, and Ally Golo of Chad, my Chief Administrative Officer (CAO). At Entebbe Airport, I had a chance meeting with Ms Glynne Evans, a most accomplished British lady diplomat who had just visited Kigali. She was charming and extremely well informed. She reminded me of beautiful Memsahebs dressed for *shikar* (hunting safaris) in pre-independence India. She told me that throughout her stay in Rwanda she had carried a sleeping-bag as an emergency kit. Soon we were on our way by helicopter to the Rwandan border.

During the flight, as we flew over the beautiful and vast Lake Victoria, the Canadian pilot signalled to me in sign language that he was receiving an important message. He then exchanged his earphones with mine and I found the BBC World Service coming through. In the news summary, the BBC announced that Rwandan government forces had vacated the capital, Kigali, which was now entirely in RPF hands; also that Butare, Rwanda's second largest city, had fallen to the RPF. I realized that, as I landed for the first time on Rwandan soil, a qualitative change in the political and military situation had occurred with the fall of the capital to the RPF and that the impact of this development would be felt well beyond Rwanda's borders.

Arrival scene in Kigali

On my arrival at the border, I was met by a Bangladeshi colonel commanding UNAMIR's Military Observers Unit in the area. I was later to meet and establish warm personal relations with Bangladeshi officers serving as Military Observers (Milobs) with UNAMIR. The colonel at the border was from Sylhet and knew all my Sylheti friends in Bangladesh, notably Humayun Rasheed Chowdhury, recently elected Speaker of the Bangladesh National Assembly, his brother, the late Kaiser Rasheed, and Faruq Chowdhury.

Before starting on the final leg of our journey to the capital Kigali by road, I was fitted with a bullet-proof jacket and provided with an escort of jeeps that drove ahead and behind us with UN flags flying. The 90-minute drive from the border was my first introduction to Rwanda. As everyone had said, the weather was perfect – about 70°F – and the road excellent. The countryside was fertile and extraordinarily picturesque. We first passed through a game-park, where lush grassland was interspersed with light forest and those beautiful, flat-topped trees that are typically African. After about half an hour, we were into cultivated land with delightful undulating hills and valleys. It was only after an hour's driving that I realized that I had seen no human beings on the roads or in the fields! The villages we passed were totally deserted and the little farmyard huts were mostly destroyed and pillaged. The crops lay unharvested and I was told that the capture of this territory by the RPF had meant that the mainly Hutu farmers had either fled or been herded into camps. It was a strange feeling that, in the world's second most densely populated country,[1] there was no one to be seen, mile after mile, as we drove through this beautiful, fertile terrain.

At 6.00 pm, we reached Kigali and went directly to the stadium, adjacent to which was UNAMIR's military headquarters located at the Amahoro Hotel. The building was well guarded and sand-bagged. It was the hostel where visiting sports teams were normally lodged and would have rated one star as a hotel. In the compound, I was received by Major-General Romeo Dallaire, the Canadian Force Commander who had performed heroically in impossible conditions and was now a recognized television personality. General Dallaire fitted exactly the description I had of him: open, frank, friendly, spry and intrepid. I took the Ghanaian guard of honour and was soon whisked away to follow, in military style, a programme that had been drawn up for me.

First, I was shown my office on the third floor and was informed, somewhat apologetically, that the office was also my bedroom! There was a desk, two chairs and in the corner, an iron bed. The room was spare but clean. Next door was a bathroom with two buckets of water, informing me of my daily ration to include washing, bath, ablutions and cistern. I had been forewarned by Iqbal Riza about the spartan conditions in Kigali with more than a mischievous chuckle. But he also knew that I was used to doing without creature comforts, especially as at home, in Malir, on the outskirts of Karachi, I take a voluntary bucket bath, even though the shower does work, albeit temperamentally.

I was now in my headquarters, both residence and office. Shortly afterwards we had a briefing, then a welcoming dinner which consisted of German army rations served in packets, warmed up. I quickly examined my share to make sure there was no pork, and we ended with the dessert of apple puree, also served in a packet. My introduction to camp life was now complete. Frankly, I relished the change from diplomatic life and, returning to my 'suite', my thoughts drifted back to London, especially to Ali, my third son, who was recovering from a bout of typhoid. Before my departure, he had treated me with such loving care – packing my clothes, reading out the instructions on my medicine kit (malaria pills every Tuesday, screamed a sticker in my briefcase); then careful folding of all my documents into neat packets and putting me early to bed in prepa-

---

[1] With the exception of island states, UN population reports consider Bangladesh to be the world's most densely populated country.

ration for my journey. He made sure I had all my reading material and my toiletries. My other children love and care for me just as much, but none of them treat me like a hapless child as Ali does. Within two months, Ali would be on his way to neighbouring Somalia where he served a term with UNICEF.

The first night, I hardly slept – new bed, one mosquito, hard pillow, strange environment, no one I knew. I wondered how my diabetic condition would bear up to this spartan existence. All these anxieties led to a restless night.

The next day, 5 July, was to be a memorable day. We started with more briefings by General Dallaire. We then went to the adjacent stadium. It had about 10,000 people living in the open – mainly Tutsis and moderate Hutus, guarded by a few Ghanaians. They had suffered nightmares of fear with murderous militia marauding the city, threatening to kill them with machetes. We next went to the airport which was a modern building but now a vacant carcase, badly hit by mortar as the key military target. We lunched with the Ghanaian contingent and then General Dallaire took me on a tour of the town.

Kigali was obviously a beautiful city, built on several hills and with petite villas, a shopping mall, good roads and a quiet, dignified residential area. But now, it seemed to have been hit by a neutron bomb. There was no sign of life. The buildings were mostly wrecked, pock-marked by mortar and machine-gun fire. Every shop, every house had been looted. We looked in on the Canadian Ambassador's residence. It had been looted bare – even the light bulbs had gone. Only a golf club had been left behind and also a desolate-looking dog. The marketplace was destroyed and deserted. There was not a kiosk in the entire ghost city that sold a Coke or a box of matches. As General Dallaire drove me past places where massacres had taken place, there were corpses and skeletons lying about picked bare by dogs and vultures. The scene was macabre, surrealistic and utterly gruesome. Worse was to follow.

We went to the ICRC (International Committee of the Red Cross) hospital where hundreds of bodies lay piled up in the garden. Everywhere there were corpses, mutilated children, dying women. There was blood all over the floors and a terrible stench of rotting flesh. Every inch of space was taken up by these patients. Inside, there was one doctor and one surgeon, the bravest, kindest people in the world who worked 24 hours round the clock. The day before, as government forces (the RGF) left, they had fired mortars indiscriminately and one had hit the casualty ward of the ICRC hospital, killing seven patients. Outside, under a tent, lay those who required amputation. Further up the compound was another tented ward. These patients had no hope of survival and were left to die silently. Further still were those who had an outside chance. The hospital only took life-threatening cases. I have never witnessed such horror, such vacant fear in the eyes of patients, such a putrid stench. I did not throw up, I did not cry: I was too shocked. I was silent. My colleagues who had lived through the massacres were hardened: they had seen worse, much worse.

Colonel Tikoca, the brave Fijian colonel who was head of the Military Observer Unit told me that on the morning of 7 April, the day after the air crash that killed President Habyarimana and triggered the massacre of Tutsis and moderate Hutus, three Tutsi families from neighbouring houses rang his gate-bell. They pleaded with the colonel to hide them in his house. He let them enter and made all 15 fugitives hide under beds. Soon, the murderous Presidential Guard arrived with machine guns cocked. Colonel Tikoca stood outside his house in his blue UN beret. The murderers had been to the houses of the Tutsis, found they had fled and were now checking them out with neighbours. The intrepid colonel did not let the killers in. So they went to the next, marked, Tutsi house. Here, the family had not taken the precaution of escaping or hiding. The colonel heard five shots. He ran to his neighbours' house and found father, mother and three children shot in the head, blood oozing all over the floor. There were thousands of such brutal murders. Never has humanity been more depraved than in Rwanda.

After the ICRC hospital, we went to the King Faisal Hospital where conditions were equally grim. This hospital had been taken over by Médécins Sans Frontières (MSF) who were also performing a heroic role. I visited every ward and found conditions much the same as at the ICRC hospital. At the King Faisal, the doctor took me to a ward which he unlocked and after my visit, locked behind him. When I asked him the reason for the locks, he replied that he had been asked by the RPF to secure the ward as the patients in it were the suspected killers, the Interahamwe. I was struck by the fact that, even in the heat of the murderous battle, the RPF had taken prisoners and were allowing them to be treated before they stood trial. A less disciplined force would have killed off those suspected or simply left them to bleed to death. The locked ward at the King Faisal Hospital made an impression on me. We then went to the Meridian Hotel which housed 2000 refugees. As we drove up, I could smell the odour of stale urine wafting across the hall. There was no water, no electricity, the building had been shattered by mortar shelling and was now packed to the hilt with refugees. Some Russian Milobs were guarding it. Only the tennis courts stood unscathed.

The fact is that never in living history has such wanton brutality been inflicted by human beings on their fellow creatures. Not in the Hindu–Muslim riots in India of 1947, nor in the murderous conflict in Afghanistan, even the Killings Fields of Cambodia and Bosnia pale before the gruesome, awful, depravity of the massacres in Rwanda. I give the following examples only to give an idea of the unbelievable horror that my colleagues in UNAMIR had lived through.

The nightmare had begun on 6 April, when President Habyarimana's plane was shot down by a rocket as it came in to land at Kigali Airport. By an extraordinary coincidence, the plane crashed in the back garden of the presidential palace so that the President's family were almost the first to realize that he had been killed. Who fired the rocket that blasted the President's plane is not known. Some accuse the RPF, others state that it was the extremists around the President's party who then launched their reign of terror. Gerard Prunier in his excellent book *Crisis in Rwanda* has examined five scenarios, leaving readers to reach their own conclusions. Within an hour of the crash, the Presidential Guard, the militia and the Interahamwe had started their meticulously planned, murderous rampage.

The Interahamwe made a habit of killing young Tutsi children, in front of their parents, by first cutting off one arm, then the other. They would then gash the neck with a machete to bleed the child slowly to death but, while they were still alive, they would cut off the private parts and throw them at the faces of the terrified parents who would then be murdered with slightly greater despatch. Radio Mille Collines and the frenzied genocide perpetrators would call on patriotic Hutus to 'kill Tutsis in their homes, their parents, their grandparents and their children and don't forget the unborn foetus'. Civilized people cannot believe such depravity, but I have heard the tapes myself. Friend murdered life-long friend, Hutu husbands of mixed marriage killed Tutsi wives and venerable priests betrayed thousands of refugees who sought sanctuary in their churches. The dean of the faculties of Butare University personally murdered five of his fellow professors.[1]

It is an extraordinary irony that these killers went on to control the camps of Goma, Bukavu and Ngara and to be sheltered and fed by humanitarian aid. They showed no remorse, no repentance and maintained that the killings were part of a civil war that began with the RPF attack on the Rwandan government in 1990. I cannot begin to explain such savage brutality among human beings; it is more than frenzy, panic or fear. I can only quote my admirable counterpart in Burundi, Ambassador Ahmed Ould Abdullah of Mauritania, who told me, 'I am an African. Throughout Africa we have tribal feuds which lead to wars and deaths. But the Hutu–Tutsi hatred outweighs all of them put together.'

Gerard Prunier has described the sheer horror and brutality of the genocide in the following words:

> The killings were not in any way clean or surgical. The use of machetes often resulted in a long and painful agony and many people, when they had some money, paid their killers to be finished off quickly with a bullet rather than being slowly hacked to death with a *panga*. Sexual abuse of

[1] For detailed accounts of the genocide see Rakiya Omar and Alex de Waal, *Rwanda: Death, Despair and Defiance* (London: African Rights Publications, 1994) and Alison des Forges, *Leave None To Tell the Story: Genocide in Rwanda* (New York: Human Rights Watch, 1999).

women was common and they were often brutally killed after being raped. If some children joining the Interahamwe became killers, others were victims, and babies were often smashed against a rock or thrown alive into pit latrines. Mutilations were common, with breasts and penises often being chopped off. In some cases, they became part of macabre rituals which would have puzzled a psychiatrist. Brutality here does not end with murder. At massacre sites, corpses, many of them those of children, have been methodically dismembered and the body parts stacked neatly in separate piles.

Survivors emerging from piles of bodies were often tracked down, such as those from the massacre of 800 people at the headquarters of the Kibungo diocese who were sought out from among the corpses by the militiamen and systematically clubbed to death. Sadism linked with racism could reach unbelievable extremes. On the campus of Butare University, a Hutu teacher whose Tutsi wife was in an advanced state of pregnancy saw her disembowelled under his eyes and had the foetus of his unborn child pushed in the face while the killers shouted 'Here! Eat your bastard!' In some cases, militiamen tried to force women to kill their children in order to save their own lives. Some people were burnt alive as their relations were forced to watch before being killed themselves. In other cases the *Interahamwe* told families that if they would kill a certain relation the rest of the family would be spared.[1]

During the massacres, Rwanda also saw some extraordinary feats of heroism by the ordinary folk who hid their persecuted friends for weeks in attics and shallow graves, running the risk of a murderous penalty. One such incident bears repetition. When President Habyarimana's plane was shot down, the button was pressed to start the slaughter. The victims had been pre-determined and were to be hunted down. One of the first on the list was the Prime Minister, Mme Agathe Uwilingiyimana, who was a moderate Hutu. There is a chilling tape of her talking on the telephone to a foreign radio correspondent when she says, 'I have to leave my house now. I can hear footsteps. They are coming to kill me and my family. Please tell the world to help us against these murderers.' Mme Uwilingiyimana then ran across her back garden into the American First Secretary's house. She then moved to an adjacent cluster of villas occupied by UN diplomats. There, she was hidden by one of the UN families. The Presidential Guard pursued her and searched room after room until they found her, whereupon they bludgeoned her and then dragged her away to an even more painful death. They also disarmed and butchered ten Belgian soldiers who were guarding the Prime Minister. Not content with this ghastly deed, the killers returned to murder her small children. At that point, an African family among the UN diplomats took over Mme Uwilingiyimana's children and bravely passed them off as their own so that the children survived. There were many such heroic deeds, including the escape of the

---

[1] Gerard Prunier, *Rwanda Crisis. History of a Genocide* (Kampala, Uganda: Fountain Publishers, 1995).

former Prime Minister, Faustin Twagiramungu, another Hutu moderate. He took refuge with UNAMIR and was then wrapped up in a blanket, camouflaged as cargo by the Bangladeshi contingent and loaded on to a Canadian Hercules cargo plane. Mr Twagiramungu frequently reminds us that he owes his life to UNAMIR and to the brave Bangladeshi and Canadian officers. Prunier describes one such incident as follows:

> Sometimes, even the simplest gesture of common decency could mean death, as with the Hutu family who could not bear the sight of the naked body of their Tutsi neighbour and went to cover it with some banana leaves, and were all killed by the *Interahamwe*. Some went beyond simple courage to attain something like sainthood, like the Hutu Catholic lay-worker Felicite Niyitegeka in Gisenyi who systematically helped hunted people cross the border. Her brother, an army colonel, wrote to tell her that the militia were aware of her activity, but she refused to stop. When they finally came to get her, she had 30 refugees in her house. The *Interahamwe* said that she would be spared but that her charges would have to be killed. She answered that they would all stay together, in life or in death. To make her recant, the militiamen then shot the refugees one by one before her eyes. When the slaughter was over, she asked to be killed. The militia leader then told her she would die and asked her to pray for his soul before shooting her.

So ended my first 48 hours in Kigali. The horror, the sheer depravity of the massacres, the sight of the dead and the dying in the hospitals, the ghost town of Kigali, skeletal carcasses of cars hit by machine guns lying on the roads, along with dead dogs fattened on human flesh and killed by pistol shots, provided a macabre backdrop. I came on 4 July, the night peace broke out in the capital. My colleagues and compatriots had lived through a nightmare since hell had broken loose after the air crash on 6 April. They were hardened, almost inured. For me the baptism was shocking and gruesome.

Negotiations for a ceasefire

The fortnight between 5 and 19 July was critical in Rwanda's history. My primary task as Special Representative was to negotiate a ceasefire between the rampaging RPF and the retreating 'interim government' (the RGF). The RPF now held the capital Kigali, while the interim government first holed up in Gitarama and then fled further west to Ruhengeri and finally to Gisenyi on the border with Zaire. On 6 July, in Kigali, I held my first meeting with the leader of the RPF, Major-General Paul Kagame. The general already had a growing reputation as a remarkable military leader whose forces, numbering 15,000, were in the process of routing the government army of 40,000. General Dallaire told me that military staff colleges all over the world would be returning to the drawing-board to examine the strategy and tactics of this remarkable military campaign. A neat explanation of Kagame's RPF's triumphal progress was not readily at hand, but the fact was that the RPF was scything through RGF defences like a knife through butter!

My first meeting with Major-General Kagame was fixed to take place at the shell-torn VIP lounge of the airport where every window-pane lay shattered. Kagame entered the room, gaunt and stern. Regrettably, my predecessor, the former Cameroon Foreign Minister, Dr Jacques-Roger Booh-Booh had been accused by the RPF of being biased in favour of the former government. Kagame was obviously sizing up Dr Booh-Booh's successor. Kagame was 37 years old, tall, pencil thin, with glasses and a high forehead, very Tutsi in appearance, soft-spoken and scholarly looking. He was frank and sparing in his words. After a brief review of the situation, I argued passionately in favour of a ceasefire. I urged General Kagame to recognize that the RPF's superiority on the battle field gave it the advantage of translating its gains at the negotiating table. I reasoned that the presence of France's Operation Turquoise in the west could affect the existing balance on the ground. To continue the battle with unnecessary loss of life would lose the RPF the immense goodwill that it had gained internationally.

Kagame gave me a patient hearing and replied that he could not negotiate with the 'criminals' who had perpetrated the massacres. He would, instead, announce a unilateral ceasefire along with conditions which he would convey to me shortly. I continued to press for an agreed ceasefire, offering to act as the intermediary between the two sides. Eventually, Kagame agreed that I should inquire as to conditions for a ceasefire from the 'other side'. Meanwhile, he would draw up his own ceasefire conditions. I gained the impression that Kagame was playing for time to consolidate his military gains. I pleaded that a confrontation with the French should be avoided, to which General Kagame replied that he was not seeking one. My first meeting with Kagame was a good one and when we parted he smiled and shook my hand warmly.

The next day, 7 July, I set off for Gisenyi to meet the leaders of the interim government. After a drive in a jeep across the bumpiest road imaginable, as the main road, being mined, was not safe, we drove for about two hours to a UNAMIR post near Kabale on the Ugandan border. I then boarded a helicopter to fly to Goma, on the Zaire side of the border from Gisenyi, where the French had their Operation Turquoise headquarters.

The 40-minute helicopter ride took us over Uganda into Zaire, flying over the most gorgeous scenery. Undulating, green terraced mountains merge into beautiful valleys and lagoons, making it into a tourist paradise. We flew past huge volcanic mountains where the famous 'gorillas in the mist' are found. The mist is created by the volcanoes, which come to life once every 30 years or so and I was told that one of the volcanoes, Mount Nyiragongo, is active and, as night falls, an orange rim around the crater reflects its luminous glow on the overhanging clouds, providing an extraordinary, thrilling sight. In Goma, we were whisked away to Operation Turquoise's headquarters where I met the kindly, urbane and highly impressive French commander, General Jean-Claude Lafourcade. Operation Turquoise's diplomatic adviser was the French career diplomat Yannick Gerard who, to my pleasant surprise, spoke to me in Urdu! He was a scholar of the language and subsequently served with great distinction in Pakistan as France's Ambassador. Despite divergent mandates, UNAMIR and Turquoise had established the most cordial co-operation and after a productive discussion, we were driven back across the border to Gisenyi where the Foreign Minister, Jerome Bikamumpaka, received me at the border post.[1]

My first meeting with the Foreign Minister was also a sizing-up visit. After a lengthy discussion on the merits of a ceasefire, he suggested that I should return two days later so that I could meet the President and Prime Minister. At least my neutral credentials had been accepted and I was now recognized as the official channel of communications between the two sides. When I returned to my car, my chief escort Colonel Tikoca told me that a group of militias had grabbed my driver and threatened to kill him. He had been saved by Tikoca drawing his pistol. Danger lurked in the background whenever we stepped into RGF territory because UNAMIR was not popular with the interim government who blamed their abject defeat on 'General Dallaire's bias in favour of the RPF' and Uganda's support for them. I returned the same evening to Kigali, having at least established meaningful contact with the leadership on both sides.

After my briefings and preliminary exchanges, I drew up a five-point plan of action to address the immediate situation on the ground. The first point was to persuade both sides of my complete neutrality. This was important as both my predecessor, Dr Booh-Booh, and the Force Commander, General Dallaire, were viewed as having strong, if opposing preferences. Dr Booh-Booh had been publicly criticized by the RPF as being 'hand-in-glove' with the Habyarimana government. The RPF's substantive accusation was that Dr Booh-Booh had withheld from the UN reports of the plans of imminent genocide by the Habyarimana government that had been conveyed to UNAMIR on several occasions. Dr Booh-Booh was also accused of being specially close to the Habyarimana clique, enjoying long weekends as the President's guest which, in the eyes of the RPF, made him biased in favour of the former government. Conversely, General Dallaire was viewed by the interim government as leaning in favour of the RPF. In fact, the pro-government radio began to publicly criticize Dallaire for 'easing the path' of the RPA during the war.

---

[1] Jerome Bikamumpaka has since been arrested and is to be tried at the International Criminal Tribunal for Rwanda.

Given the background of these subjective accusations from both sides, it was important that I should underline my transparently neutral credentials. Being an Asian with no historic, ethnic, religious or linguistic connections with either side helped to establish this neutrality.

The second point was the critical issue of seeking an agreement for a ceasefire. Before I left New York, the general feeling was that the civil war would continue for some time and would probably end in a stalemate through exhaustion. No one expected a quick, decisive victory. The RPF had an ill-equipped army of about 15,000 and was taking on a government force of 40,000 that had been well equipped and had found itself supported by French and Zairean forces during a similar RPF incursion in 1990. The RPF's gains in the eastern sector and now in Kigali appeared to represent their high-water mark and further advance could stretch the RPF's limited resources. Now that Operation Turquoise had been launched, it was anticipated that the RGF would gain moral support from their presence and hold on to the western sectors. As always, the timing of a ceasefire depended on the emergence of a military equilibrium on the ground. Given the fact that the RPF were continuing to achieve military successes, I doubted, in my mind, that an equilibrium was at hand as no military leader will agree to a ceasefire if he finds his opponents on the run. Nevertheless, in accordance with my mandate I had to try.

Basically, my arguments were that an agreed ceasefire was better than a unilateral one. As a fall-back position, I reasoned that a unilateral ceasefire was better than none! With General Kagame, I underlined the need to retain the international goodwill which was in the RPF's favour. I argued that there was a danger that this goodwill would be dissipated if a humanitarian catastrophe occurred through the absence of a ceasefire. My second argument in favour of a joint ceasefire was that the RPF had probably gained as much militarily as was likely, particularly as Operation Turquoise was now launched in the south-western sector, and that the iron was now hot for the RPF to translate its military gains into political ones through negotiations.

My task of persuading the interim government (the RGF) for a joint ceasefire was less difficult as they were losing ground and had a weak negotiating hand. They were clearly desperate and on the run. Anything that would stop the RPF advance, allow the RGF to retain a foothold in Rwanda and enable the rapidly discredited leadership to maintain some representational respectability was acceptable. Therefore, it was not surprising that after some 'brave talk' about lofty principles, recovering lost territory and RPF 'treachery', the RGF leadership gave me carte-blanche to negotiate terms for a joint ceasefire.

The third point of my plan was to persuade both parties to the conflict to allow humanitarian aid to flow smoothly for the benefit of the population in the sectors controlled by them. After the gruesome television images, a huge humanitarian effort was building up and it was important that no hindrances were placed in the distribution of aid.

My fourth point was that, once a ceasefire was achieved and the bloodshed ceased, it was important to return to the negotiating table. The Arusha Accords provided a framework for these negotiations. The consolidation and implementation of Arusha was therefore the basic structure on which a durable settlement could be built.

My fifth point was to seek national reconciliation through justice and fair play: justice not only to punish the criminals of genocide but justice also for returning refugees, both new and old, for the restoration of their land and properties; justice and compassion, also, for those who had been materially or psychologically affected by the genocide.

Armed with these five points, I intensified my shuttle between Kigali and Gisenyi to negotiate a ceasefire with both parties. Major-General Kagame, whom I met again in the shattered VIP lounge of the airport, responded to my ceasefire proposal by repeating that he would not dignify the criminals by negotiating with them and that, instead, he would shortly announce terms for a unilateral ceasefire. However, he readily agreed to the unrestricted flow of humanitarian aid and also the need for justice and reconciliation. He accepted the Arusha Accords as a basis for the future, adding that they would need to be adjusted to the new realities on the ground, mentioning particularly that the MRND's role would need to be reviewed. Finally, Kagame stressed to me the importance of UN assistance to rebuild a totally shattered infrastructure.

Returning to Gisenyi, I met the entire leadership of the interim government, consisting of President Sindikubwabo, Prime Minister Kambanda, Foreign Minister Bikamumpaka, Defence Minister Bizimana and Chief of Staff Major-General Augustin Bizimungu. I had the unpleasant task of conveying to the RGF leadership that Kagame would not negotiate with them and that the ceasefire negotiations would have to be conducted through me. I was first informed that the RGF's withdrawal had been strategic and that though the RPF's advance and takeover of Kigali was a reality, the RGF would soon recover their losses. The immediate need, however, was for an agreed ceasefire and for a return to the Arusha Accords, with minor modifications. The RGF leadership insisted that they were still a significant force and represented the majority of the Rwandan people who had decided to follow them to the western region. The RGF complained bitterly of Dallaire's 'bias'. In the end, they agreed to my five points, confirming the carte blanche regarding terms for an agreed ceasefire.

After this intensive round of discussions, I came away with an impression that the RGF's brave talk was really whistling in the dark and that they were facing a military defeat which even the arrival of

Operation Turquoise had not helped to contain. General Bizimungu, the RGF's Chief of Staff, informed General Dallaire that he no longer had a headquarters and that his army was operating 'from trenches'. Another blow to RGF morale came on 6 July, when nine senior RGF officers, headed by Brigadier-General Rutasira and Brigadier-General Gatsinzi and including Major Emmanuel Habyarimana (who was later to become a member of the National Assembly), issued a declaration from a village called Kigeme in which they denounced genocide and distanced themselves from the former government, thereby causing an apparent split in the RGF.

My impression of the RPF's response, on the other hand, was that while they paid lip service to the concept of a ceasefire, their victorious march towards the west was likely to continue and by keeping the ceasefire ball in the air, they were playing for time.

During these shuttle negotiations, I was also able to establish cordial and meaningful contact with General Lafourcade who headed Operation Turquoise. Although the presence of Operation Turquoise, armed with a Chapter VII mandate was somewhat incongruous when set against UNAMIR with a Chapter VI mandate, it was necessary that the relationship between UNAMIR and Turquoise should be co-operative and based on mutual understanding.[1] The RPF naturally viewed Operation Turquoise with deep suspicion, but an exchange of messages had led to them accepting Turquoise's presence at face value. In turn, Turquoise had assured the RPF that its role would be strictly humanitarian. UNAMIR and Turquoise soon developed a good relationship, appointing liaison officers and with Dallaire and Lafourcade frequently talking to each other on the telephone. As a result of this deliberate policy on both sides to respect and co-operate with each other, a number of political flash points were pre-empted and resolved amicably. I was gratified to note that, despite their reservations towards Operation Turquoise, the RPF was careful to avoid confrontation with it. Kagame was insistent, however, that Operation Turquoise withdraw at the appointed time, on 22 August, and that UNAMIR take over its humanitarian role on schedule.

When one is in spartan and hazardous conditions as in Kigali, especially as there was always a whiff of danger of which we were reminded by our constant wearing of flakjackets, one particularly values the friendships one forges. My immediate colleagues at that time will be part of my life for ever. Dr Abdul Hamid Kabia, of Sierra Leone, is an outstanding diplomat and a superb human being. Big, tall and strong, he has a basso profundo voice reminiscent of Paul Robeson or Chaliapin. He is a civil servant par excellence, wise,

[1] Chapters VI and VII refer to the chapters of the UN Charter that prescribe the degree of authority required in the implementation of UN resolutions. Resolutions under Chapter VII are mandatory and give those involved in the implementation of the resolutions, e.g. peace-keepers, a pro-active role – for example, in certain circumstances they are authorized to use arms. Resolutions under Chapter VI are non-mandatory and a peace-keeping force may use arms only in self-defence.

balanced, immensely friendly and with mature judgement. Then, on the military side, there were extraordinary men like Major-General Romeo Dallaire. He is brave and decisive, a leader of men, full of humour and good cheer. General Dallaire loves chocolates which I invariably brought back for him whenever I travelled. The Deputy Force Commander, Brigadier-General Henry Anyidoho of Ghana, a mountain of a man, is also a magnificent human being, loyal, disciplined and dedicated. Brigadier-General Anyidoho was respected by all parties and headed a superb Ghanaian contingent. Colonel Tikoca, head of the Military Observers Unit deserves special mention. He is Fijian, an open, brave, immensely popular, buccaneer of a man. He loved talking rugby with me, showing the scars where vicious opponents had trampled on him. He has seen military observer action all over the world – dodging bullets in Lebanon and in Somalia. At the time we were in Rwanda, Colonel Tikoca was kept away from home because he had once led a coup attempt in Fiji, against his friend the President, which did not succeed. These differences have since been amicably resolved and Tikoca went home to receive a well-deserved medal for his peace-keeping role, from his friend, the President!

By my second week in Kigali, the interim government was installed in Gisenyi and the battleground had moved to Ruhengeri, the home and bastion of the late President Habyarimana. Meanwhile, General Dallaire had acquired a couple of goats at headquarters as the UNAMIR contingent's mascots. He explained that he wanted to see some life amidst the sea of dead bodies that he came across in Rwanda. Since my arrival on 4 July, Kigali had been peaceful and the only shots I heard were when General Dallaire fired his pistol at some dogs that had attacked his precious goats. He missed!

During the second week of July, General Dallaire drove me about the town for another round. The city was still totally deserted. We first went to a UN vehicle depot. It had been broken into and looted. I was told that 96 vehicles had been stolen by the RPF, the UN white painted over with camouflage. Our drivers recognized the cars, but it was too early to intercept and ask for their return. We next went into a government building and, as we entered the rear garage, we saw the grim sight of five twisted, dead bodies lying in a corner. The men had been executed recently and there was no one to identify or bury them. The carcasses just lay there, waiting to be eaten by vultures and predatory dogs. We then went to the Parliament building which had been the RPF's headquarters in the city. The building had been smashed by mortar fire and shelling. As we entered its dark and eerie chambers, we were greeted by a dog snarling from the depths of a room. Dallaire drew his pistol and hurriedly ushered us out. Rabid dogs feeding on human flesh were an unusual menace to contend with!

We then made a round of the poorer sector of the town which was also badly devastated. I got off at the Central Mosque, which had been especially targeted as snipers had mounted machine guns on top of the minaret. The mosque had been devastated and when I returned to headquarters, I urged the Muslim contingents – the Tunisians and Bangladeshis – to join me in cleaning up the debris so that we could say our Friday prayers there. We also helped to clean up the churches. Rwanda has a Muslim population of approximately 5 per cent, though the Muslim members of the National Assembly claim the figure to be higher. Generally, the Muslim community was recognized to have conducted itself honourably during the genocide. Gerard Prunier describes the role of Rwandan Muslims in the following terms:

> The only faith which provided a bulwark against barbarity for its adherents was Islam. There are many testimonies to the protection members of the Muslim community gave each other and their refusal to divide themselves ethnically. This solidarity comes from the fact that 'being Muslim' in Rwanda, where Muslims are a very small (1.2 per cent) proportion of the population, is not simply a choice dictated by religion; it is a global identity choice. Muslims are often socially marginal people and this reinforces a strong sense of community identification which supersedes ethnic tags, something the majority of Christians have not been able to achieve.

On 14 July, Faustin Twagiramungu, the Prime Minister-designate under the Arusha Accords, arrived in Kigali in our C-130. By then, we had cleared two floors of the Meridian Hotel. The Prime Minister-designate was given 'a suite' on the fifth floor and was provided security by UNAMIR soldiers. His suite had a gaping hole made by a mortar shell and splintered window-panes, but it was the best we could arrange for him. I called on Mr Twagiramungu immediately after his arrival and impressed on him the urgent need for an agreed ceasefire. He told me that he had visited France, Belgium, Uganda and Tanzania before returning to Kigali. All four governments were strongly in favour of a ceasefire. President Museveni of Uganda had sent a message to General Kagame advocating a ceasefire. Kagame had agreed in principle, but had informed Museveni that his military High Command wanted to achieve its military objectives first. Twagiramungu agreed that another message from the Ugandan President was necessary as, otherwise, a humanitarian tragedy was inevitable, with adverse consequences for a successor government. After his tête-à-tête meeting with me, Mr Twagiramungu proceeded to his first meeting with the RPF leadership.

By 14 July, the civil war was drawing towards its denouement. The RGF had abandoned Ruhengeri and retreated to the border town of Gisenyi. This was the proverbial corner in which the former government was now painted, waiting for the coup de grâce. On 15

July, accompanied by General Dallaire, I held a critical meeting with General Kagame and made the following points to him:

a) The Security Council had issued a Presidential Statement calling for an immediate ceasefire. The RPF's delay in implementing the ceasefire, even a unilateral ceasefire, would be counter-productive and would lose the RPF international goodwill.

b) While recognizing that the RPF wanted to press ahead for an outright military victory, it was vital to halt and reverse the impending humanitarian tragedy.

c) A broad-based transitional government on the lines of the Arusha Accords, was needed to facilitate international recognition and contribute to national reconciliation. Non-criminal elements associated with the former government could be inducted into such a government.

Kagame responded by stating that a ceasefire was imminent and would be announced 'tonight or tomorrow'. He showed me a map and drew a line along the territory that the RPF intended to hold, leaving a narrow strip near Gisenyi for the former government. He stated that there should be no mention of the 'other party' in the ceasefire agreement and that UNAMIR should monitor the ceasefire. He added that the door was open for opposition civil and military elements to join the new government, as only the criminal elements associated with the former government would be prosecuted. RGF returnees would be screened and retrained before being integrated into the national army. They could give themselves up to UNAMIR should they so wish. General Kagame agreed that Brigadier-General Rutasira and Brigadier-General Gatsinzi – the leaders of the RGF splinter 'Kigeme' group – could be flown in from Bukavu to support the ceasefire. Kagame also indicated that a broad-based government, 'probably' with Faustin Twagiramungu as Prime Minister, would be sworn in during the following week. He assured me that Hutu refugees would be encouraged to return and treated with compassion and justice. He also urged that the vitriolic propaganda by Radio Mille Collines that continued to be broadcast from movable transmitters should be stopped. He again requested the UN's help in the revival of Rwanda's shattered infrastructure.

Finally, I presented a ceasefire document to Kagame. He read it carefully and indicated his broad agreement to the original document with the following meaningful amendments. Kagame omitted references to (i) Twagiramungu as Prime Minister, (ii) to the RGF, in maintaining the ceasefire and (iii) with reference to the Arusha Accords he struck out the word 'framework', leaving reference only to its 'spirit'. Before I left, Kagame appeared relaxed and confident. His parting remarks were, 'Let it be clear that there is only one locomotive that will pull this train. We shall put everything right that has been wrong with this country for so long.' In the end, he agreed to my going public on the ceasefire. On return to UNAMIR headquarters, I made the announcement to the swarm of about 80 media representatives that habitually thronged the hall of the Amahoro Hotel from morning to night.

The next day, 16 July, the news of an imminent ceasefire was carried by CNN and the BBC, but no actual announcement was forthcoming from RPF headquarters. I tried desperately to find General Kagame, but he told me frankly, at a later date, that he had deliberately avoided meeting me. Evidently, his young Turks had not agreed to let the opposition off with Gisenyi at their mercy. Meanwhile, the interim government and the RGF High Command had capitulated and were crossing over, helter-skelter, into Zaire, taking with them anything that they could lay hands on: weapons, cash, furniture, vehicles, spare parts. Military defeat had turned into a rout.

Over the following weekend, events moved fast. The world seemed to hold its breath, waiting for the mass exodus from Gisenyi. It was expected that most people would go to Goma, a town in Zaire under the protection of Operation Turquoise. The French were obviously tense as some shells fired by the RPF had hit the airfield in Goma. I received a message from General Lafourcade which sounded like an ultimatum. It stated that unless the RPF stopped shelling Goma, France would be obliged to 'retaliate with force'. An armed confrontation between the advancing RPF and the French would engulf the entire region, adding a new dimension to the war. I sent a written message to General Kagame imploring him to keep his promise of avoiding confrontation with the French. Kagame replied that he had ordered his forces to avoid targeting the area where the French were deployed. I then relayed this reply to Lafourcade. These were tense hours and by sunset, Gisenyi had fallen and the mass exodus to Goma was on. The ceasefire was then announced, 48 hours too late to prevent the humanitarian tragedy which then ensued in Goma.

During these tense, grim negotiations a shaft of humour made a contrast. It was evident that with military defeat staring them in the face, the RGF leadership had a weak negotiating hand. They knew that they could hardly insist on any conditions for a ceasefire. They did, however, ask me to convey one condition. They called for the return of the dead body of their President which the RGF leadership claimed was in the hands of the RPF – in Kigali – 'the least they can do is to hand us back the body of our beloved leader so that we can give him a decent burial'. On return to Kigali, I dutifully conveyed this request to General Kagame who remarked with some consternation 'What body? We don't have his body, they carried it with them when they fled. They even drove the Kigali Airport ambulance across to Goma!' Several weeks later, I noted that the late President was given a ceremonial burial in Gbadolete by President Mobutu!

The human drama of Goma has been vividly chronicled in TV and media images that were seen in every drawing-room of the world. A ceasefire, as promised to me by General Kagame 48 hours earlier, might have saved the worst of the tragedy, but the RPF was intent on conquering the last RGF stronghold. The defeat of the RGF was now complete and their leadership scurried for shelter in Zaire, like an army of mice abandoning a sinking wreck. Now the media focused on the humanitarian tragedy of Goma which overtook the earlier holocaust of the premeditated massacre of an innocent population. We had entered the syndrome of cholera, disease, horror and death in Goma.

Before moving on, I shall attempt to answer a question that is frequently asked of me. How could a rebel bush army of 15,000 with limited support from Uganda, so easily defeat a 40,000-strong government army fully equipped by France and possessing infinitely superior logistic and fire-power capability? As General Dallaire remarked, the RPF's victory would make military staff colleges throughout the world go back to the drawing-board to study General Kagame's campaign. My response to the question is, however, superficial and its military element gleaned from General Dallaire and his colleagues.

The main difference between the RPA and RGF was one of discipline and commitment to a cause. For a guerrilla force, the RPA's discipline was commendable. It speaks volumes for their training that, long after their victory, the RPA generally retained an extraordinary discipline in their conduct. In contrast, the RGF soldier was not battle trained and was often described as lazy and pleasure-seeking. Only the Presidential Guard maintained quality discipline. The RGF soldier was often written off as a fighter by describing his familiar demand of 'no beer, no war'. In terms of commitment, the RPA soldier was fighting for a cause – a return to a homeland from which he felt he had been unjustly banished. This commitment gave the RPA a determination that was singularly lacking in the RGF.

As regards military tactics, the RPA would frequently encircle military targets for long periods, using as little ammunition as possible. After the siege had led to desperation, the RPA would open up withdrawal outlets through which the RGF would gratefully retreat to their next stronghold. This deliberate easing of an escape route meant that few pitched battles were fought (which would have depleted the RPA's strength and fire-power). It also meant relatively few war casualties. Moreover, constant retreats by the RGF led to a lowering of morale. A deeper analysis of the RPA's military success will, I am sure, ensue in due course, perhaps with a paper from General Dallaire.

The Broad-Based Government of National Unity (BBGNU)

19 July was a very special day because the RPF's victory had been completed and a new government was to be announced. For the ceremony, we went to the charred building of the National Assembly and there, on the lawn, a tent had been pitched for the occasion which was witnessed by a crowd of about 200 people and an impressive array of military security. We sat in the front row and soon the 18-member Cabinet of the new Broad-Based Government of Nationality Unity was sworn in – each Minister taking the oath in Kinyarwanda (the local language). The top four posts were: Pasteur Bizimungu, President; Major-General Paul Kagame, Vice-President; Faustin Twagiramungu, Prime Minister and Colonel Alexis Kanyarengwe, Vice-Prime Minister. Three of these top four posts were held by Hutus and only one by a Tutsi – Vice-President Kagame. The Cabinet also had a fair ethnic mix and two women were included. I delivered the Secretary-General's message in French. The only other foreign dignitary to make a speech was the Prime Minister of Uganda. Tanzania and the OAU had been invited, but did not have sufficient notice to attend.

By 19 July, as news of the RPF's military victory spread across the country, the first signs of life emerged in Kigali. Looking out of my bedroom (office) window at dawn, I saw the first few families leaving the Amahoro Stadium with their belongings stacked on their heads and children strung across their backs. The first day there were two or three families, next day 50 or so and within a week the entire stadium had emptied. Small kiosks and markets were now springing up with women selling bananas and vegetables. There were also signs of movement in the communes and villages. Seemingly, Rwanda had risen from the dead.

Through July into mid-August, Kigali hesitantly took the first steps back to revival. From a totally deserted city, with every windowpane smashed, every house pock-marked by shell fire and looted, markets, shops, restaurants and petrol pumps began to sprout. The population began to trickle back to their houses and even a nightclub was opened. There was no curfew in Kigali, whose citizens appeared only too eager to put behind the horror of the recent past. As the weeks went by, a large number of 'Burundi' Tutsis could be seen driving around in their swanky cars.

The Burundi Tutsi is French-speaking, business-oriented and hedonistic. Their women are tall, languid and beautiful and have the most exotic hairstyles. They claimed to have financed the war and had returned for their share of the booty. The Ugandan Tutsi is English-speaking, disciplined and frugal. They formed the major part of the victorious army and quietly sat in the driving seat. The arrival of old case-load (Tutsi) refugees led to the forcible occupation of the large number of abandoned properties and farms. In Kigali, some Hutu families were forced to vacate their homes under duress, exercised usually by unpaid RPA new recruits who willingly obliged their predatory paymasters with a show of strength. Gerard Prunier aptly describes this phase in the following terms:

> The RPA now felt the full impact of its hasty recruitment in the early summer. Raw recruits with guns acted as bushwhackers in the hills, grabbing properties for their relatives coming out to Burundi. There were to be several consequences of this. On the one hand, tales of RPF violence tended to paralyse any return to normal international relations with a regime still regarded by many – not only in Paris – with some reserve, and this at a time when normalization was vital in order to restart the economy. These tales also gave comfort to the militia and MRND cadres in the camps of Zaire and Tanzania, who were trying to keep the enormous mass of refugees under their control and especially to prevent them from returning home. Tales of violence coming out of Rwanda were a boon to the killer bourgmestres.

During this period, we were inundated with visitors. General Dallaire and I took a mischievous delight in inviting them to our candlelight dinners at headquarters, serving them with our special menu of tinned mackerel, followed by heated German army rations and ending up with the inevitable packet of apple puree. One of the more memorable visitors was President Mary Robinson of Ireland, a most dignified, caring and warm personality. The late Jim Grant, head of UNICEF, who was a legend in his own lifetime, came twice. Racked by serious illness, he was on the go 18 hours a day, so kind, so humane, so dedicated. When Jim lifted an emaciated child in his lap, it was not for effect: you knew that he genuinely cared for that child. His dedication was infectious and he headed a wonderful band of servants for humanity in UNICEF. The dignified, efficient and humane Mme Sadako Ogata, the High Commissioner for Refugees, whom I had welcomed in Pakistan when she toured the Afghan refugees camps, was another welcome visitor. We also received the ebullient and charming Baroness Chalker, the brilliant and graceful Catherine Bertini, head of the WFP (World Food Programme), Jan Pronk, the Netherlands Minister for Development, who was also highly impressive in his command of detail and had a remarkable incisiveness in finding the nub of an issue, and Dr Ganns, head of the Africa Department of the German Foreign Office, who was a most knowledgeable, sensitive and experienced visitor. We also had our fair share of flag-wavers seeking the TV spotlight, readily available in Kigali from the gathered horde of media representatives.

The deluge of foreign visitors soon became overwhelming as neither UNAMIR nor the newly formed government had the logistic capacity to handle the impromptu visitors who expected everything laid on for them. I sent a telegram to UN headquarters remonstrating at this unending swarm of visitors who sought seats on our C-130s, appointments with Rwandan leaders, transport, accommodation, protocol and security. I illustrated our difficulties by indicating that a group of European parliamentarians, a group of African dignitaries, a Belgian delegation, a British delegation, a Tanzanian delegation, a US Assistant Secretary of State and the High Commissioner for Refugees would be visiting Kigali in the next two days. I conveyed our difficulties in receiving these visitors with UNAMIR's threadbare resources and considering that in Kigali there was no transport, no water, no electricity, no taxis, no shops, no accommodation, no telephones, no security and no services of any kind. Government ministers were unable to talk to each other on the telephone or have secretaries to process their daily programme. They had no cars, no letterheads or typewriters to type a letter. In such dire conditions, neither UNAMIR nor the government was able to service the deluge of visitors.

Significantly, President Bizimungu and Vice-President Kagame did not receive the French delegation led by Secretary-General Dufourq. Nor did President Bizimungu meet Prime Minister Balladur when he invited the Rwandan President to meet him in Cyangugu during a stop-over with Turquoise. The Rwandan President may have felt slighted at being invited by a foreign head of government to a town which was part of Rwandan territory!

2. July – August 1994

Goma
A vision of hell

By 19 July, the massive human exodus to Goma had begun. Within a few days, over a million Hutus swarmed across the border in Gisenyi, urged on by Radio Mille Collines and the RGF's cadres (prefects, sub-prefects, *burgomestres*) who acted as their shepherds. They went across in cars, buses and ambulances but mainly on foot, providing the media with an opportunity to project another side of the human tragedy in Rwanda. TV journalists now vied with each other to catch the most gruesome frames of cholera, dysentery, despair and death. The international humanitarian community mounted a huge relief operation and poured in aid to feed and shelter this mass of humanity that had arrived on the hard, black, lava-coated soil that had gushed out from the volcanoes around Goma over centuries.

By 20 July, an impressive delegation led by the Under Secretary-General for Humanitarian Affairs, Peter Hansen, gathered in Nairobi to proceed to Goma to see what could be done to provide relief to this desperate cauldron of suffering humanity. I arrived in Nairobi to meet up with this delegation suffering from a terrible cold which I found, later, to be a blessing in disguise. We then took an early morning flight on 21 July to Goma.

We landed alongside a battery of enormous US planes that disgorged food, milk, transport, mobile water purifiers, medicines and a vast array of the logistic support that only the United States of America can put together, as it were, 'in a jiffy'. Here was a striking example of the world's greatest superpower acting at full throttle. It was hugely impressive and made all the other nationalities look like church wardens on a picnic. We were received at Goma by General Lafourcade and then we began a 15-minute ride through the town that, for its sheer horror, will remain a recurring nightmare for all of us who piled into the motorcade.

The road from the airport into town was full of starving, sick and dying refugees. Scores of dead bodies lay strewn about rotting in the sun, with people simply stepping over the dead carcasses. Everyone, including those of us in the cars, held handkerchiefs or some cloth, against their noses to prevent the putrid smell of dead bodies raising nausea. Dead children lay next to mothers who were also dying of cholera, of hunger or simply of exhaustion. As we drove through the town, I noticed a small makeshift hospital. Outside lay about ten people, either dead or dying, and I recall one man – thin as a stick, foaming at the mouth – making a final gesture of despair by a faint movement of his arm. He was still barely alive. When we returned half an hour later, he was dead. There is one frame that still haunts me. It is of a woman who had died of disease or sheer exhaustion, lying on the pavement with a distraught two-year-old daughter trying to revive her. That journey was the most horrifying experience of my life – the death, the horror, the stench, the sheer indifference to the dead who lay strewn all over the streets was like a vision of Hell. I would have been physically sick but for my appalling cold which prevented the stench passing through my nostrils.

Later, we went on a helicopter tour of the camps where hundreds of thousands of refugees were being sheltered. The bleak, lava-coated terrain under the volcano of Mount Nyiragongo was littered with makeshift huts stretching as far as the eye could see. Refugees carrying children, pots and pans, some with blue UNHCR sheets, were pouring into this landscape, which seemed to depict a surrealist painting of doom. The horror of Goma was a terrible denouement of the massacres that Rwanda had seen in the preceding weeks. Surely humanity had not known anything as awful, as gruesome or as savage as the Rwandan tragedy!

In Bukavu, to the south of Goma, we met the Governor of South Kivu and also the brave, dedicated UN and NGO workers who had given of their best to save humanity from this disaster. These men and women deserved the highest praise for their incredible fortitude and commitment. The Governor was a pasteur. He told us that his province had been the breadbasket of the region. It was larger than France and Italy put together. Its population was only 3 million and yet the refugees had drained all his resources. There was no food or water, only cholera, dysentery, hunger and death. By the afternoon, we were back in Kigali and I was surprised to receive a telephone call from the Secretary-General himself. He wanted a personal report from me of our tour. He is a dynamic personality, a man who will not be hemmed in by red tape. It was refreshing to work for Mr Boutros Boutros-Ghali.

That evening, back in Kigali, Peter Hansen and I took stock of the appalling tragedy that had overtaken Rwanda. Nearly a million people had been savagely slaughtered after 7 April. A million frightened Hutus had sought refuge as Internally Displaced Persons

(IDPs)[1] in the Humanitarian Protection Zone (HPZ) protected by Operation Turquoise and now over a million Hutus had poured into Goma in the most horrifying conditions; 50,000 deaths were eventually recorded from the refugee camps in Zaire. Surrounded by this tragedy, we pieced together a strategy which we outlined in a telegram sent to the Secretary-General after meetings with President Bizimungu, Vice-President Kagame and Prime Minister Twagira-mungu.

We commended the international effort for bringing succour to the refugees in Goma, but felt that a solution to the problem lay in the early return of the refugees to Rwanda. We noted that the refugee camps were being controlled by the Interahamwe and the former government militia and that UN facilities for refugee return and the BBGNU's assurances of fair treatment were not reaching the refugees. We recommended that the UN humanitarian effort should be Rwanda based to encourage refugees to return and that every effort should be made for the return to normality of a totally devastated country by reviving such facilities as water, power, transport, the airport and telecommunications.

After our closed-door meeting with the Vice-President, General Kagame addressed the media and made the following comments. First, the Broad-Based Government of National Unity would encourage refugees to return home. They need not fear persecution. Refugees returning from Goma would not be screened. Secondly, abandoned farms and properties would be restored to those who had left in panic. (When a questioner asked what would happen if a new case-load returnee (Hutu) found his property occupied by an old case-load returnee (Tutsi), Kagame replied, 'The old case-load have been unjustly banished from their country for decades. They deserve every sympathy. We shall help them. But they cannot be assisted against the legal rights of other Rwandan citizens.' Thirdly, criminals would be prosecuted according to a process of law and the UN should appoint a commission of experts which should urgently begin its work to identify and punish criminals. Finally, the new government would encourage RGF civilian and army personnel to rejoin the fold.

In their meetings with Peter Hansen, the Rwandan leaders expressed sincere appreciation for UN support and especially for the provision of aircraft for President Bizimungu's visits to Zaire and Tanzania. They also offered full co-operation to the UN's efforts to encourage the return of refugees, reopen Kigali Airport and establish UN radio broadcasts, and would facilitate access to UN personnel in carrying out their functions.

---

[1] An internally displaced person (IDP) is someone who has sought refuge within his or her native country. The definition of a refugee, on the other hand, is a person who has sought refuge outside their country of origin.

The Rwandan government attempts pacification

By now, it was apparent that, spurred on by the horrific images of Rwanda, a vast amount of international humanitarian aid was being poured headlong into the refugee camps in Zaire and Tanzania. At its height, this humanitarian aid reached an expenditure of US$2 million a day.[1] The dispensation of this aid was not placed in any political framework because no thought seemed to be given to the fact that the bulk of the refugees were not in any real danger. They had fled partly at the behest of their extremist leaders and partly in expectation that the victorious RPA would inflict the same terror on them that they had seen their own militia and the Interahamwe unleash toward the Tutsi and the moderate Hutu. At the time of the crisis, no one stopped to think that providing a permanent abode for refugees so close to the border could also lead to their militarization, with obvious destabilizing consequences in the region. Moreover, it seemed incongruous that, while the international community was very willing to spend US$2 million a day on feeding and caring for refugees, there seemed to be no provision, no budget head, no pot of gold available to revive a totally devastated country, rebuild its shattered infrastructure or assist the victims of genocide. Above all, no steps were taken to prevent extremist leaders rearming and retaining control over the mass of refugees in the camps.

The Joint Evaluation of Emergency Assistance for Rwanda (JEEAR) has referred to this anomaly in the following terms:

> Of the more than US$2 billion estimated to have been spent on the Rwanda crisis since April 1994, the vastly larger share has gone to the maintenance of refugees in asylum countries. Independent analysis of UN/DHA financial tracking figures and financial information from key individual donors broadly confirms this point. Although such a disproportionate allocation is understandable – refugees must be supported – it appears to Rwandese who have lived through the horror of genocide that the international community is more concerned about the refugees than the survivors.

During the Goma crisis, the UN Secretary-General had spoken to Rwanda's neighbouring heads of state with a view to seeking their co-operation in halting and reversing the flow of refugees. President Bizimungu sent a message to the Secretary-General appreciating his intercession and himself went on visits to all four neighbouring capitals, of course in UN aircraft which were placed at the President's disposal whenever he decided to travel abroad. (Similarly, a helicopter was provided to Rwandan leaders whenever there was a request for internal travel.) At that time, Rwandan leaders frequently expressed their gratitude and appreciation for the support provided by UNAMIR. Gradually, this appreciation ebbed away and turned to

---

[1] The JEEAR states that US$1.4 billion were spent on refugee relief in the first nine months of the humanitarian operation.

bitterness at UNAMIR's inability to support the government's effort for revival and repair of the infrastructure.

Immediately after its installation, the new government made a supreme effort to convey its message of reassurance to its people. Almost twice a week, the entire Cabinet would take off for one of the major towns and address the people gathered in the local football stadiums. I went to several such meetings in, for example, Byumba, Ruhengeri and Gikongoro, where about 10,000 local people would be addressed, first by the Interior Minister, Seth Sendashonga, who took a dynamic lead role in the proceedings, then by Prime Minister Faustin Twagiramungu, Vice-President Paul Kagame and finally President Pasteur Bizimungu. After speeches in Kinyarwanda, members of the public would be asked to come forward with their complaints and questions. I noted that the questions were not 'sponsored' by the local administration and seemed genuine because some of the complaints were harsh. For example, a Hutu woman said that she and her family had helped some Tutsis to hide during the genocide, but other neighbours had denounced her sons as collaborators and they had been taken to prison only because the denouncers sought to occupy their land. Was this the justice that the government promised?

Another example was of a recently returned Tutsi who said, 'We heard your appeal for all Tutsis who had been banished by the former government to return to their homeland. I did so and found my old house empty. So I reoccupied it. Now, one month later, the Hutu who had unlawfully seized my house has returned and reclaimed it. The prefect says that I must give it back to him. Where am I to live? And why did you ask me to return if you cannot promise me housing and work?'

For hours on end, the President would patiently reply to the questions from the people gathered in the stadium. I was impressed by the sincerity and simplicity of these meetings. There was no effort to gloss over difficult issues, nor an attempt to exaggerate the government's successes. The country and people had lived through trauma and tragedy; the return to sanity, harmony and stability was going to be long and hard. The message was that there was no easy way out, but the direction was clear.

Perhaps the most dangerous and dramatic meeting was the one in Kibuye that I attended with Seth Sendashonga before the French left the Humanitarian Protection Zone. This meeting was part of a deliberate effort to gradually introduce the new government in the hostile triangle covering the south-western corner between Gikongoro, Cyangugu and Kibuye where 1.2 million IDPs had taken refuge under the protection of Operation Turquoise. It was known that remnants of the Presidential Guard and the Interahamwe were still operating in the HPZ.

I went with Seth Sendashonga to the Kibuye stadium where about 10,000 hostile supporters of the RGF were gathered. As we entered the stadium under the guard of a tense French protection unit, we were received by boos and catcalls. We had entered the lion's den but, undaunted, Seth set about delivering his message of reconciliation on the microphone. 'This is the stadium where 6000 innocent people were bludgeoned to death,' he said. 'Their mass graves are outside this arena. But we come to you in peace and reconciliation. We are all one people. I am a Hutu. I am a minister in the new government of National Unity. Let us turn away from war and massacre. No one will be persecuted. Even known criminals will have a right to justice. You need not panic. Stay and cultivate your lands.' Seth was courageous in facing the hostile gathering. Gradually, the crowd's hostility abated and at the end, they asked questions – difficult, hard questions like 'How can we be sure that you can prevent the RPA from murdering us in revenge?' But the Interior Minister had managed to establish a rapport.

When I was asked to address the crowd, I did so in French, grabbing two children from the audience and telling the crowd that Rwandan people must never let their children face another holocaust. The UN was there to help the people of Rwanda, not to take sides in a political dispute. We would provide food, shelter, clean water, healthcare and transport for the needy. As I made this commitment, a WFP truck loaded with sacks of food drove up to the stadium with perfect timing. I told the crowd, 'We come as friends with food and when that lorry is unloaded, you can ride back on it to your villages.' They gave me a round of applause and as we left, an old woman took the microphone and said, 'I am glad you came. We were told by the radio that you were monsters, like the devil. I now see that you are like any ordinary people. We might still find peace.' When we were safely back in the helicopter, Colonel Tikoca whispered to me, 'The French caught a guy with a grenade at the gate of the stadium'. 'Thanks for telling me,' I replied. We both laughed.

UNAMIR take over from Turquoise

By mid-August, it was time for Dallaire to hand over the charge that he had so brilliantly and courageously handled to his successor – another French Canadian, Major-General Guy Tousignant. Emotional farewells were made and new faces replaced the familiar ones that we had known throughout the difficult days. General Tousignant is in a different mould to Dallaire – quiet, low-keyed, immensely calm and a brilliant logistician. He made his mark immediately.

As the changeover was due to take place on 19 August, a major dilemma was staring us in the face. It had been agreed that UNAMIR should take over the HPZ from Operation Turquoise and the Rwandan government were insisting on France's departure on the due date, 22 August. However on 9 August UNAMIR had only 1025 personnel on the ground, a fifth of its promised strength (5500). With every passing day, the situation began to look more desperate, especially as the Rwandan government had expressed formal reservations to the idea of the Franco-African contingent of Operation Turquoise (comprising units from Senegal, Chad, Mali and Guinea) joining UNAMIR.

The contrast in deployment effectiveness between UNAMIR II and Operation Turquoise was embarrassingly stark. While three months after the Security Council resolution UNAMIR could muster only 20 per cent of its formed troop strength[1] and had to wait several months longer for its full complement of equipment, France was able to deploy, within a week of the relevant resolution, 2500 men with 100 armoured personnel carriers, two Gazelle and eight Puma helicopters, a battery of 120 mm mortars, four Jaguar fighter bombers, eight Mirage fighters and reconnaissance planes!

Our troop strength was wholly inadequate to take over the HPZ from Turquoise and the promised additional battalions from Ethiopia, Malawi, Zambia and Tunisia were delayed because of logistic, air transport and budgetary difficulties. In short, bureaucratic wheels were turning too slowly to meet a critical zero hour situation on the ground. On 13 August, I was directed by New York to inquire whether the Rwandan leadership could agree to a brief delay – no more than a week or two – for the takeover. I called on Vice-President Kagame on 15 August and pleaded with him for more time. He reluctantly agreed to a week, but took the opportunity to inform me that, according to his information, the French were allowing the HPZ to be systematically looted by the militia and the RGF. He said that the French were making no effort to control the vitriolic propaganda from the 'hate' radios and that Rwandan government vehicles were being freely used by the RGF to transfer Interahamwe and militia from the HPZ to the refugee camps in Zaire. Kagame added that, in contrast with the negative attitude shown by Turquoise, the Rwandan government had co-operated with the UN by (a) accepting the transfer of the Franco-African battalion from Turquoise to UNAMIR, (b) not moving immediately into the HPZ as was their right and allowing UNAMIR to stabilize the situation, and (c) co-operating with the UN agencies and NGOs in allowing the free flow of humanitarian aid and human rights observers into the HPZ.

The same night, 15 August, I received a message at 9.00 pm asking me to meet the President. I hurried to his residence (where the fuselage of the former President's Falcon still lay wrecked beside the garden wall!) and found Vice-President Kagame and Prime Minister

---

[1] Formed troops are army contingents from member states performing a military role. They carry arms and need to be contrasted with unarmed Military Observers who perform a monitoring role.

Twagiramungu in attendance. The President came straight to the point and said he was concerned at the prospect of even a week's delay in the takeover from Turquoise. He suspected that it could be the thin end of the wedge for the French to have an excuse to stay on. He repeated the criticisms of French behaviour in the HPZ made earlier by General Kagame, adding that every passing day was creating problems for the government. He requested that, despite UNAMIR's threadbare resources, it should take over on schedule. In short, President Bizimungu was withdrawing General Kagame's earlier agreement for a week's delay.

At the meeting, the President also underlined the importance that his government attached to the appointment of a commission of experts to inquire into the genocide in Rwanda. Finally, he repeated his government's request for immediate, up-front, financial aid so that the wheels of state could begin turning again.

President Bizimungu's demand magnified our dilemma. Moreover, General Dallaire was in the process of being replaced by General Tousignant and it seemed unfair to ask General Tousignant, who had barely taken over, to make such a vital decision. Nevertheless, a decision had to be made both on military and political grounds and I admired the cool, calculated, logistic-oriented analysis that Tousignant gave of his military options. I too weighed up the political options and both of us agreed that, on balance, we should not seek an extension. Despite our scant resources and the highly unfair burden being placed on the Ghanaian battalion, which had lived through the worst horrors of the genocide and deserved a less onerous deployment, we felt we should proceed with the takeover on 22 August. The Deputy Force Commander, Brigadier-General Henry Anyidoho, was a pillar of strength at this critical juncture, bringing to bear the amazing commitment and discipline of the Ghanaian contingent. So, despite headquarters' doubts and against the firm advice of our American and European friends, Tousignant and I took the decision to take over from Operation Turquoise on the appointed date.

In desperation, I sent a telegram to headquarters to outline the scenario:

a) UNAMIR's successful replacement of Turquoise in the HPZ was crucial: success could stabilize Rwanda; failure would lead to a catastrophe worse than Goma.

b) To a population generally loyal to the former government, Turquoise was seen as saviours, UNAMIR regarded as hostile. Turquoise had elite troops, fully equipped and operated under a Chapter VII mandate. In contrast they were being replaced by jaded Ghanaians and troops (Ethiopian, Tunisian) that had not even arrived in Rwanda. UNAMIR operated under Chapter VI with threadbare logistic support.

c) It was vital that the UN humanitarian agencies should give their full support to UNAMIR so that they could win over the HPZ population's goodwill while replacing Turquoise.

d) At all costs, a second Goma had to be avoided.

Miraculously, the long-delayed Ethiopian battalion arrived on 18 August, literally dropping in from the sky unannounced. The Rwandan government had also agreed to the staying on of the Franco-African battalion which had been part of the French Operation Turquoise and, amazingly, on 22 August we had scraped the barrel and produced just enough troops to take over from Operation Turquoise. Of course, it meant vacating the rest of Rwanda of UNAMIR's presence, but our honour was at stake and we took over from the French on schedule.

The situation at the time was that the media were expecting another Goma-style blow-out at Bukavu, the southern exit point from Rwanda, as hundreds of thousands of displaced persons in the HPZ were by then on the move. There was general anticipation of 'Après France le déluge' as the media gathered, like vultures at a kill, to record another cataclysmic disaster. This time, UNHCR and the humanitarian agencies were not going to be caught flat-footed and had prepared to receive a million refugees across the border. It was a tense time for UNAMIR. However, we too had put everything into preventing a crisis. The specialized agencies and NGOs co-operated magnificently with UNAMIR to urge the population to stay behind and not to plunge, lemming-like, towards cholera, dysentery and abject deprivation as at Goma. For a tantalizing week, we held our breath as the brave Ghanaian and Ethiopian forces of UNAMIR took over from the French. They disarmed the militia, reassured the people and generally exuded an aura of calm security. There was not a single incident. The agencies provided shelter, food and solace to the mass of humanity on the move and eventually succeeded in turning most of them back. Only 20–30,000 crossed into Bukavu, thanks to the remarkably successful preventive action mounted by UNAMIR and the UN agencies. The press departed, UNHCR folded its tents on the Zaire side and the moment of crisis passed with a deep sigh of relief from everyone.

Looking back, UNAMIR's takeover from Operation Turquoise was one of its most successful operations, achieved through exemplary co-operation with the Rwandan government, the specialized agencies and with the departing Operation Turquoise. The Rwandan government was, naturally, straining at the leash to establish its sovereignty over territory that was its own but that had been under French protection. General Dallaire, General Tousignant and I pleaded long hours with the Rwandan leadership and with the RPF High Command to hold back their military forces from a precipitate entry into the sector which we felt could lead to violence and a 'second Goma'. Instead, we counselled that UNAMIR should, first, take over from the French and after providing appropriate assurances, the government should send in its civilians (customs officers, prefects, *burgomestres*) and only gradually introduce its military force into the sector. After long discussions and with some reluctance, the government agreed to our plan of action.

Persuading the UN's specialized agencies to co-operate with UNAMIR in the takeover proved an unexpectedly difficult task. This was due in part to my inexperience of UN 'internecine turf wars' and in part to the latent antagonism between humanitarian and military cultures. My simple argument was that the population in the HPZ saw Turquoise as its friendly saviours and UNAMIR as unsympathetic opponents. When UNAMIR solders went into the sector to take over from the French, it was important that they should arrive with 'goodies' with which only the humanitarian agencies and NGOs could provide them, in the form of food, blankets, medicine, clean water and other humanitarian items. At first, quoting from their book, the specialized agencies declined, but when I sat with their local heads of agencies and explained the sensitivity of the takeover and the common gain for all of us, they willingly agreed to co-operate. It was a perfect example of co-operation at the local level.

The end result was that a second Goma was averted and the eventual takeover of the HPZ by the Rwandan government was remarkably peaceful and incident free. UNAMIR helped to disarm those of the former government's militia and gendarmerie who decided to stay on in Rwanda. This process was also achieved voluntarily and peacefully. By the end of September, the whole of Rwanda was firmly under the sovereign control of the Rwandan government.

The Rwanda Emergency Normalization Plan (RENP)

From my first meeting with General Kagame on 6 July and in subsequent meetings with the President and Prime Minister, a recurring theme was the Rwandan government's fervent hope for UN support to quickly revive the shattered infrastructure of the country. I had, independently, come to the conclusion that, if peace, harmony and stability were to be re-established in Rwanda, its basic needs had to be addressed immediately. The destruction in Rwanda was total. There was no water, no power, no telecommunications, no banks, no transport, no petrol, no municipal services, no police, no government offices, no civilian government vehicles, no markets, no shops, no schools, no food. A government did exist, but it had no means or tools to govern. Cabinet members could not even contact each other on the telephone. Some ministers walked several kilometres each day to the office, which was usually a burnt-out shell of a building. The immediate need to revive the basic infrastructure of the country was writ large on every wall, which led to the formulation of my Rwanda Emergency Normalization Plan – RENP.

I divided the RENP under the following three heads:

a) An immediate loan/credit so that government could start functioning by paying salaries, importing essentials and opening hospitals, to be started in days.

b) Restoration of power, water supply, radio, telecommunications, agricultural needs and airport, to be started in weeks.

c) Training of police/gendarmerie, prison services, reopening of Central Bank, schools, municipal services, de-mining, repair of roads/bridges, revival of public transport, to be started in the coming months.

I had launched the RENP by the end of July and had refined it by mid-August. In a telegram to headquarters, I vented my frustration at vast sums of money being allocated to the refugee camps while no prospect was discernible for immediate relief internally, to a devastated country. I pleaded for a small fraction – even 1 per cent of the funds earmarked at a Geneva pleading conference – to be made immediately available in Rwanda to prevent further crises like Goma. I recommended that this liquid fund should be made available, in the form of a Secretary-General's Trust Fund, to provide the fuel for launching the RENP.

With the passage of time, my discomfort, even embarrassment, at the abundance of UNAMIR and NGO vehicles, supplies, telecommunications, etc compared with the government's lack of resources became progressively more acute. While our Milobs, secretaries, plumbers and clerks insisted on each having a car and a mobile phone, I would watch Rwandan ministers walk to their offices, their shoes covered in dust. While we could move about in helicopters and freely utilize our numerous vehicles, General Kagame told me that 70 per cent of his patrols were carried out on foot. On several occasions, the Prime Minister would travel to our headquarters in one of our borrowed four-wheelers, climb up the three floors to my office and request the use of my telephone to contact his family living abroad. He would then lean out from my office balcony and note a sea of gleaming white UN vehicles of every shape stationed in the compound. 'Can't we have a few of these – you know we don't have any vehicles for the government, not even one to receive foreign visitors,' he would ask. Strictly speaking, the UN rules did not allow the lending of our vehicles to the government, but we stretched them as best we could.

Sometime in July, one of our Canadian communication engineers came to my room and informed me that although the building housing the telecommunications unit that connected Rwanda with the international telephone system had been badly damaged, the unit itself was intact. The Canadian major said that he could repair the system if a new cable could be bought from Nairobi. In fact, Rwanda's telephone link with the outside world could be restored within hours. I asked the major the cost of the cable, to which he replied, 'Approximately US$1500'. I was delighted and promised him the cable on the next UNAMIR flight. Imagine my horror when my administration informed me that there was no budget head to pay for such development expenditure. Such expenses would be borne by the UNDP! I lost patience and handed over $1500 from my wallet, but the harsh reality dawned on me that as Special Representative of the Secretary-General, I could not even use my budget, which was financing UNAMIR operations in Rwanda to the tune of $15 million a month, to buy a $1500 cable to assist the Rwandan government. The rules stated that 'assessed' peace-keeping funds were exclusively to finance the peace-keepers. Revival of the country's infrastructure would be financed by 'voluntary' funds processed through the special agencies over which the Special Representative had no control whatsoever. This appalling reality was, in my view, the fundamental reason for UNAMIR losing ground with the Rwandan government so that, from an atmosphere of appreciation and warm cordiality in August 1994, we had descended into rancour and bitterness by the time of our departure in April 1996.

Soon after the government was formed and the National Assembly nominated, I was asked by its President (Speaker) whether UNAMIR could assist in repairing the roof of the building of the Parliament chamber, which was the only building where the National Assembly could meet and without which government business could not begin. As with most buildings in Kigali, the Parliament building had been badly hit by mortar and shell fire. The National Assembly was due to meet in ten days and with only US$2 million in the Trust Fund that Jan Pronk, the Netherlands Minister for Development, had delivered, I arranged for a Habitat representative from Nairobi to have a quick look and survey the building.[1] The excellent Dr Kuhl of Habitat arrived and saw our dilemma. Even the most urgent emergency operation by Habitat could not possibly meet our deadline. I then took the initiative and after consultation with Dr Kuhl, the UNDP Resident Representative, the Rwandan Minister for Works, UNAMIR organizers and the Dutch government representative, we gave the contract for the repair of the roof of the Parliament chamber to a local construction firm after looking at three estimates. This entire exercise, in which I was assisted by UNAMIR engineers and technicians, took about two days. The process was transparent and up front with all parties consulted. The roof was repaired in time for the Assembly to meet. We had not proceeded strictly in accordance with

---

[1] Habitat is the UN agency for housing, located in Nairobi.

UN regulations and had taken several short-cuts, but there was transparency and accountability in our decisions and actions.

Of course, the Parliament was only one of a large number of government buildings across the country that had been destroyed and needed urgent repairs. The UNDP and Habitat had recognized the importance of repairing these and just before my departure in April 1996, Dr Kuhl made the following comment to me:

> Ambassador Khan, I have good news. An emergency rehabilitation programme worth US$12m has been approved for Rwanda. Habitat will be repairing all major government buildings not only in Kigali but in all the major towns for the next 12 months. This is the breakthrough we had been working for.

I shared Dr Kuhl's delight at the 'emergency' programme having been approved and sponsored. The critical point is that it took 20 months for the emergency programme to come through after surveys, feasibility reports, approvals by committees and the seeking of appropriate financing. With a trust fund, UNAMIR peace-keeping forces could have jump-started the building-repair programme 20 months earlier and handed over to Habitat at the appropriate time. The positive impact and goodwill created might have made the difference between the success and failure of the mission.

Another example of UNAMIR peace-keeping having the capability to jump-start a damage-repair process related to the revival of Kigali Airport. It had been heavily rocketed and its instruments looted before the RGF withdrew. Even the fire engine and ambulances had been driven away so that the airport consisted only of a runway and a shattered building. One of UNAMIR's first tasks was to make the airport operational. We immediately approached the ICAO (International Civil Aviation Organization) representative in Nairobi, Dr Baliddawa, who had a team of experts flown out within 24 hours. The preliminary report indicated that the airport would require power, the restoration of basic instruments, equipment, communications and trained technical staff before it could become operational for military aircraft. Commercial traffic would follow later. The first report stated that the ICAO would assist but even an emergency programme would take three to six months. While we accepted the ICAO's emergency plan for the repair to the airport, we set our own engineers and communications experts to work. A large generator was installed by UNAMIR which provided the power. Our engineers cleared the runway and installed essential equipment which was manned by a Bangladeshi team of Milobs who controlled air movements in co-operation with our own Canadian air traffic control and helicopter unit. Within days, the airport was functional, providing an essential link with the outside world. As promised the ICAO emergency assistance came through and within six months, Sabena followed by other airlines were flying into Kigali, controlled by trained Rwandan air traffic controllers.

I will cite three further examples to illustrate how UNAMIR was capable of immediately jump-starting the process of recovery in a time-frame that, with the best will in the world, the specialized UN agencies could not match.

The first related to the request by the Rwandan Minister of Primary Education, Mr Pierre-Celestin Rwigyema, who subsequently became Prime Minister, for helicopter assistance in distributing primary school examination papers to all schools throughout the country on the same day. He explained that, the schooling system having been totally destroyed, it was essential for primary schools to start functioning again as, otherwise, an entire school year would be lost. The distribution of examination papers was the trigger that would start the process. I sympathized with the Minister and felt that there was no greater proof of normality than children going to school. With Force Commander Tousignant in full support, we worked out a meticulous schedule with the Education Minister to distribute the examination papers in a single day. It involved helicopters, four-wheelers and Milobs carrying papers to the most distant villages, but the project was successfully carried out with military precision.

Then some time in mid-1995, the Chief of Staff, Colonel Sam Kaka, telephoned me and said that, as Rwanda was now reasonably secure, he wanted the RPF's boy soldiers to return to school. He explained that the boy soldiers were, in fact, orphans of genocide victims whom the RPA had inducted into its force so that they could, at least, be provided with food, clothing and shelter. The time had now come for these children to be demobilized and return to school. There was a sufficiently large building in Butare for such a school, but it had been wrecked and looted. Kaka requested UNAMIR's help in repairing the building so that the school could become operational.

I visited the school with the Deputy Force Commander, Brigadier Sivakumar, the Minister of Education, the UNICEF representative and a representative of the RPA. There was no power, no water, the kitchen's cooking equipment was not working and sanitary outlets were totally clogged up. Since the objective of demobilizing boy soldiers was laudable, we had no hesitation in repairing the premises. Our engineers built field lavatories and repaired the water and electricity, a generator was loaned and UNICEF arranged for beds and blankets while providing basic funding for the children's housing, food and studies. Within three weeks, the school was up and running and 2000 boys were being housed in it. We were then told that a lot of pilfering was taking place from the school as it had no boundary wall. The Indian engineers agreed to erect a barbed-wire fence to secure the area, but while these engineers would do the work, the barbed wire needed to be purchased. UNAMIR had no budget for this purchase, nor had the specialized agencies. The embassies and NGOs could not help either. We drew a blank with every request. Eventually, the Indian contingent paid from its own imprest to complete the task. Thus, while we used our technicians and logistic support to repair the building, the lack of basic financing was an inhibiting factor in completing the assignment.

The third effort involved the distribution of new currency notes across Rwanda. The government had seen the former government carry across to Zaire all the currency it could lay its hands on. This currency was now the monetary unit not only in Rwanda, but also in the refugee camps. The only problem for the new government of Rwanda was that while it had virtually none of the national currency, the opposition had nearly all of it. The Rwandan government had therefore planned to change the currency with a view to neutralizing the RGF's advantage. Obviously, the exercise had to be carried out with the utmost secrecy and unerring precision. Only General Tousignant and I knew of the plan, which was again successfully completed in a single day by our excellent Canadian helicopter crew.

These successful manoeuvres were prime examples of close co-operation between UNAMIR and the Rwandan government. Strictly speaking, however, this form of assistance to the Rwandan govern-ment did not fall within our mandate. Distributing examination papers and new currency or repairing the international telephone system was not part of 'protecting civilians at risk' nor could it be justified under 'reconciliation'. Nevertheless, the Force Commander and I had not the slightest doubt that in providing these facilities we were helping the Rwandan people – both Hutu and Tutsi – in reviving and restructuring their shattered country. In the examples I have quoted, UNAMIR equipment (helicopters, bulldozers, heavy vehicles, etc) and technical manpower (communications experts, engineers, doctors, masons) were available to complete the tasks. In other important cases, equipment and technical manpower were not enough and needed to be complemented with minimal financial outlays which regrettably were not available. For instance, to repair houses, build barracks for former RGF returnees or dormitories for demobilized children, no funds were available. These vital projects that could have been justified in the mandate under the heading of national reconciliation, had to be passed over as not even US$10 million was available in the UN Secretary-General's Trust Fund, while donor countries were spending US$2 million a day in the refugee camps – money that was passing through the hands of the political leadership that stood accused of genocide in Rwanda!

All these examples illustrate that UNAMIR had the capability to repair and start up essential infrastructural services within days. The UN agencies concerned require at least three to six months for their emergency programmes to become operative. In this twilight period, there is no question of turf rivalry, as the peace-keeping engineers, logisticians and experts who are already in place as peace-keepers simply jump-start a process which they then hand over to the UN specialized agencies as soon as they are ready. What the peace-keepers lack is adequate financing and an appropriate mandate.

By mid-September, a certain calm had descended on Rwanda. The government was in full control of the country, and markets, shops and cafés were springing up all over. Deserted farmhouses were being reoccupied and ambassadors began to filter back to their posts. Sabena had opened the first commercial service since the war and a bustle of normality was apparent all over. It was now time for us to move out of the office cubby-holes that had also served as our bedrooms/dining rooms into more conventional quarters. Dr Kabia and I decided to join the military headquarters staff at the Belgian Village which is a cluster of about 12 chalets built on a hill between the Meridian Hotel and the Amahoro Stadium. The complex had been built by the Belgian government to accommodate their military experts serving in Kigali. After the murder of ten Belgian soldiers on 9 April, the Belgian Village had been abandoned and subsequently looted. General Dallaire and I had visited the village soon after the war ended and found it totally devastated. I had even smelt rotting flesh in one villa and had turned away. Nevertheless, it was an ideal location for residential quarters.

Soon the military had cleared up the mess and repaired the damage at a cost of US$300,000, and so I decided to take the plunge and move to one of the chalets. There was still no water, but at least the four-room chalet was a home with a garden and a lovely panoramic view over the hills. What specially attracted me to the Belgian Village was an excellent tennis court which promised more enjoyable exercise than the one-hour walkabout outside UNAMIR headquarters that I would undertake almost daily to keep my diabetic condition in check. So I moved to the villa and employed a Ugandan housekeeper, Loida, a hefty, cheerful woman who washed, ironed, cooked and cleaned for me with good humour.

Radio UNAMIR

From the time of my earliest reports to UN headquarters, I had felt the need for an independent UN radio station that would project the UN family's objectives and policies to the people of the region. It would also provide a much-needed public relations image in a country that was shell-shocked and war-torn. We needed to explain why we were in Rwanda, how we could help revival and normalization, where to find field hospitals, humanitarian relief centres and child immunization units, how to locate UN specialized agency units and NGOs operating in the field. This need was all the more acute in a country which was so deeply influenced by the radio culture because it had no newspapers and no television. Radio has therefore been Rwanda's main, perhaps only, source of information as was so tragically demonstrated by Radio Mille Collines during the genocide.

The UN soon agreed to start a radio station in Kigali, but obtaining the government's approval was more difficult. The Rwandan government first suggested that Radio Rwanda and the UN should combine to broadcast from one station – Radio Rwanda – which could be boosted by additional UN transmitters. I replied that amalgamating the two would lead to the UN radio station losing its independent voice. I added that projecting the objective situation on the ground, particularly to refugees in the camps, could be done with more benefit for the government through an independent UN radio station than through Radio Rwanda. The government then argued that giving permission for a UN radio station would open the door for every private radio station to broadcast from Rwanda. I responded that the UN could not be equated with private radio channels and should be given special dispensation. While these negotiations were taking place, our cause was not helped by an over-enthusiastic UNAMIR radio technician who began trial broadcasts without seeking formal permission. This strengthened the hand of those in the Cabinet – namely the hard-line RFP and also the national security guardians – who felt that UNAMIR was riding roughshod over Rwandan sovereignty. Eventually, after arduous negotiations and a helping hand from donor countries, notably the UK, the government signed a formal agreement and Radio UNAMIR went on the air on 12 January 1995, broadcasting four hours a day, two hours in Kinyarwanda and one each in French and English.

In the early days, Radio UNAMIR could be heard in about 60 per cent of the country, but with the arrival of additional transmitters donated by the UK we were able, by the end of 1995, to cover the whole of Rwanda and also the refugee camps in Zaire and Tanzania. Despite a skeleton staff and a limited budget, Radio UNAMIR made an impact. We began receiving letters from all over the country and also from the camps, asking for elaboration of information we had broadcast. The Tanzanian Foreign Minister mentioned the value of Radio UNAMIR in helping to guide refugees on developments in Rwanda and many Rwandans employed locally by UNAMIR informed us that Rwandans preferred to listen to Radio UNAMIR broadcasts because they were more objective than those of Radio Rwanda.

Our radio unit was headed by a small group of dedicated UN officials led by Zouaoui Benamadi, a distinguished Algerian journalist, and Patricia Tomé, a highly experienced and balanced radio-station operator from France who had served in Cambodia and Bosnia. These senior UN officials were assisted by an excellent staff of about 12 Rwandan journalists, technicians and interpreters. Through their commitment and zeal, they had put Radio UNAMIR on the map of Rwanda.

Training the gendarmerie

One of the first co-operative ventures between the Rwandan government and UNAMIR was to start a training programme for the gendarmerie. It was a measure of the total destruction of Rwanda's infrastructure that not a single gendarme or policeman existed when the new government took charge. Our Civilian Police (Civpol) contingent was headed by Colonel Diarra, an excellent Malian officer who had held a ministerial post in his country. He organized a two-month crash programme to train the first batch of 103 gendarmes.

The training was to be carried out by UNAMIR Civpol officers working under an RPA major at the Police Training Academy at Ruhengeri. Unfortunately, the Academy had been shelled and looted. When we inspected the premises, there was no water, electricity or telephones, no beds, no sanitation, the kitchen had been destroyed, the library ransacked and the blackboards used for fuel! However, since training the gendarmerie and police was a specific part of our mandate, we were able to divert peace-keeping funds without being questioned by the administration. UNAMIR quickly set to work to have the Academy functional and within days, we had a transformer to provide electricity, safe drinking-water, and clean latrines. We managed to repair the kitchen and provide essential utensils, books, blackboards and stationery. In collaboration with UNICEF who were fully on board regarding my RENP-oriented emergency relief programmes, we found beds, blankets and food for the young trainees. This was precisely the support that I was looking for in the repair of other sectors but which, because of bureaucratic and budgetary hurdles, we could not deliver on. We even loaned the Academy some vehicles for the staff. In this way, we had trained the first batch of 103 gendarmes by December 1994 and a further two batches of around 500 gendarmes each in two successor courses. By June 1995, UNAMIR had played a leading role in training about 1300 gendarmes.

UNAMIR's Civpol also collaborated with the Rwandan Ministry of Interior to start a programme for the training of civilian police. A building was taken over near N'Sinda and the first batch of 900 trainees was inducted under the stewardship of Major Denis Karamera, an excellent RPA officer, who was supported by 12 UNAMIR Civpol officers.

3. August – September 1994

The international community moves to justice in Rwanda

The Rwandan government's consolidation of control over its territory had been remarkably swift and effective. Though some reports of arbitrary arrests and revenge killings were received, on investigation our Milobs and human rights observers found the incidents were usually isolated cases and not part of a policy ordained from the top. In fact, one of the RPF's strengths was to admit error and not attempt a cover-up. General Kagame told me at the time that 47 of his soldiers were under arrest, eight of whom would be facing court martial for taking the law into their own hands. He added that discipline had to be maintained, but it was understandable that a young soldier, seeing someone who may have murdered his family, would lose control and seek immediate retribution. Overall, however, security prevailed, even though there were occasional killings of prefects or *burgomestres* either by Hutu hit squads, punishing moderate Hutu 'collaborators', or Tutsi extremists who felt the district officials were being too accommodating to the new returnees (Hutu) at the cost of the old (Tutsi).

The Gersony report

On 14 September, we were suddenly faced with a major crisis on our doorstep. It surfaced with a telephone call from Iqbal Riza, Assistant Secretary-General, Peace-Keeping, at headquarters, who inquired if I knew anything about a disturbing report from a UNHCR official called Robert Gersony. When I told him that neither my colleagues nor I had the slightest knowledge of Mr Gersony or his report, Riza asked me to proceed immediately to Nairobi to intercept Kofi Annan, head of the DPKO, who was on his way to Somalia. Riza added that the Gersony report was sufficiently serious for Kofi Annan to include

50

Rwanda on his way back from Somalia. On 15 September, I met Kofi Annan at Nairobi Airport where he informed me that Gersony, a senior and experienced UNHCR official, had sent a report to High Commissioner Mme Ogata in which he claimed that the RPA had carried out massive revenge killings of Hutus in Rwanda's southern belt bordering Burundi and Tanzania. Gersony claimed that the killings had taken place since June 1994, i.e. after the RPA had taken over the region. Mme Ogata had indicated to the Secretary-General that the report would shortly be made public, with highly damaging repercussions not only for the Rwandan government but also for UNAMIR. Kofi Annan stated that he would be visiting Kigali on 18 September accompanied by Gersony to inquire into the background of the report.

Back in Kigali, I was informed by Roman Orasa, the local UNHCR representative, that Gersony had been operating in the border regions with Tanzania and Burundi between June and August. In fact, his presence had only recently been known to Orasa. Gersony had not discussed his conclusions with him, but had given his report directly to the High Commissioner who had naturally been shocked by its conclusions. She had conveyed the conclusions of the report informally to the Secretary-General, sending shivers of concern all the way across the 38th floor of headquarters and down to Kigali. It was agreed that the report would be held over until after Kofi Annan's investigations and the Rwandan government's comments, particularly as it stood squarely indicted.

Kofi Annan, Gersony and Kamal Morjane of UNHCR arrived in Kigali on 18 September and were immediately conducted to UNAMIR, where General Tousignant, Dr Kabia and Brigadier-General Anyidoho joined me in listening to Gersony's conclusions. He briefed us for about two hours from detailed notes that he carried in his dossier, but did not show to us. The burden of Gersony's case was that, between June and August, he had spoken personally to victims of RPF massacres who had escaped, visited the sites where the killings had taken place and carefully counter-checked evidence. He was convinced – and he would stake his reputation on the line – that deliberate revenge killings of Hutu civilians, on a massive scale, had taken place at the hands of the RPA, operating in the southern belt bordering Tanzania and Burundi. Gersony's conclusions were that the RPA had engaged in the calculated, systematic, pre-planned killings of around 30,000 Hutus. He further concluded that the killings could only have been part of a policy emanating from the highest echelons of the RPF. The main difference between the Hutu massacre of Tutsis and the revenge killings described by Gersony was that the RPA acted with subtlety and finesse, covering their tracks with greater dexterity than the RGF militia and Interahamwe. Gersony then described several instances in detail: how people hiding in the swamps had been lured back with assurances of safety and murdered with machetes; how they had been gathered in churches and blasted by grenades. He stated that the killings had mainly taken place with machetes, hoes and blunt instruments, as gunfire would attract attention. As proof of his conclusions, Gersony pointed to the continuing exodus of Hutus from the southern belt to neighbouring countries.

We heard out Gersony in horror and with some disbelief, as his description ran counter not only to the government's professed policies but to the reports that our Milobs, UN agency field representatives, NGOs and human rights observers had been sending us.

After the briefing Kofi Annan, accompanied by Gersony, Morjane and myself, called on the Minister of the Interior, Seth Sendashonga, the Minister of Foreign Affairs, Jean Marie Vianney, and the Prime Minister, Faustin Twagiramungu. The President and Vice-President were out of the country at the time. Gersony gave a full account of his findings to his interlocutors. The Prime Minister and the two ministers heard out Gersony's indictment with politeness and equanimity. They expressed shock at Gersony's findings, rejecting them as being based on planted evidence. They did not question Gersony's bona fides. The immediate points that were made by the Prime Minister and the Minister of the Interior were:

a) While the government itself acknowledged that some individual acts of revenge had taken place, it would not be possible for the government to massacre 30,000 people without attracting the attention of the international community.

b) It was highly unlikely that the RPA would travel around with hoes, clubs and machetes to carry out its massacres, as contended by Gersony.

c) The President and Cabinet ministers had themselves been concerned at press (*Le Monde*) reports of RPA atrocities along the Tanzanian border. The President had stayed in the area for three days to observe conditions but had found that it was mainly Hutu extremists, operating from camps in Tanzania, who were killing returnees to incite fear among the refugee population. The President had seen no evidence of shallow graves or bodies floating down the Kagera River with hands tied behind backs.

After Gersony's briefing, we held an internal discussion related to his findings and conclusions. Brigadier-General Anyidoho and Colonel Tikoca (Chief of Military Observers) agreed that the incidence of revenge killings was higher in areas where the UN and NGOs were sparsely represented (e.g. Kibungo and the Tanzanian border). However, they rejected the contention that 30,000 Hutus had been massacred by the RPA in a systematic, preordained campaign. They added that several journalists had published such `sensationalist` reports but when Military Observers had examined the evidence in detail, the reports had invariably been found to be exaggerated. They were convinced that Gersony had also been subjected to such 'planted and dramatized' evidence.

Charles Petrie, Deputy Director of the United Nations Rwanda Emergency Office (UNREO) had visited the area recently and had heard rumours of massacres. He had therefore carried out a careful investigation with NGOs operating in the region. Petrie rejected the conclusion that there had been systematic, preordained massacres by the RPA. His explanation of the Hutu exodus was that the region had seen a large number of Burundi/Tanzania Tutsis return to Rwanda, especially to the border areas. These old case-load refugees had occupied lands and homes, etc and were now intent on staying on in Rwanda. These Burundi Tutsis were not like the disciplined fighting-force Tutsis of Uganda, but a more acquisitive, business-oriented group. They had carried out activities to frighten the Hutu population, probably with the connivance of local RPA commanders. The fact that there were hardly any UNAMIR blue berets or NGOs in the region had enabled this group to carry out its activities unchecked. Petrie concluded that the zone may have seen intimidation by returning Tutsis, but discounted massacres on the scale described by Gersony.

The following day, i.e. 20 September, Kofi Annan and I visited several sites in the border region. Without referring to the Gersony findings, Kofi Annan asked the UN blue berets (doctors, engineers, etc) who were working at the grassroots level in the communes about the treatment of returning Hutus to the region, The blue berets replied that about 80 per cent of the Hutu farmers from the region who had left in panic had returned. They were being absorbed and well treated by the new RPA administration. Their return had generally been smooth and peaceful. Kofi Annan then inquired about an alleged massacre in a village which had been pinpointed by Gersony. A UN major (an Australian doctor) replied that he too had heard of rumours of a massacre in the village and had gone down to investigate. He found that in fact a massacre had taken place in late July (i.e. after the formation of the new government), but it had been commissioned by a rabid Hutu extremist *burgomestre* who had been operating in the HPZ region even in late July, as there were pockets of territory still under the control of the former government. Eventually, when the RPA took over, the *burgomestre* fled to Zaire, but several of his henchmen had been apprehended. These alleged criminals were now in custody. They were being correctly treated as prisoners and their names had been given to the ICRC. At least in this case, the description given to Gersony was accurate, except that the identity of the perpetrators and victims was transposed.

Later in September, I visited a team of US and Canadian doctors operating near Kibungo from the region that Gersony had identified as the 'massacre belt'. The doctors told me that they could tell from the treatment of their patients that the killings had subsided and had been replaced by relative calm. During the April–July period they had treated patients with fresh wounds made by machetes and the like. Now their patients were coming not with wounds but with post-conflict ailments like dysentery and diarrhoea. There were practically no patients with fresh wounds.

Kofi Annan and Gersony were scheduled to leave Rwanda at 1.00 pm on 21 September. That morning, I had a meeting with Seth Sendashonga, the Minister of the Interior, and Patrick Mazimpaka, the Minister of Youth. I impressed on them that, however outrageous and incorrect Gersony's accusation may appear to them, the government's Achilles' heel was that a continuing exodus of Rwandan Hutus to Tanzania and Zaire was actually taking place and also that UN access to this region had not been readily forthcoming. After consultation with the Prime Minister, the ministers agreed that the government would announce a joint investigation in the region where Gersony had gathered his evidence.

Accordingly, at noon, Seth Sendashonga arrived at Kigali Airport and met Kofi Annan before his departure for Nairobi. It was agreed that a joint investigating team consisting of four Rwandan ministers and four UN representatives, one each from UNHCR (the minister stated that Gersony would be welcome to join the team but Gersony declined), UNAMIR, the Human Rights Commission and the ICRC, should visit the region. Gersony, who had still not given any documents in writing, was asked to identify the villages where he had gathered his information. He sat down in the VIP lounge with Seth Sendashonga and wrote out the names. The joint team visited these villages the following day and found no evidence except a mass grave dating back to April or May.

On the flight to Nairobi, Gersony expressed his complete satisfaction at the manner in which his report had been received by UNAMIR and the Rwandan government. He said that UNAMIR had treated it with due seriousness and the Rwandan government had reacted positively by appointing a joint investigating team. He could not have expected more. Kofi Annan's conclusion was that the report, 'if there was in fact a written report', should now be referred to as information which would be investigated further and that, meanwhile, it should stay in the drawer as a public airing would result in sensationalizing conclusions that had not been verified.

Regrettably, two days later, the international press was referring to the 'Gersony report' and the UNHCR spokesman was also commenting on its conclusions and the High Commissioner's directives to UNHCR staff. Subsequently, the High Commissioner addressed a formal letter to President Bizimungu in which she attached an unsigned document which, in fact, was a resumé of Gersony's allegations. Thus, instead of keeping the lid on, the 'report' fuelled more speculation, with predictably damaging results.

As expected, the President was furious with the accusations that were now public knowledge and addressed a press conference, indicting UNHCR in particular and the UN in general. He addressed a letter to the Secretary-General stating that all senior members of his Cabinet had felt deeply anguished and let down at the public airing of the 'Gersony report'. He stated that, despite the 'false accusations by Gersony, the government had demonstrated its good faith by appointing a joint investigating team in which Gersony had declined to participate. Notwithstanding, the report had been made public without even the courtesy of a written document being conveyed to them. The Rwandan government felt specially aggrieved that there was no attempt to check or verify Gersony's findings and an uncorroborated, verbal report was given credence, against the tide of general opinion by people on the ground. The UNHCR had acted like prosecutor, jury, judge and executioner rolled into one.' Although most of the Rwandan government's wrath was aimed at UNHCR, some of the anger, especially at the middle and lower levels of the governments, spread across to all the UN agencies. Most of the agency representatives reported to me that their work and standing had been undermined by the public airing of the 'Gersony report'.

From the outset, we had given Gersony the respect that he deserved as a professional. His findings were regarded as honest. We disagreed with his conclusions, but accepted the integrity of his assessment based on the evidence that he had collected. In the end, when he had pronounced himself satisfied with the reaction of the UN and the Rwandan government to his report, there was a clearly expressed understanding that the matter would await verification and should not proceed further. We shared these conclusions with a visiting US delegation. Subsequently, the public airing of the Gersony information (to date there is no written report) was therefore extremely regrettable and damaging to the UN cause in Rwanda. Incidentally, the International Commission of Experts specifically pronounced themselves against the conclusions of the Gersony findings.

My own assessment is that the Kibungo and southern border region had seen a heightened incidence of revenge killings and atrocities by Burundi Tutsis aimed at preventing the return of Hutu refugees. It is possible that these atrocities were carried out with the connivance of some RPA elements operating at a more senior level than the normal revenge killings which took place at a lower, personal level. Nevertheless, I do not accept Gersony's conclusion that the killings were part of a 'pre-ordained, systematic massacre ordered from the top'. If that were so, the ministerial visits to the HPZ, during which Cabinet ministers implored the mainly Hutu audiences in Kibuye, Gikongoro and Cyangugu to return and reconcile, would have to be regarded as a cleverly mounted facade behind which the government was ordering a massacre! Only a few days before Gersony's visit, the Minister of the Interior had asked me to procure large quantities of seeds and farm implements so that when President Bizimungu visited Cyangugu, his pleas for Hutus to return from the refugee camps in Zaire could be encouraged by promising them seeds and farming tools to restart their lives as farmers. Such requests, made privately, negate the concept of a preordained campaign of genocide.

There is a final, ironic twist to the 'Gersony report'. After Faustin Twagiramungu and Seth Sendashonga left the government in August 1995, each made statements from abroad, accusing the RPA of massacring Hutus in the region identified by Gersony. Mr Twagiramungu placed the figure as high as 300,000, and suggested that the massacre might, after all, have taken place! The irony is that these two personalities were the leading opponents of the Gersony findings when they were initially made!

The UN Experts Commission on Genocide

Understandably, the issue of crime and punishment had a deep resonance in Rwanda. Following the genocide, the need for justice and banishing 'the culture of impunity' pervaded the entire national psyche of the Rwandan people. To them, deliverance from the scourge of genocide required that its perpetrators should immediately be tried, whether they were within or outside the country. For those criminals who were in Rwanda – the small fish – the existing system of justice was inadequate. Rwanda had no laws relating to genocide. Moreover, the entire judicial system, like everything else in the country, had been totally destroyed. There were no judges, prosecutors, magistrates, court officials (greffiers), gendarmes or police. There were no prison officials to guard the growing number of prisoners. Nor were there buildings that could serve as courts. The entire system of internal justice needed to be restructured quickly to start the trials. Of course, there were no funds to even begin the start-up of the judicial process. Yet the clamour for the judicial process to start delivering was very loud.

The major figures accused of genocide – the big fish – were now outside Rwanda. They were living in neighbouring countries like Zaire, Cameroon, Gabon, Togo, Tanzania or Kenya. The more affluent had taken up residence in Western cities like Paris, Brussels, Montreal or Geneva. Few of these personalities sought the shadows of anonymity. The majority lived ostentatiously, visiting restaurants, giving statements and publicly questioning the accusation of genocide. Their line was that Rwanda had seen a civil war in which killings and atrocities had taken place on both sides of the ethnic divide. Both sides were guilty.

It was against this background that Rwandan leaders expected international support for a tribunal to try criminals accused of genocide. They also anticipated financial aid to start up their internal judicial system. For an international tribunal to be created on the lines of the recently formed International Criminal Tribunal for former Yugoslavia, it was necessary, as a first step, for the UN Security Council to officially examine whether genocide had been committed in Rwanda. In fact, member states had been reluctant to accept that genocide had taken place and the first reference from the Security Council to the term 'genocide' did not occur until 27 May. Against this background, the government pressed hard for the Secretary-General to nominate the Commission of Experts that the Security Council had called for in its Resolution no. 935.

The Experts Commission was announced by the Secretary-General on 26 July and comprised Ambassador Atsu Koffi Amega of Togo, as Chairman, Mme Habi Dieng of Guinea and Mr Salifou Fomba of Mali. As soon as I learnt the names of the Experts Commission, I realized that Rwanda would react negatively as all three nominees belonged to francophone African countries. Sure enough, on 5 August, President Bizimungu expressed to me his profound concern at the Secretary-General's choice, indicating reserve not only at their nationalities, but also because at least two – Mme Dieng and Mr Fomba – were not regarded by him to have sufficient experience and seniority to perform the task. It took all my powers of persuasion to dissuade the President from rejecting the Commission.

The Experts Commission paid several visits to Rwanda, held discussions with Rwandan leaders and UN officials and travelled to distant villages where massacres had occurred. Unfortunately, the Rwandan government's reservations regarding their nationality and experience had filtered through to them and Mme Dieng and Mr Fomba remonstrated with me at the government's attitude towards them. They stated with commendable maturity, however, that the government's negative remarks would not prevent them from fulfilling their mandate and from reaching an objective verdict. The Chairman, Mr Amega, was a particularly mature and learned personality who managed to soften the jagged edges of the Commission's sensitivities.

On 1 October, the Commission of Experts issued its interim report which it confirmed later. The following conclusions of the report are particularly relevant and read as follows:

a) Individuals from both sides to the armed conflict have perpetrated serious breaches of international humanitarian law, in particular of obligations set forth in Article 3 common to the four Geneva Conventions of 12 August 1949 and in Protocol I additional to the Geneva Conventions and relating to the Protection of Victims of Non-International Armed Conflicts of 8 June 1977;

b)   Individuals from both sides to the armed conflict have perpetrated crimes against humanity in Rwanda;

c)   Acts of genocide against the Tutsi group were perpetrated by Hutu elements in a concerted, planned, systematic and methodical way. These acts of mass extermination against the Tutsi group as such constitute genocide within the meaning of Article II of the Convention on the Prevention and Punishment of the Crime of Genocide. The Commission has not uncovered any evidence to indicate that Tutsi elements perpetrated the acts committed with the intent to destroy the Hutu ethnic group as such.

d)   The Commission of Experts has recommended that the Security Council take all necessary and effective action to ensure that the individuals responsible for the foregoing grave violations of human rights in Rwanda during the armed conflict are brought to justice before an independent and impartial international criminal tribunal.

e)   In order to enhance the far and consistent interpretation, application and adjudication of international law on individual responsibility for serious human rights violations and to achieve the most efficient allocation of resources, the Commission has further recommended that the Security Council amend the Statute of the International Criminal Tribunal for the Former Yugoslavia so that it can consider crimes under international law committed during the armed conflict in Rwanda.[1]

The report – particularly sub-paragraph (c) – appeared to fully vindicate the government's position that genocide had been perpetrated by elements of the former government. It also recommended the setting up of an International Criminal Tribunal for Rwanda (ICTR). Subsequently, I did not hear of complaints from the government against the selection of the team of experts. Curiously, however, the government never fully exploited the conclusions contained in the Commission's report.

The International Criminal Tribunal for Rwanda (ICTR)

Following the report of the Commission of Experts, the Security Council was under pressure from all sides to appoint an international criminal tribunal for Rwanda. The Rwandan government had conveyed to the UN that they wanted the tribunal to be located in Rwanda, the death penalty to be retained, criminals to serve out their sentences in Africa, Rwandan judges to be appointed to the tribunal and Rwanda's own jurisdiction over all criminals to be accepted. In conveying these points, I recognized that the Rwandan government was grandstanding a bit for the benefit of strident public opinion and that these demands were their maximal positions and were negotiable.

---

[1] Interim report of Commission of Experts presented to Security Council Document no. S/1994/1125, dated 4 October 1994.

When the draft resolution outlining the ICTR's constitution was presented to the Security Council in the fourth week of October, it contained a number of points that were at considerable variance from Rwanda's maximal stand. I was concerned, however, that the Security Council intended to vote on the resolution within a few days, on 4 November. I felt that without adequate explanation of the rationale for the ICTR's constitution, Rwanda could easily vote against the resolution. I immediately telephoned New York, suggesting a postponement of the Security Council vote in order to enable basic discussions to take place with the Rwandan government. I was told that there were still four days before the vote and there was adequate time for the Rwandan Permanent Representative to discuss the issues beforehand.

I could not help feeling that UN headquarters and the Security Council were being insensitive and unfair to Rwanda. First, the new Rwandan Permanent Representative, Ambassador Manzi Bakuramutsa, had taken over charge only a few weeks earlier and was hardly in a position to discuss complex legal issues in depth.[1] Secondly, instructions that could enable him to have a meaningful discussion at UN headquarters were hardly likely to be sent 'in four days' considering that the Prime Minister had no telephone, no residence (he still lived on the fifth floor of the Meridian Hotel) and a one-man office. The Foreign Minister was in no better position to exchange detailed briefs with his Permanent Representative. It was typical of the world to pay little heed to the total devastation that existed in Rwanda and expect it to function like a smooth, well-oiled machine running on all cylinders!

For the only time during my tenure as SRSG in Rwanda, I used my national connections and briefed Ambassador Marker, Pakistan's Permanent Representative at the UN, on the folly of the Security Council hurtling towards a resolution on the ICTR without discussing the issue with the Rwandan government. I explained to Ambassador Marker, who was also on the Security Council, that out of about eight points on which there were differences between the UN and Rwanda, at least five could be resolved by a thorough dialogue explaining the rationale of the UN's legal stand. The points of difference that would remain were the death penalty and the ICTR's location but, even on these, I felt Rwanda would agree to disagree and not vote against the resolution. I argued that it would be regrettable if Rwanda voted against a resolution that concerned it directly. Marker spoke to his colleagues on the Council, notably the US Permanent Representative, Ambassador Madeleine Albright, who quickly agreed to a short extension, until Tuesday 8 November. Meanwhile, I urged the Rwandan leadership either to send the

---

[1] Ambassador Bakuramutsa assumed charge as Rwandan Permanent Representative on 24 August 1994.

Minister of Justice to the Security Council or to receive a senior legal expert from the UN. They agreed to the latter.

By a strange twist of fate, the senior legal official who was scheduled to arrive for discussions in Kigali on Wednesday 2 November had an accident while bicycling to his office. He was replaced by the head of the Legal Department, Dr Hans Correll, who was not able to arrive in Kigali before the afternoon of Friday 4 November. The Rwandan Cabinet (Conseil d'Etat) meets every Friday and by the time Correll met the PM on the morning of Saturday 5 November, the die was cast. Rwanda had decided to vote against the resolution on the International Criminal Tribunal for Rwanda, which was passed on 8 November. The irony is that when Judge Goldstone paid his first visit to Rwanda on 11 December and explained the reasons for the decisions that the tribunal could not have the death penalty and that the location of the tribunal's site would be in Arusha but that the Deputy Prosecutor's office would function from Kigali, the government of Rwanda publicly gave its support to the tribunal. Greater sensitivity towards Rwanda would certainly have led to Rwanda abstaining, if not voting in favour of Resolution 935 setting up the ICTR.

The human rights mission

On 2 August, the High Commissioner for Human Rights, Mr Ayala Lasso, visited Rwanda, responding to the clamour for a large contingent of human rights observers to be assigned to Rwanda. Ayala Lasso had a difficult and delicate task ahead of him which he handled with skill and composure. On the one hand, he had to quickly find the funds, the personnel and a team leader in order to respond to media and foreign government pressure for an effective team of human rights observers to be assigned to Rwanda. The pressure had built up after the Gersony report and other media criticism that only three human rights observers were assigned to Rwanda and had been operating without financial or logistic support. This was largely true as Karen Kenney, the Irish leader of the three-member team, lived in UNAMIR accommodation, used our military vehicles and telephones and shared our military rations because they had been given practically no budget. In exasperation, Karen Kenney resigned and made a statement to the press highly critical of the human rights operation in Rwanda.

On the other hand, Ayala Lasso had to convince the Rwandan government of the need for a large human rights mission in Rwanda. The first questions that the Rwandan leaders asked of human rights representatives were: 'Where were you when we were being mercilessly slaughtered during the genocide? Now you want to send hundreds of monitors to ensure that we behave correctly, despite the massive provocation? Should your monitors not be reporting on the activities of the perpetrators of genocide who are still active in the refugee camps?'

Ayala Lasso answered these questions tactfully. He identified three broad tasks: the first, to look back and examine the evidence of genocide which would be shared with the government and with the ICTR; the second, to ensure that human rights were observed and any violations duly investigated and recorded; the third, to train the judicial cadres – magistrates, prosecutors, defence attorneys, etc – in order to revive the judicial system that had been totally devastated.

Mr Lasso obtained the government's approval and, by the end of October, over 100 human rights observers had arrived in Rwanda. The head of the team was an Australian, William Clarence, who had long experience in human rights issues and also with UNHCR. My advice to Ayala Lasso was to ensure proper funding and logistic support for the monitors as the media would be ready to pounce on any shortfall that made them appear unable to perform their duties effectively. I noticed the difficulty Clarence was having with his monitors: many of them seemed either to be university dropouts looking for jobs or idealistic crusaders who did not easily conform to office discipline and teamwork. After a year in the post, Clarence left in some acrimony and was replaced by Ian Martin, a highly skilled, experienced and focused officer who had already served as head of Amnesty International and had led the Human Rights Observer Mission in Haiti.[1] By the time Martin took over, the number of observers had risen to 147, but the problem of funding had not been effectively resolved, leading to breakdowns in future planning.

The Special Rapporteur on Human Rights

The Human Rights Commission had also appointed René Degni-Segui of the Ivory Coast as its Special Rapporteur to Rwanda. Mr Degni-Segui was a regular visitor to Rwanda who made a comprehensive assessment of events through visits, discussions and interviews. His method of inquiry was extremely thorough and he produced reports that were objective, incisive and balanced.[2] These reports confirm the view of the International Commission of Experts that genocide was committed in Rwanda. They also severely criticize the politicization and militarization in the refugee camps while, at the same time, they take the government to task over the Kibeho incident (see Chapter 6) and the appalling overcrowding in the prisons.

I found Mr Degni-Segui to be a man of wisdom and high integrity. It is extremely difficult for an outsider who comes on occasional visits

---

[1] Ian Martin was subsequently appointed SRSG in East Timor.
[2] Report of Special Rapporteur on situation of human rights in Rwanda, S-C Document no. A/50/709-S/1995/915, dated 2 November 1995.

to a theatre of operations to fully comprehend the deep undertow of sentiments. In my experience, two outstanding personalities, René Degni-Segui and Richard Goldstone (who would be the Chief Prosecutor of the ICTR), possessed the rare gift of feeling the real pulse of the Rwandan people and seeing issues in sharp focus. Their ability to make these assessments was as much due to their experience and sagacity as to their propensity to spare no effort in seeking the truth.

Nyarbuye

In early September, I had taken a helicopter trip to Rusumo, the border crossing-point between Rwanda and Tanzania. Having completed my visit to the local UNAMIR regiment, I found we had time to spare so the helicopter pilot inquired if I would like to drop in at a village called Nyarbuye which was a ten-minute flight from the border. My helicopter party consisted of six UNAMIR staff and included the RPA Liaison Officer, Major Frank Kamanze, who, like me, had never been to Nyarbuye, but had heard of it as one of the worst massacre sites in Rwanda.

We were soon circling over an imposing hilltop church – an impressive structure commanding the heights over the rolling valleys in one of the poorer regions of Rwanda. As the helicopter landed in a field adjacent to the church, I became aware of an eerie silence that surrounded the church and its outhouses. There was absolutely no sign of life.

My unscheduled visit to Nyarbuye turned out to be one of the most defining moments of my life. During my stay in Rwanda, I had seen shallow graves, dead bodies scattered on the ground, in hospitals or in housing compounds, mass deaths in Goma through cholera and exhaustion, but none of these macabre experiences could compare with the sheer horror that I witnessed in Nyarbuye.

The massacre at Nyarbuye took place soon after the genocide started on 6 April. As news of marauding killers spread in the prefectures, about 4000 Tutsis living in the region sought sanctuary in the church at Nyarbuye, the only safe haven in the vicinity. It was not long before the Interahamwe surrounded the church, intent on carrying out their evil intentions. At first, the priests negotiated with the killers who seemed willing to discuss a safe outlet. Unknown to the priests, however, was the reckoning by the Interahamwe that they needed reinforcements to carry out their task efficiently. So they played for time while calling up the Presidential Guard and the armed militia from Kibungo, the provincial capital. When the armed reinforcements arrived, negotiations were abruptly aborted and the priests given half an hour to save their skin or suffer the same fate as the beleaguered Tutsis. At 5.00 am, the priests abandoned the church, which was the signal for the massacre to begin. The killers moved in, hacking with machetes, axes and hoes. They spared neither women nor children and leaving nothing to chance, they first cut the tendons around the ankles to stop the able-bodied from running away. The slaughter continued for two days and when the killers got tired of killing with axes, they resorted to filling rooms with women and children and blowing them up with grenades.

As we entered the courtyard next to the church, we found hundreds of corpses of men, women and children lying scattered about or piled up in a corner. The flesh was still on their bones and most of the bodies still wore the clothes that they were wearing at the time of the massacre. As we entered this macabre, nightmarish scene, the smell of decaying flesh was overpowering. We then entered the church itself. There, inside this impressive building, lay the remains of around a hundred corpses. The dead bodies were scattered around the alter, in the aisles, on the benches and all around the church. The bodies were lying unclaimed, rotting, part eaten by dogs.

Dazed and horrified at this gruesome scene, we moved on to a small medical centre next to the church. As we approached it, two fat dogs padded out of the room. By then, two of my colleagues were overcome by the horror that they had witnessed and opted out of the rest of the walkabout. In the small room at the medical centre, I saw the massacred bodies of about 40 children, all between the ages of three and ten. They had been slaughtered in the room with machetes and axes. Some were locked arm-in-arm and were presumably brothers and sisters. The dogs we had disturbed were obviously feeding on the rotting carrion.

As we left the church, numbed and horrified, we saw a group of five women standing at the edge of the field. They were the first human beings we had sighted since arriving at the church. I approached and spoke to them with Major Kamanze interpreting.

This was what they told us. The group considered themselves lucky to have escaped the massacre. They were heading for the church when they saw the Interahamwe encircling the compound, so they shrank back and hid in the surrounding swamps. On the fateful day, when the killings started, they could hear the screams, the sound of gunfire and explosions. For two days, the slaughter continued until, having completed the job, the Interahamwe left the site. So horrific was the scene that no one dared go back to the church for months. The compound had been completely deserted and the bodies had lain there unclaimed and unburied.

One woman in the group was a survivor. She was young and well built. She had a gash in her neck and another on her forehead. She said she had been left for dead in the courtyard after the Interahamwe had attacked her with machetes. Two of her small children had been killed. She had lain unconscious, bleeding profusely, under a heap of dead bodies. Fortunately, that night rain fell which revived her and as the killers had left, she crawled out of the church into the swamps where she was 'saved' by the women who were already hiding there. Our visit to Nyarbuye was impromptu as was the chance meeting with the survivors. I have no doubt that their story was authentic.

When the Secretary-General visited Rwanda in July 1995, I insisted that he visit the church at Nyarbuye. By then, most of the bodies had been buried and those that had been left for visitors to see were now skeletons with their flesh picked bare by carrion eaters.

Sainte Hélène

In stark contrast with the awful, gruesome experience of Nyarbuye, I was given the following account of a brave, 12-year-old Hutu girl whom I shall call Sainte Hélène. It happened around June 1994. During the frenzied massacre of Tutsis by gangs of marauding Interahamwe, houses had been marked out for the bestial killings that were triggered by the air crash that killed President Habyarimana. During the weeks that followed, bloodthirsty gangs of Interahamwe mercilessly hunted down their prey.

At the height of the massacres, in a middle-class household of Kigali, a Tutsi family was undecided whether to seek shelter in a UN-guarded sanctuary or to make a run for it to Burundi when the Interahamwe arrived outside their home. Seized with panic, the elders had just enough time to hide the wife and four small children in the attic before the gang of killers burst into the house. They asked about the rest of the family and were told that the wife and children were visiting friends. Seeing enough of a quarry among the elders to satisfy their murderous lust, they lined the family up against a wall and murdered them. Their corpses were then dragged into the pick-up that had brought the gang of killers and dumped in a mass grave on the outskirts of Kigali. Peeping through narrow cracks in the loft, the mother and the four children watched this gruesome scene, in a cold, petrified silence. The Interahamwe did not stay to search the house, probably because they had others marked to visit. They moved on, leaving the mother and her children paralysed with fear, hiding silently in the loft.

Hours passed. Night fell and morning came, but the mother was too frightened to take any risks because, all day long, she could hear the chants of the crazed gangs of the marauding killers rampaging through the streets. Besides, their neighbours were Hutu who could easily betray their presence to the killers. So they stayed in the loft. Night fell again, but no one dared descend to the living quarters. By next morning the children were hungry and thirsty, not having eaten for 48 hours. The mother was now desperate and could not stand the deprivation any longer. So, at 5.00 am, she crept down to the kitchen, taking care not to switch on a light. In total darkness, she opened the refrigerator and lit the stove to cook some food. The smoke and smell of cooked food wafted into the adjoining house, occupied by the Hutu family. Either out of innate hostility to the Tutsis or to ingratiate themselves with the Interahamwe, the neighbours immediately alerted the local militia to signs of life in the Tutsi neighbour's home. Within minutes, the killers swept into the house, grabbed the Tutsi mother and led her away to the mass grave where, after being hacked to death, she was thrown into the pit where the rest of the family had been dumped. All this unbelievable horror had been witnessed by the four small children who remained hidden and starving in the loft. Hungry, dehydrated and petrified, the children stayed numbed in the attic.

Next door, in the Hutu family who had betrayed their Tutsi neighbour to the Interahamwe, lived Hélène, one of three daughters. Hélène was 12 years old. She had known and played with the Tutsi children next door. She had seen the bodies of her Tutsi neighbours thrown into the van and she had heard her father call in the Interahamwe to murder the Tutsi mother. Having taken a count of the bodies, Hélène realized that the children were probably hiding in the house. That night, as it grew dark, Hélène prepared some food, stole out of her house and entered the eerie silence of the house next door. She could see the congealed blood still lying on the floor, but she crept in, laid the food in a prominent place and tiptoed back to her home.

The following night, Hélène went back with more food and was gratified to see that the plate that she had left the night before had been taken. She now realized that her little friends were hiding somewhere in the house. She dared not call out to them in case their presence became known to her parents or to the Interahamwe. So, every night, Hélène would come to the dark house, leave a plate of food and then kneel in prayer for the lives of the children.

Soon, the tide turned. The interim government and the murderous Interahamwe were being defeated in battle and were now on the run. The Tutsi-dominated RPF began converging on Kigali and it was now the turn of the Hutus to leave their homes and run. Hélène's family saw the writing on the wall. They decided to make for Goma. That night, Hélène made her last visit to her neighbours' house, left a plate of food and prayed for their salvation. Above, in the loft, the Tutsi children were unaware of the drama in the streets. Hélène and her family, like thousands of others, abandoned their house and headed for Goma. Soon afterwards, Kigali fell to the RPF; the Tutsi children were saved and were adopted by their aunt who arrived from abroad.

Hélène's family now began their trek to Goma, on foot. They walked hundreds of kilometres without food or water, following the swarm of fleeing Hutus. The journey was horrendous. People lay by the wayside dying of exhaustion or dysentery. Children roamed

about abandoned by their families. The same Interahamwe that had
bludgeoned Tutsis to death now demanded the last franc of 'protection money' from fleeing Hutus. Somehow, Hélène and her family
reached Goma alive. There, among half a million other refugees they
were surrounded by horror, squalor, disease and death. And today,
somewhere in Rwanda, or perhaps meandering in the forests of
Congo, lives an 18-year-old saint called Hélène.

'What was the underlying reason for the genocide in Rwanda?' is a
question that has frequently been asked of me. I have no plausible
answer. Historians, sociologists and political analysts who have a
deep knowledge of the region have analysed the causes of this most
gruesome human catastrophe and have put forward their reasons
and theories. I claim no such profound knowledge. My views are
simply those of a close observer of the Rwandan scene for nearly two
years.

I believe there is no single explanation for the genocide, but a
confluence of several factors that came to a head in April 1994. The
over-population analysis, projected by some sociologists, was clearly
a contributing factor, but not, in my opinion, the sole explanation for
the genocide. This view assumes that Rwanda had reached a point of
over-population that, given the sudden decline in international cash
crop values, made genocide inevitable. This explanation for the
genocide does not stand up to close scrutiny. If it were so, countries
like Bangladesh and parts of India and China would have seen
genocide several years ago. Moreover, Rwanda under Habyarimana
had been one of the more successful countries of Africa and was
considered a model state in terms of development. The 'cheese and
mice' theory (in which experiments with a constant amount of cheese
being given to an increasing number of mice leads, after a given point
of 'population density', to the mice killing each other) does not offer
the sole explanation for the genocide.

A second contributing factor was the intrinsic tension between the
two ethnic groups. Hutus and Tutsis had lived in relative peace in
Rwanda and Burundi, but the previous four decades had seen an
escalating incidence of massacres and civil wars that had left deep
scars of hatred and suspicion between the two communities. However, similar ethnic divisions within a geographic unit have existed
throughout the world, causing tensions and conflicts but rarely
leading to genocide, as for example, the Berber and Arab in North
Africa, the Aryan and Dravidian in South Asia, the European and
African in Southern Africa. The fact is that the Hutu and Tutsi
shared the region in relative tranquillity for centuries, inter-
marrying, following the same religion and adopting the same customs, language and traditions. Ethnic rivalry cannot, by itself, be
viewed as the cause of genocide in Rwanda. Clearly this hostility was
primed and fanned by other forces.

A third factor that ignited the tragedy was the influence of the colonial powers, particularly during the previous 50 years when Western norms and moral standards were force-fed to a traditional African society. The demands of impeccable democracy, of multi-partyism and of modern, western norms of governance provided a destabilizing influence on the established social and political structure that led to anarchy and chaos, in which the influence of an evil, vengeful elite provided the match that ignited the volatile mix.

A fourth factor is the extraordinary docility and compliance to command of the Rwandan people. Nowhere in the world could such hardship, such torture, such unbearable pain be suffered in silence and with such fatalistic acceptance. Traditionally, the Rwandan people have silently obeyed the command of their leaders. The call of the shepherd is followed by the flock without demur, as though it were an order from God. I have seen this resignation in the over-crowded prisons of Rwanda, on the hilltop at Kibeho, in the festering camps of Goma, where this mass of humanity moved compliantly to their doom on the orders of their immediate leaders. This attitude was perhaps an important contributing factor in the genocide, when the narrow, ruling elite called on the masses to eliminate the Tutsi and those who supported them (the moderate Hutus). Unquestioningly, the communes, the villages and towns followed the edict of their leaders. Unquestioningly, the Tutsis walked silently to their slaughter. Unquestioningly, the mass of Hutus followed their leaders into the camps in Goma. There was an almost hypnotic compliance with the commands of their leadership.

Each analyst would give his own weightage to the various factors in play. In my opinion, all four basic factors outlined above converged to trigger the genocide in Rwanda.

4. October – December 1994

Persuading refugees to return home

Rwanda begins recovery

By October, three months had passed since my arrival and the gruesome, turbulent period of Rwanda's recent past was over. Pain and anguish had given way to a stunned, numbing silence. The civil war had ended with a clear military victor. A new government had been formed to grapple with the deep problems created in the wake of genocide. Over two million refugees had moved to Zaire, Tanzania and Burundi. Nearly half a million of the old refugees (Tutsis) had returned, but there was a continuing exodus of Hutus out of Rwanda. Some of those who left in panic – the new case-load (mainly Hutu) – had returned, but the refugee camps were increasingly becoming a source of tension and violence. Rwanda itself was shattered, physically and psychologically, its anger sharpened by the international community's inability or unwillingness to provide it with basic cashflow aid that would help begin the task of reconstruction.

In UNAMIR, we were now able to lift our eyes from the immediate crisis and assess the tasks that lay ahead. It was a time for stocktaking. On the positive side, while reports of banditry, revenge killings and overcrowding in prisons were a source of concern, the overall climate of security was as welcome as it was unexpected. Credit for this achievement was due, mainly, to the discipline and motivation of the RPA whose cadres, even in the flush of victory, showed commendable composure and restraint. This relative tranquillity helped to lower tension and to build a base of co-operation between UNAMIR, the UN specialized agencies and NGOs on the one hand and the Rwandan government on the other.

On the negative side was the realization that the bulk of the two million refugees were not returning. This was partly due to the intimidatory hold of the extremist political cadres who had been allowed to dominate the refugee camps, and partly because the refugees feared retribution on return to Rwanda. Reconciliation could not be contemplated until the bulk of the refugees decided to return home and face transparent justice.

By October, UNAMIR was nearing optimum strength and the long-promised equipment in the form of armoured personnel carriers, heavy vehicles, generators, computers, etc was finding its way into Rwanda from distant peace-keeping operations like Somalia, Mozambique, Kuwait and Cambodia. The transportation of this material to land-locked Rwanda was a particularly tortuous and expensive exercise which had been one of the reasons for the long delay. Ironically, however, the troops and the equipment reached full throttle only when UNAMIR's peace-keeping operations were hardly necessary and the need of the hour was for a post-conflict, peace-building effort.

I wondered how 5500 fully equipped UN troops would keep themselves occupied if they did not have a peace-building mandate. I therefore renewed my efforts to revive the RENP and for authority to expand the mandate towards peace-building. My UN colleagues told me that UN peace-keepers had dug tube wells in Somalia, built roads and bridges in Cambodia, de-mined in Kuwait and helped train cadres in Mozambique. I was hopeful that, in addition to their role as peace-keepers, UNAMIR could engage in a similar peace-building exercise in Rwanda. For the present, however, our formed troops had their hands full helping the RPA to establish law and order, transporting prisoners, refugees, agricultural seeds and food from one corner of Rwanda to another, treating the sick and the injured, helping in communications and assisting the specialized agencies in distributing humanitarian aid.

On 12 and 13 October, President Mary Robinson of Ireland came to Rwanda. I accompanied her to Goma where she visited all the Irish charities operating in the camps. President Robinson was a most dignified, gracious and dynamic personality whose caring and humane approach left a deep impact on all those who met her. She was well informed and completely focused on the problems being faced by the people of Rwanda. I recall the incident when her Zairean hosts asked the President to meet the Committee for Social Welfare in the Goma camps which consisted mainly of the RGF extremist representatives. President Robinson sized up the group immediately and whispered to me, 'This will be the quickest and coldest handshake ever!' I also recall President Robinson meeting two Irish lads who had come out to Goma to help with one of the charities. At the height of the Goma cholera crisis, there were hundreds of dead bodies that no one wanted to bury. Every charity agency, NGO, even the Zairean government declined to touch the decaying cadavers. Not even financial reward could induce private contractors to carry out the gruesome task. Then, up stepped these two Irish boys and volunteered to do what had to be done. They rolled up their sleeves, dug up the shallow graves and buried the bodies deep enough to avoid contamination. It was typical of President Robinson that she recognized and greeted these young heroes.

Operation Retour

As the dust settled in Rwanda and some semblance of order and elementary governance was becoming discernible in the country, the main preoccupation of the international community, Rwanda's neighbours and Rwanda itself was the need to persuade the refugees and the IDPs to return home. The voluntary return of these refugees and IDPs in dignity and safety was the central political issue in Rwanda. Durable peace and reconciliation could not be conceived without the return of the bulk of this population. Of the two categories, urgent priority was given to the 1.2 million IDPs who had gathered in the south-western corner of Rwanda formerly secured by Operation Turquoise – the Humanitarian Protection Zone. The reason for this urgency was that the Rwandan government was eager to take full control over its territory. It did not want to see protected 'no-go zones' in its own backyard. Moreover, the RPF was convinced that these IDP camps were hotbeds of guerrilla activity and that remnants of the RGF militia and Interahamwe were operating from them. The government was eager therefore to close the IDP camps and root out the anti-state elements. For the UN and its agencies, priority in addressing the IDPs also made sense because it was easier to mount repatriation campaigns from within Rwanda than from outside.

Accordingly, UNAMIR evolved a plan called Operation Retour, aiming to persuade the IDPs to return home voluntarily. The plan was discussed with the UN agencies and NGOs and once their approval had been obtained, it was explained to the Rwandan government who, despite some scepticism, came on board. The plan consisted of a joint UN–government operation in which the IDPs would be informed of arrangements and facilities for their return home. These facilities included housing, transportation and humanitarian welfare through the setting-up of way-stations and welcome centres in the communes. All this data was collected at the computerized Integrated Operations Centre (IOC) located in the Ministry of Rehabilitation.

Operation Retour was an important forerunner to the task of persuading refugees living in neighbouring countries to return home. This would be more difficult because the element of intimidation was greater than in Rwanda and the government and UN's capacity to influence less. It was felt that the success of Operation Retour could later be used to persuade refugees in neighbouring countries to travel down the same road. Despite the Rwandan government straining at the leash to forcibly close the camps, they co-operated with UNAMIR and the agencies in the combined operation.

After a slow start, Operation Retour built up significantly so that by December 1994, about 300,000 IDPs had gone back to their villages in transport provided by a combined UN–Rwanda operation. These were heady days in which the RPA and the UN were co-operating closely with positive results. There was a voluntary melt-down of IDP camps in the Cyangugu and Kibuye areas which saw only a few IDPs travelling across the lake to join the refugees in Zaire. Some hard-core militia moved to other IDP camps in the Gikongoro region, but the majority of IDP camp-dwellers went home to the 13 communes that had been identified as the ones from which they had originated.

By the end of December, Operation Retour was beginning to slow down and the RPA's impatience to move in and forcibly close the remaining camps surfaced again. There were ultimatums bandied about ('We shall take over IDP camps by the end of December,' said Radio Rwanda; '17 December,' said the Prefect of Gikongoro). Accordingly, in a meeting with Vice-President Kagame on 24 December, I pleaded strongly against ultimatums and precipitate action for a forcible closure of the camps. I argued in favour of reinvigorating joint efforts for a voluntary melt-down of the camps. In the most positive and co-operative meeting with Kagame so far, he agreed not to insist on forcible closures and to increase the joint effort at voluntary persuasion. The ambience at the meeting was specially relaxed and we ended up talking of playing tennis. General Kagame accepted General Tousignant's invitation to dinner.

Given the boost of the Vice-President's support, Operation Retour saw a further rapid melt-down of IDP camps in the former HPZ. The IDP population was reduced to about 250,000 that now gathered in eight camps near Gikongoro. Thus, nearly 700,000 IDPs had gone home voluntarily in one of the most successful but unheralded episodes of Rwanda's post genocide history. The success story of re-settling these 700,000 IDPs in their communes was due mainly to the excellent co-operation between UNAMIR, the specialized UN agencies, and NGOs on the one hand, and between the Rwandan government and the UN family on the other. This successful operation went unrecognized, which only underlines the truism that good news is no news.

Tension in refugee camps
Proposal for separation and relocation

By October, the refugee situation in Zaire, Tanzania and, to a lesser degree, Burundi had become the main cause of tension and concern for the region. This was because the refugees were regrouping and organizing themselves under the former leadership into a credible military threat to the new government in Rwanda. UN agency and NGO representatives began to report a new militancy from the camps and also military training among the former RGF militia and Interahamwe who were licking their wounds and straining to resume battle with their adversaries. Alarm bells began to ring in the capitals of Rwanda's neighbours and also with the humanitarian agencies who were seeing relief supplies being partially used for politico-military purposes.

The Rwandan government was also uncomfortable with UNHCR, because of a long history of perceived indifference to the Tutsi refugee as compared with the 'generosity' to the Hutu and also because UNHCR had allowed the refugee camps to be administered by the RGF's political leadership and had publicly questioned the climate of security in Rwanda for returning refugees. Rwanda's criticism of UNHCR was reflected in the following extract from a letter addressed to the President of the Security Council by its Permanent Representative:

f)   In particular we would like to express our disappointment about the manner in which UNHCR has behaved *vis-à-vis* the problem in our country;

g)   At the height of the genocide in April–May this year UNHCR officials dared make a false report that RPF forces were responsible for the genocide. Yet the whole world witnessed the militias of the Mouvement révolutionnaire national pour le développement/Coalition pour la défense de la république (MRND/CDR) and the former RGF butchering innocent people in broad daylight;

h)   UNHCR accepted and widely publicized false reports by MRND/CDR militias in the refugee camp in Ngara, United Republic of Tanzania, which alleged that RPF forces had killed people at a church in Kibungo. When these reports were cross-checked by the United States Committee for Refugees and by independent journalists, they were found to be false. The dead bodies alleged to be the work of the RPF were proved to have been those of persons who had died long before the RPF appeared in the area.

The Rwandan government's main preoccupation now turned towards the increasing intimidation and militarization that they claimed was taking place in the refugee camps of Zaire and Tanzania. The goodwill generated by President Bizimungu's early visits to neighbouring capitals began to wear off as accusations of complicity, particularly against Zaire, for allowing 'genociders' to hold political sway in the camps, were made public. Rwanda's leaders raised this issue several times with me and President Bizimungu addressed a letter to me in which he accused Zaire and Tanzania of 'permitting intimidation and of harbouring criminals'. He called for the separation in the camps of the political elements from the general mass – as it were, the wolves from the sheep. The following is an extract from President Bizi-mungu's letter addressed to UNHCR on 1 September 1994:

> The Interahamwe and their leaders, including those suspected of having been the brains behind the genocide in Rwanda, freely, openly, and publicly carry out propaganda inciting the population to hate, hunt and kill others on ethnic lines. Those refugees who dare to voice dissenting views are ruthlessly suppressed and those who dare to return to their homeland are actively hunted down and harassed if not killed. All this is done by people who at the close of day return to refugee camps run by the UNHCR.

The Security Council took note of these tensions and shortly afterwards, the Secretary-General directed me to proceed to Zaire and Tanzania as his Special Envoy with a view to seeking a solution to this growing problem. During the two following months, I visited Zaire and Tanzania several times to discuss with their leaders the issue of separating the political leadership from the mass of camp-dwellers and the relocation of the camps at a distance from the borders.

My first visit to Tanzania took me to Zanzibar, an enchanting island that was a sheer delight for me and my delegation who had lived through such horrific times in Rwanda. Zanzibar exudes charm and serenity through its beautiful, pastoral surroundings, its warm, courteous people and its glorious climate. There are no traffic lights in Zanzibar and the charming island has its own distinctive character. For almost a century, it was part of the Kingdom of Muscat and the Sultans were so taken by the languorous beauty of the surroundings that they transferred their capital from Muscat to Zanzibar. The island is therefore a mixture of Arab and African cultures which is apparent from the architecture, the winding souks, the exquisite wooden doors and the customs of the Zanzibarian people. Simplicity and affability seemed the hallmark of the Zanzibarian people. It was typical that I first met President Mwini at Friday prayer where he arrived at the mosque without fanfare or security. Dotted around the town are relics of old palaces, tombs of Iranian and Turkish Sultanas and, of course, the famous church where Livingstone declared the end of slavery. We stayed at an old house that had recently been converted into a new hotel. The house had been built by the Dinshaw and Cowasjee families, two of the most distinguished Parsee families living in Karachi.

President Mwini, his Foreign Minister and Cabinet colleagues spoke with one voice. Tanzania had traditionally settled wave after wave of African refugees. They had all been welcomed in the spirit of African brotherhood and the Tanzanian people had accepted them with open arms. Some had settled permanently in Tanzania and had even been given Tanzanian nationality. The current influx of Rwandan refugees was, however, an exception. The Tanzanian people resented their presence and wanted them to return to their homeland. The refugees could not be absorbed socially or economically into Tanzania and had caused damage to the environment and to the ecology of the country. Moreover, general elections were due and the presence of the refugees would cause serious embarrassment to the government party. The Rwandan refugees should therefore return to their homeland as early as possible. Tanzania preferred that the refugees should be relocated in UN-protected areas on Rwandan soil. Tanzanian leaders suggested that the ideal way to achieve an early return was for the Rwandan government to announce a general amnesty.

I responded that the idea of a general amnesty was anathema to the Rwandan government because it would appear to condone genocide. A forcible return of refugees was also against UN principles. Instead, I suggested that the UN would support Tanzania in encouraging a voluntary return. This would entail suppressing intimidation in the camps by separating the political elements from the ordinary folk, along with guarantees of justice and fair treatment by the Rwandan government to the returning refugees. After some discussion, the Tanzanian leaders agreed to the concept of separation and relocation of refugees, but insisted that the UN's financial support was essential in implementing this manoeuvre. They were firmly of the view that the real issue was the fair and humane treatment of returning refugees in Rwanda, rather than intimidation in the camps, which they felt their forces were capable of controlling.

My visits to Tanzania left me impressed by the discipline and capability of the Tanzanian police and army and also the clear-sighted approach of their leadership, which was determined to put its weight behind inducing as many refugees as possible to return to Rwanda. They did, however, require logistic and financial support from the international community to carry out the difficult process of separation and relocation of the camps. The refugee camps in Tanzania were well organized and comprised mainly of refugees who had left during the early part of the outbreak of genocide and hostilities in Rwanda. Separation, however, would be a difficult, even violent, task as was made clear when an attempt was made by the Tanzanian authorities to arrest the notorious *burgomestre* of Murambi, Remy Gatete, from one of the camps. The attempt led to a much-publicized riot and the Tanzanian police had to lay off Gatete.

My visits to Zaire (since renamed the Democratic Republic of Congo) took me to Kinshasa and then to the President's outpost in Gbadolete which was roughly half-way back to Rwanda. Zaire is one of Africa's richest countries with immense, untapped wealth in hydro-electric power, minerals, oil and precious stones. It is also extraordinarily fertile. It is, however, one of the most bizarre and misgoverned countries imaginable. Civil servants and school children in Kinshasa walk for two to three hours to the office or school because public transport has been dragooned by VIPs. Diplomats travel with US$20 cash in their cars to pay tolls at road barriers suddenly erected by the army or police who compensate in this way for unpaid salaries. Diamond mafiosi in dark glasses, Gucci suits and with armed guards fly to Paris for haircuts, while every morning thousands of city-dwellers scrounge for scraps in the city's numerous rubbish dumps. This volatile mix provides a febrile, garish and unpredictable ambience to the most routine and mundane daily chores of life. Yet the Zairean people are extraordinarily talented, in art, music, sport and literature.

I first met the Zairean Prime Minister, Kengo wa Dondo, followed by the Ministers of Foreign Affairs, Defence and Interior. The Prime Minister was a most impressive personality, urbane, articulate and rational. The Defence Minister, Grand Admiral Mavua Mudima was also a striking figure, open and friendly. In their different ways, they made it clear that, despite Zaire's political and ethnic sympathies with the former government, it wanted the earliest possible return of the refugees to Rwanda as they were causing unbearable ecological, social and economic damage on Zairean territory. Moreover, elections were imminent and the presence of refugees would be harmful for the government parties. The Zairean leaders in Kinshasa were firmly of the view that the onus for the early return of refugees lay squarely on the Rwandan government, which needed to take effective steps to induce the refugees to return home.

I then proceeded to Gbadolete for an audience with President Mobutu. He received me in imperious style, wearing a leopardskin hat. He was brutally frank. He said that the refugees who had come to Zaire had ethnic affinities with the Zairean people and he himself had been supportive of President Habyarimana. This did not mean that Zaire was willing to permanently host 1.5 million refugees who had destroyed the region's agriculture, polluted the cities and taken over the entire region. Schools could not open in Goma and Bukavu because refugees had occupied them and were burning chairs and desks for fuel. Their presence had placed an impossible burden on the Zairean people. In his view, Rwanda should declare a general amnesty and, except for a few known criminals, take back its population. Moreover, the UN should provide compensation to Zaire for the damage that the refugees had caused to the environment and to the economy. Finally, elections were due shortly and the presence of so many refugees would have an adverse effect on pro-government parties. The President felt that the real reason for refugees not returning was not the alleged intimidation in the camps but the fear of persecution and retribution on their return. He urged the Rwandan government to go much further in treating returning refugees fairly and humanely.

The message from Tanzania and Zaire was clear. Despite political or ethnic sympathies for the former regime, both governments were, in my assessment, genuine in seeking an early evacuation of the refugees back to Rwanda. The political, economic and social damage that the refugees were causing to both governments, as they neared elections, was overwhelming. Both were therefore eager to stop and reverse the flow of refugees, which they could only achieve with the help of the international community and the United Nations. They both felt that the quickest way was for the government of Rwanda to engage in some form of public reconciliation with its opponents, and suggested a general amnesty or negotiations with non-criminal elements of the former government. In my view, which I conveyed to the two presidents, this suggestion was premature, given the depth of feeling in Rwandan government circles about the recent genocide. Tanzania and Zaire were also agreeable to the separation of the political elements in the camps from the ordinary folk. They understood, however, that separation would be a difficult task with the likelihood of violence. They also accepted the concept of relocating the refugee camps at some distance from the border so as to avoid friction and tension with Rwanda. President Mobutu recalled that it had been decided at the 1969 OAU Summit to locate refugee camps at some distance from the frontiers.

It was therefore apparent from my first round of discussions in Tanzania and Zaire that both governments accepted that the likeliest way of inducing the voluntary return of refugees was to separate the hard-core political elements in the refugee camps from the ordinary folk. Simultaneously, the government of Rwanda should be persuaded to implement a high-profile campaign, on the lines of Operation Retour, to persuade the refugees to return. Once it was decided to separate the 'wolves from the sheep', there was consensus among the asylum countries, Rwanda, the donor states and the UN that the refugee camps would need to be relocated at some distance from the borders. Clearly, this operation of separation and relocation would require significant financial support and also the presence of an armed force, because the manoeuvre was likely to lead to violence.

Having found agreement in principle from all parties concerned and after discussing details with UN HQ, I embarked on my second round of visits to Zaire and Tanzania, carrying with me proposals for a detailed plan of action to separate and relocate the refugee camps. I took with me to Kinshasa and Dar-es-Salaam experts in the military, logistic, humanitarian and communication fields, who formed joint commissions with their opposite numbers in each country to work out a plan of action.

The first task was to define the refugees into various categories. In Zaire, the following four divisions were agreed by the joint commission:

— *Category A*: The top leadership, identified as 228 in number, who, with their families, consisted of around 1000 persons. This category were easily identifiable and were mostly living in hotels and hired accommodation.

— *Category B*: The former RGF, comprising 30,000 military personnel, of which 16,000 were in camps near Bukavu and 14,000 near Goma. The former retained their military status while the soldiers in Goma had mainly taken on civilian gear in order to qualify for UNHCR humanitarian aid. Along with their families, this group consisted of around 50,000 people.

— *Category C*: The former militia and Interahamwe. By far, the most politicized and dangerous group who acted as the spearhead of the sabotage and guerrilla campaign inside Rwanda. This group, which was equated with the extremists, was estimated at between 10,000 and 15,000. The Zairean Defence Minister assured me that it would not be difficult to distinguish this group from the ordinary folk.

— *Category D*: The ordinary folk, 850,000 in the Goma (North Kivu) region and 450,000 near Bukavu (South Kivu).

In our discussion with Zairean leaders, it was felt that the problem of separation related mainly to Categories B and C as the top leadership (Category A) was expected to move, voluntarily, to francophone African countries like Gabon, Cameroon, Senegal and Togo. In Category B, 20 to 30 per cent of former RGF soldiers were expected to return to rejoin a united army in Rwanda, leaving about 30,000 and about 15,000 militia and Interahamwe (Category C) to be separated and relocated at some distance from the border. As regards Category D, the Rwandan government was to mount a major campaign to induce the ordinary folk to return home from the refugee camps.

Of course, in Tanzania the complexion of the refugees was different. Categories A and B were barely represented in the Tanzanian camps because they had not crossed over with a retreating army. The Tanzanian component therefore comprised Category C (the former prefects, *burgomestres* and political cadres) and Category D. The total number of refugees in Tanzania was estimated at 650,000.

The next question was where to site the new camps. The Zaireans, particularly, inclined in favour of relocating the camps at 'some distance' rather than within 100 kilometres of the border. They argued that even though transporting the refugees to a nearer location would be cheaper, they wanted to avoid any accusation by Rwanda of complicity with cross-border sabotage. Secondly, the people of the region were already so fed up with the Rwandan refugees that to keep them in the same province would lead to greater tension. The Zaireans therefore opted to locate the camps in the central districts which were over 500 kilometres away from the Rwandan border.

In Zaire, the joint commission went out to actually inspect the possible sites for suitability. The journeys to the prospective locations were harrowing, one site being visited after an eight-hour journey in a raft. Our members on the joint commission came back with amazing accounts of the interior where airports were covered by wild growth through non-use; where railway tracks existed, but no trains came because there was no fuel; of roads and bridges destroyed by lack of maintenance; of villages that once had electricity and telephones but now had to do without! Eventually, they shortlisted three sites, Lokandu, Irebu and Kongolo, with a marginal preference for Kongolo – because it could be serviced by an airfield, which though currently disused and overgrown with weeds, could be revived. Otherwise, chaperoning train- or truck-loads of resentful, violent Interahamwe across vast distances seemed more like a nightmare than a reality.

Tanzania also decided to move the refugees some distance away from the border to ensure that they could not filter back to the region. The Tanzanian government, in its organized way, had already pinpointed several sites to which the camps could be moved.

Once the leadership of Zaire and Tanzania had agreed in principle to the separation and relocation of camps, we went on to discuss with them the crucial questions of how this difficult operation was to be completed and the financial outlay required for it. The response was different in each country. Tanzania maintained that its own security forces could perform the task without outside help, but would require logistic support and financing. Zaire, on the other hand, wanted a UN contingent to secure the relocated camps.

In Kinshasa, the joint commissions burnt the midnight oil discussing, in the minutest detail, the salaries to be paid to the Zairean force and the required logistics and equipment, which ranged from mosquito nets to helicopters, from riot gear to transport vehicles.

In a nutshell, the proposal agreed with Zaire was that the government would recruit a specially trained, crack unit of three battalions (2500), which would be assisted by a UN force of 500. This combined force would secure the camps, one by one, starting in the north and working southwards down to Bukavu. The force would then escort the refugees to relocated camp sites in the interior where it would also ensure security. It would be made up of formed troops, Milobs and logistic and communications units. It would be deployed in both North and South Kivu, acting under a UN Force Commander and a Zairean Deputy.

In Tanzania, the complexion of the agreed force was slightly different. No UN force was deemed necessary as the contingent would be drawn exclusively from the Tanzanian army and police. However, a 20-member UN liaison presence was considered acceptable by the Tanzanian government. The main area of support required from the

UN by the Tanzanian government was in the form of logistics, communications and financial back-up.

Over a six-month period, the total cost, which included purchase of equipment, movement of personnel – both national and foreign – deployment of communications, equipment, etc was estimated as follows:

For Zaire   Cost in US$ million

	Zairean Force 2500 personnel	UN support for 500	Total
Fixed costs	32.7	5.6	38.3
6 months sustainment costs	8.4	7.2	15.6
Total	41.1	12.8	53.9

For Tanzania   Cost in US$ million

	Tanzanian Force 2600 personnel	UN support	Total
Fixed costs	40.3	0.8	41.1
6 months sustainment costs	8.9	0.4	9.3
Total	49.2	1.2	50.4

These proposals, which had been hammered out in the joint commission and were agreed by Tanzania and Zaire, were sent to UN headquarters in New York in the second half of December.

Within a week, I was informed that there was no possibility of the proposals even being considered, as donor and troop-contributing countries had flatly refused to provide personnel or to finance the operation. I was informed that out of more than 60 countries approached, only one had given a half-positive response. All the others had been negative. Frankly, I was surprised at the speed and decisiveness with which our proposals, had been turned down. For instance, none of the donor country ambassadors represented in Kigali had been asked for their comments on the proposal. What made my position acutely embarrassing with the governments of Zaire and Tanzania was that I had negotiated the agreements in Kinshasa and Dar-es-Salaam with the full knowledge and support of UN HQ and, yet, when the package was agreed by all parties, it was summarily rejected. Either donor country reluctance to fund such an operation should have been known beforehand to prevent extended

negotiations, or the UN should have made a greater effort to persuade donor countries to have a closer look at the plan.

In the end, I had to inform the leadership of all these countries
that the plans we had so meticulously worked out in the joint commissions had been summarily rejected. To this statement President
Bizimungu replied, 'Mr Ambassador, I think the UN headquarters
have got their facts wrong on the troop-contributing offers. There is
one country that has offered its troops.' To my quizzical look, he
added, with a twinkle in his eye, 'Rwanda!'

Subsequently, the Secretary-General handed over the problem to
UNHCR. The High Commissioner Mme Ogata circulated an alternative plan of action aimed, essentially, at curbing intimidation in the
refugee camps. The Zaireans agreed to provide a limited force which
was complemented by a mainly Dutch police contingent. This contingent began operating early in 1995 and its efforts improved the
discipline in the camps. The plan did not, however, address the core
issue of separation and relocation. The UNHCR operation was a
worthy effort but remained, essentially, a palliative.

Two years later, in December 1996, after vast amounts of humanitarian aid had been poured into the refugee camps, the tension
caused by guerrilla activity and cross-border sabotage led to another
blow-out in Eastern Zaire. Again, horror frames of fleeing refugees,
disease and dying children appeared on television screens. There was
a renewed public outcry to prevent another humanitarian disaster
while donor countries vacillated on the action to be taken. Eventually, when the Security Council had almost agreed to a UN force of
10,000 being despatched to the region, the problem subsided: a local
Tutsi rebel force led by Laurence Kabila gained control of the situation, thereby relieving the international community of the need to
send out an international force. The irony is that the international
community was prepared to undertake the vast expense of sending
out a 10,000-member UN force, but had rejected preventive action
with the 500-member contingent proposed two years earlier. If the
10,000-member force had been despatched, tax-payers of donor
countries would surely have had a right to question why the earlier
proposal had been summarily dismissed.

UNAMIR deployment

By November, a remarkable change had come about in Rwanda.
Towns, villages, communes were now alive with activity. Pillaged
houses and farmyard huts were being repaired, children skipped
back to school, fields were being cultivated and office workers
returned to work. Most of this activity was in the private sector
because the government still did not have funds to pay salaries. In
fact, the Prime Minister told me that it was becoming increasingly

difficult to maintain discipline in an army that had been victorious, but had not been paid for four months! The Rwandan leadership was now increasingly plaintive about the international community and the UN, which imposed every kind of conditionality on the government without providing the means to achieve these objectives.

After meetings with the Rwandan leadership, I made yet another attempt with headquarters to generate a basic minimum fund that would crank up the broken-down machinery of state. I pointed to the fact that the army had not been paid for four months, that the Prime Minister had no residence of his own and there was scarcely any transport available to the government. I pleaded for a diversion of 10 per cent of the funds being spent in the refugee camps so that the government could address vital issues of law and order, reconciliation and the revival of the country's devastated infrastructure.

Except for the Indian battalion that was expected in December, UNAMIR was now at full strength with a battalion deployed in each of the five main sectors. The heavily overworked Ghanaians were moved to Kibungo, one of the less stressful regions; the Nigerians were in Byumba, usually trouble-free, RPF-dominated territory; the Indians were to take over in Kigali, having indicated in advance that they would prefer to stay in the capital; the Ethiopians were in Cyangugu, the Tunisians in Gisenyi and the French African battalion (Chad, Guinea, Mali, Senegal) in the difficult Kibuye sector. Finally, the Zambians were in Gikongoro. Of the rest, the British logistic contingent, the Australian medical unit, Civpol and the Canadian headquarters and communications units were located in Kigali.

The 320 Milobs who had their headquarters in Kigali were now operating from every prefecture and provided a ground-level link with the RPA and the civil administration. They also co-operated closely with the UN specialized agencies and NGOs operating in the field. While Milob presence in the prefectures was reassuring to the agencies, the NGOs and the local community, the basic sense of security could best be provided by the UNAMIR formed troops that were assigned to the more difficult regions. There was, in fact, a distinct difference in the security climate in regions where our armed, formed troops were present as opposed to those where only unarmed Milobs were posted. For example, in Gitarama, where only Milobs were present and occupied, along with other UN agencies, a large church compound, 13 attempted thefts and break-ins were reported in a single month. In the compounds occupied by our formed troops in other regions, not a single such attempt was reported.

Generally, the differences in the UN's military and humanitarian 'cultures' did not surface at times of danger and insecurity because there was an essential bonding and togetherness between the military and the civilian agencies operating in the field. For instance, they frequently lived in the same compound, used the same office premises and communications and preferred to go out on patrols together. It was only when danger receded that the differences in the military and civilian cultures began to emerge with the civil and humanitarian agencies distancing themselves from the security umbrella of the military. Therefore, as the security climate improved, the distance between UNAMIR and the civilian agencies also began to increase.

By December 1994, the Indian Gurkha battalion had arrived, comprising around 900 personnel. Most of the soldiers were Nepalese Gurkhas, but their officers came from all parts of India. The engineers, communications, medical and logistic units were also mainly non-Gurkha. The most senior officer of the Gurkha battalion was Brigadier Sivakumar, a Madrasi Brahmin who first assumed the role of Chief of Staff at UNAMIR headquarters, i.e. no. 3 in the military hierarchy. He then succeeded Brigadier-General Anyidoho as Deputy Force Commander when his tenure ended in August 1995 and finally, when Force Commander Major-General Tousignant departed in December 1995, Brigadier Sivakumar took over as the Acting Force Commander for UNAMIR's final four months.

Although there were a score of Bangladeshi and five Pakistani Milobs, the arrival of the Gurkhas brought a substantial South Asian dimension to UNAMIR which, apart from the Canadians, British and Australian units, was essentially African. The Gurkhas soon showed their mettle, being highly disciplined, efficient and courteous. They earned the respect of their colleagues, as indeed of the Rwandans, for their discipline and general helpfulness.

General Sivakumar – a vegetarian – and a number of other officers of the Gurkha regiment took up residence in the Belgian Village and became my neighbours and fellow tennis players. Three of the young Indian officers belonged to my old school, the Royal Indian Military College in Dehra Dun, and brought me news of developments since I was a schoolboy there, 50 years ago!

Mention of the Gurkha regiment would not be complete without reference to their extraordinarily able doctor, Major Karan, who quickly established a reputation which made him unique in Rwanda. Everyone, from diplomat to Rwandan minister, wanted only to be treated by Dr Karan who never turned back a patient whether he was a poor Rwandan or an ambassador. He became something of a legend in Rwanda with his extraordinary diagnostic skills as a doctor.

For their efficiency, discipline and military proficiency, the Gurkha regiment lived up to the high reputation that they have earned internationally as professional soldiers. Brigadier Sivakumar proved himself a remarkably able successor to Major-General Tousignant, successfully completing the difficult and complex task of phasing out UNAMIR from Rwanda with dignity and honour.

Signs of tension between UNAMIR
and the Rwandan government

The relatively relaxed atmosphere in the country with no curfews and few road blocks was welcome relief from the grim and dangerous period that UNAMIR had lived through. The Belgian Village where some of us had taken up residence was a delightful spot. It was well protected, clean and surrounded by gardens. It had a tennis court, swimming pool and a small restaurant which became the hub of social activity for UNAMIR and agency personnel. The Ghana band, a remarkably versatile group that could play music ranging from military tunes to high life and jazz, was a special favourite. It would play late into the night on Saturday evenings with young people dancing and relaxing over barbecues. From December onwards, the Ghana band had competition from the excellent Gurkha band who were also extremely versatile, mixing Scottish bagpipes with western dance music and the latest Indian hit parade songs that were rendered in a male and female voice by the same singer! At about this time, UNAMIR organized various sporting activities with marathons, athletics, volleyball, football and tennis being contested between various regiments and civilians. We even got together a cricket team which played in Uganda and Kenya.

Now that UNAMIR's military component was almost at full strength and our overdue logistic support was flowing in by air cargo, UNAMIR began to exude its full panoply of power, bestriding a devastated, impoverished Rwanda like a colossus. The UN was omnipresent in Rwanda with its fleet of white cars, its well-equipped force and its impressive communications. It was the richest employer and the biggest tenant for houses. Daily, it flew in vast quantities of food, equipment and humanitarian aid which was stocked in enormous warehouses. Its aircraft were the only link with the outside world and its helicopters the only means of reaching the furthest point in Rwanda from Kigali in less than half an hour. More than 80 per cent of the vehicles on the road were painted UN white and they included every kind of vehicle, from saloons to dump trucks, from coasters to fork-lifts. Every foreigner seemingly had a mobile telephone, every NGO and agency a fleet of cars at their disposal. In stark contrast, Rwandan ministers, parliamentarians, civil servants walked to offices that had no telephones, no typewriters, no files, no vehicles and one or two secretaries who had probably not been paid a salary. All this public demonstration of strength, capability and abundance stood out in embarrassing contrast with Rwanda's devastation, its government's lack of resources and its abject penury.

Although, at the time, relations between the RPA and UNAMIR, especially at the senior level, were friendly and co-operative, I could sense that friction, born of anger and envy, would develop if the UN and the international community did not quickly provide essential aid to Rwanda. Soon, unpleasant incidents between UNAMIR and the RPA, especially at the lower levels, began to take place with increasing frequency. UNAMIR was also becoming the target of abuse from citizens and Radio Rwanda would pick up the smallest incident, like a traffic accident, and blow it up as an example of UN insensitivity to Rwanda's sovereignty. When taken up at a higher level, these incidents were smoothed over, but I became aware of a growing restiveness towards the UN. Ambassador Dillon who was the Secretary-General's Special Envoy to the region, placed Rwandan attitudes in correct perspective when he reported that while Rwandan leaders appreciated UNAMIR II's contribution, they viewed the UN as a whole in a negative light. Conscious of this sensitivity, I deliberately stopped using helicopters to attend public meetings in distant towns because it was embarrassing for me to arrive in a helicopter when the Rwandan leadership would drive for hours in ramshackle jalopies to reach their destinations. We in UNAMIR also kept our offices spartan and functional while most other UN agency offices were being fitted out with wall-to-wall carpeting, modern furniture and the usual trappings associated with diplomatic offices. I felt that so long as the government remained deprived, it would not be appropriate for us to be surrounded by luxury. All my military colleagues agreed with this view and though we had now graduated from military rations to normal fresh food, our living conditions remained simple and frugal.

Francophone versus anglophone

At around that time, one event brought home to me the depth and relevance of the divide between francophones and anglophones in Africa. In 1994, the French Francophone Summit was held in Biarritz. France, the host country, did not invite Rwanda, even though some non-francophone African leaders like President Mugabe were invited as guests. During one of the bilateral summit meetings between Rwanda and Zaire, President Mobutu offered to look after Rwanda's interests at Biarritz. The message was clear. Rwanda, a predominantly French-speaking country, was seen to be dominated by an English-speaking elite and so it was to be treated as an outcast from the francophone fold! On several occasions, for example elections for international posts, Africans have divided sharply on the basis of francophone versus anglophone and it takes time for a non-African to realize how deep this schism has become in Africa.

In my opinion, Rwanda adopted irrational policies towards francophone countries, treating them with undue suspicion. France, and to a lesser extent Belgium, were regarded as permanent adversaries, unable to turn a new page in their relations with the new government. Rwanda constantly spurned genuine initiatives by these

. ABOVE. UNAMIR
Headquarters at the
Amohoro stadium Hostel,
Kigali.

2. RIGHT. General Dallaire.

3. ABOVE. General Tousignant addressing officers of the former RGF (Hutu armed force) at Gako re-education centre. In October 1995 a new regiment of former RGF was re-integrated into the Rwandan national army (RPF).

4. BELOW. Shaharyar M. Khan and General Tousignant, December 1995.

5. ABOVE. Kibeho. The scene inside the medical centre.

6. BELOW. Goma, Zaire, 25 July 1943. Rwandan refugees set up camps outside Goma.

7. LEFT. The prison at Gikongoro.

8. BELOW. Nyarbuye Church – scene of massacre.

RIGHT. Mosque at Kigali.

0. BELOW. Mary Robinson visiting refugees in Goma.

11. ABOVE. Secretary General's visit, 14 July 1995.

12. LEFT. Gen Paul Kegame, vice President, talking to Gen Tousignant before the ceremony at Mount Ribero, 7 April 1995

13. RIGHT. President Pasteur Bizimungu of Rwanda holds a press conference at the United Nations headquarters, 7 October 1994.

14. RIGHT. Julius Nyerere, former President of Tanzania and Chairman of South Centre, addresses a press conference concerning the Agenda for Development, United Nations, New York, June 1994.

15. LEFT. Prime Minister Faustin Twagiramungu of Rwanda addresses a press conference where he urges the international community to help stabilize the situation in Rwanda, United Nations, New York, 2 December 1994.

16. BELOW. Secretary-General Kofi Annan (second right) meeting with Paul Kagame (shaking hands), Vice President, and Pasteur Bizimungu (right), President of the Rwandese Republic.

countries to establish cordial, co-operative relations. It seemed that Rwanda was hurting itself by adopting such a stridently anti-French policy because even if they were convinced of French mala fides, tactically it would have been wise to establish minimal normal relations. My efforts to persuade the RPF's senior echelons for an improvement in Rwanda's relations with France and Belgium fell on sceptical ears, though some senior government ministers like Prime Minister Faustin Twagiramungu and Foreign Minister Anastase Gasana, were in favour of improving relations with France and its friends in Africa.

The co-ordination of UN activities

In mid-November, I was summoned to Geneva for a meeting with Secretary-General Boutros Boutros-Ghali who was accompanied by Marrack Goulding, head of the DPA, and Peter Hansen, head of the DHA. UN agency heads also attended the meeting. The agenda for discussion had three major issues relating to Rwanda: national reconciliation, the return of refugees and co-ordination between agencies. On reconciliation, the Secretary-General wanted the Rwandan government to demonstrate greater commitment and openness, particularly by involving non-criminal elements of the former government who were living abroad. As regards refugee return, I briefed the Secretary-General on the success of Operation Retour with the IDPs and the need to apply the same formula with even greater intensity to refugee return. I added that though all concerned governments had made commitments regarding preventing intimidation in the camps and giving fair treatment and justice to returning refugees, there was only limited implementation on the ground. Unless a synchronized effort took place on both sides of the border, the flow of returning refugees would continue to be desultory. Zaire and Tanzania had pleaded lack of finances and personnel to control intimidation and to relocate the camps. Rwanda's record, though laudable in resettling IDPs, continued to be suspect, in the light of negative reports of revenge killings and arbitrary arrests. Prison conditions in Rwanda were also an inhibiting factor for refugee return.

The issue of the SRSG's co-ordinating role in relation to the specialized UN agencies was then raised by the Secretary-General, with a profound sense of frustration, when he sought answers from his senior colleagues and his Special Representatives in Kigali and Bujumbura to the perennial problem of internal co-ordination between the SRSG and the UN's specialized agencies. The Secretary-General made it clear to agency heads gathered at the meeting that he regarded his SRSG as the leader responsible for all UN efforts in the field. He expected full co-operation from the agencies. He considered the SRSG's role to be like that of an ambassador who presides over a mission in the field encompassing different departments with their separate budgets.

After the meeting, in a *tête-à-tête*, the Secretary-General inquired how inter-agency co-ordination could be improved and asked me specifically which agencies were the more recalcitrant. I replied that the problem was essentially institutional and hierarchical. The UN had no institutional framework which gave the SRSG control and authority over UN inter-agency activity, with the result that co-ordination in the field had to be achieved through reasoning, cajoling and persuading at the ground level rather than invoking hierarchical authority. I had no complaints with local heads of agency in Rwanda who had been extremely co-operative, as was apparent from the Turquoise takeover and Operation Retour. However, I could not insist on an institutional response when none was ordained in the UN system. I added that, as a long-serving diplomatic officer who had been an ambassador and dealt with embassies, I found it unbelievable that the responsibility for carrying out the Security Council's political mandate should rest squarely on the SRSG's shoulders, but that he was given neither funds nor hierarchical authority over his sub-units to implement his task.

The issue of co-ordination within the UN system is both simple and complex. The simple part of the problem is easily stated. The SRSG carries with him into the field no funds whatsoever to deploy in the country of assignment. Secondly, though designated as head of the UN family, the Special Representative has no rules of business, no hierarchical authority and no institutional control over his sub-units, the UN specialized agencies. Both these problems require elaboration.

Whenever the Secretary-General appoints his Special Representative – a decision that is invariably endorsed by the Security Council – it is the Special Representative, alone, who is charged with the responsibility of implementing the political objectives that the Security Council decides upon. Thus, the SRSG is not a *primus inter pares*, but the head of the UN family operating on behalf of the Secretary-General, usually in a crisis situation, carrying with him as his brief a mandate decided upon by the apex political body in the world – the Security Council. In Rwanda, for instance, the SRSG's mandate required him to negotiate with the Rwandan government and deliver on political issues such as national reconciliation, security and fair treatment for returning refugees, holding back on an immediate takeover after the departure of Operation Turquoise, the creation of an International Commission on Kibeho, co-operation on Operation Retour, improving conditions in prisons, negotiating new mandates, the creation of Radio UNAMIR, accepting the International Criminal Tribunal and the handover of equipment, to mention only the most prominent examples.

In order to influence the government towards moving in the desired direction, the SRSG should carry the proverbial stick and carrot in his hand. Yet, he is given neither. UN regulations require that funds assessed for peace-keeping can only be spent to support, equip and sustain the peace-keepers. Assessed funds cannot be channelled towards post-conflict peace-building or infrastructure repair. Thus, in Rwanda, the UN budget for sending, equipping and maintaining 5500 troops came, at its height, to half a million dollars a day. Not a single dollar of that money could, strictly speaking, be spent on, for instance, repairing the telecommunications or the power supply in Kigali. UNAMIR medical units that we brought, at great expense, to Rwanda were also, in the strict sense, to service UNAMIR personnel and not to treat those Rwandans affected by genocide or blown up by land mines. The SRSG therefore presided over an expensive empire, but could not dispense funds for the smallest requirement to support a devastated country and its people. There was no trust fund to dip into nor an enabling clause in the mandate which could be interpreted as licence to help and build confidence in Rwanda. In such situations it does not take long for the government in question to realize that the chief UN representative is unable to respond to the most genuine requests for financial support and to move on to watering holes that are not dry. The end result is that while every responsibility and expectation to move the government in question in the prescribed direction is placed solely on the shoulders of the SRSG, he is given no financial authority to influence that government.

As regards inter-agency co-ordination, each specialized agency, whether developmental or human rights-oriented, has its own mandate, its own budget, its own headquarters, its special culture and, of course, its local representative. Usually when the Secretary-General appoints a Special Representative he writes a letter to the head of every UN agency informing him or her of his decision and seeking the agency's full co-operation to enable the SRSG to achieve targets set forth in his mandate. The Secretary-General expresses the hope that the local agency representatives will co-ordinate their policies closely with his Special Representative. In reply, the agency heads politely and vaguely respond to the Secretary-General, welcoming the Special Representative's appointment and informing the Secretary-General that he can rest assured of the agency's co-operation with the Special Representative. There the matter ends, with probably copies of the correspondence sent to the local representatives.

The simple fact is that no head of an organizational unit, whether managing director of an industrial concern, an army general or head of a hospital unit, can be expected to perform his functions without hierarchical authority, rules and regulations, lines of command and elementary control over the sub-units operating under his authority.

Yet, this is precisely the scenario that a Special Representative finds himself in when he arrives in his theatre of operation.

The issues of management and co-ordination stated above are so elementary that they beggar belief. The complex aspect of the problem is in locating the reasons for this state of affairs. Finding answers to this question requires delving deep into the labyrinthian complexity of how each UN agency has evolved with its separate constitution, specific funding, particular mandate and eventually its own different culture. From UNHCR to UNICEF, from the Human Rights Commission to the UNDP, each has its own particular relationship with UN headquarters which itself has layers of independent controls.

Turf preservation is perhaps the most obvious factor that inhibits hierarchical control and effective inter-agency co-ordination. Each specialized agency jealously guards its own turf and resents any suggestion of possible encroachment. These territorial lines are usually drawn via funding programmes that aim to control, for example, orphanages and childcare units (UNICEF), medical centres (the WHO), training institutes for magistrates (the UNDP) or the setting-up of refugee camps (UNHCR). It follows that the larger the funding capability of a particular agency, the greater the territory controlled. This, in turn, leads to turf wars, as for instance in the case of training the Rwandan judiciary which both the UNDP and the Human Rights Commission claimed the right to sponsor.

Over the years, the UN has evolved a system in which the UNDP representative acts as the Resident Co-ordinator and as a *primus inter pares*. In a crisis situation where a Special Representative enters the fray, this system becomes subject to extreme turbulence. It stands to reason that where the Secretary-General appoints his Special Representative with the mandate to co-ordinate and supervise all UN activity, no other UN official should be designated to co-ordinate UN agencies. If the UNDP representative is to carry out such functions at all, they should be performed on behalf of the SRSG, either as his deputy or delegated by him for this specific purpose. To illustrate this dichotomy, I quote below extracts from the circular letter sent out on 21 March 1995 by Mr Gustave Speth, the UNDP Administrator, to his newly appointed representative in Kigali, which he sent to me for information:

> The resident co-ordinator assumes, on behalf of the United Nations system and in consultation with the other representatives of the United Nations system, overall responsibility for, and co-ordination of, the systems operational activities for development carried out at country level.

> The resident co-ordinator system, furthermore, seeks to promote effective dialogue and interaction of the United Nations system with other multilateral, bilateral and non-governmental organizations active in development co-operation, with a view to constituency-building for national development.

> The resident co-ordinator exercises team leadership among the organizations of the United Nations system at country level.

In Rwanda, a further complicating factor was the appointment of a Humanitarian Co-ordinator. To begin with, the roles of Humanitarian Co-ordinator and Resident Co-ordinator were merged in one person – the UNDP representative. After the genocide had been controlled, the DHA maintained a separate Humanitarian Co-ordinator – Randolph Kent – who as head of UNREO was to act as post-crisis manager and co-ordinator for humanitarian aid. This appointment, again without the assignation of a clear-cut hierarchical role, resulted in a grating, complicated relationship with the specialized agencies on the following counts. First, the Resident Co-ordinator (the UNDP head) felt aggrieved that an important portfolio which he had previously held had been taken away from him. Secondly, the specialized agencies were somewhat resentful that they should be shepherded by a Humanitarian Co-ordinator who had no funds of his own, but only a broad mandate to co-ordinate the activities of the specialized agencies. Thirdly, even more confusing for the agencies was the fact that they were expected to be co-ordinated by three different personalities, namely the SRSG, the Resident Co-ordinator and the Humanitarian Co-ordinator! It seemed that the UN system suffered from an excess rather than a lack of co-ordination.

Another factor inhibiting effective co-ordination was the different cultures that had gradually evolved in the UN system. I was soon aware of the civilian culture against the military. There were also development and humanitarian cultures that had their own special dynamism and motivation. Sometimes, these cultures clashed and the SRSG – as head of the UN family – had no means of playing an overriding, decisive role, with disastrous results, as at Kibeho.

Perhaps the most incongruous element of the SRSG's office was that even the headquarters representation in his office was not formally responsible to the SRSG, but to their respective units operating from UN headquarters. For example, the Chief Administrative Officer in UNAMIR took instructions from and answered directly to the Administration (Field Administration Logistics Division) at HQ in New York. The SRSG was kept informed, most of the time, but the formal administrative chain of command did not include him. Similarly, the head of UNREO was also independent; even though he represented an arm of UN HQ, the DHA. Heads of UNREO did not even sit in the same office as the SRSG, perhaps because his humanitarian culture clashed with the military and the political! Surprisingly, he did not figure in UNAMIR's organigram even though the Force Commander representing the military was part of the SRSG's administrative structure. The JEEAR refers to co-ordination within the UN system in the following critical terms:

However, co-ordination arrangements in relation to other areas and levels of the system were less satisfactory. The fact that the roles of the SRSG, the UNAMIR Force Commander and the Humanitarian Co-ordinator/head of UNREO were limited to operations within Rwanda hampered co-ordination between the policies and operations inside Rwanda and those relating to refugees in neighbouring countries. Within Rwanda UNREO performed several useful functions, though it suffered as a result of its ad hoc status and lack of clarity over its relationship to DHA and UNDP, its relationship with operational UN agencies and its relationship to the SRSG. In addition it did not have adequate resources and some of its personnel (many of whom were UNDP and seconded NGO personnel), lacked emergency co-ordination experience. Consequently its role was limited, principally to that of information sharing.

Apart from these layers of separate and independent fiefdoms operating within the UN fold, there was another complicating factor, that of donor country funding. Perhaps the roots of this particular issue could be found in the Cold War era when the activities of the Department of Peace-Keeping Operations had to be hermetically sealed into a purely peace-keeping role. Funds for peace-keeping were collected on an assessed basis which meant that proportional contribution was obligatory on member states. These funds were available only to sustain the peace-keepers and their logistic support. For all development, humanitarian or emergency aid, the donor community provided 'voluntary contributions' to be distributed across the UN specialized agencies. The UN system kept a careful watch on operations to ensure that assessed peace-keeping funds were not diverted to domains which were the preserve of voluntary contributions. The end result of this rigid compartmentalization was that while half a million dollars a day of assessed contributions could be spent on sustaining peace-keepers, none of these funds could be diverted to post-conflict repair and emergency relief functions.

UN military peace-keepers, who had no peace to keep in Rwanda but with their engineers, technicians, logistics and communications were capable of providing immediate repair and relief, were prevented from doing so because it was not part of their mandate and even if the mandate were stretched, there were no funds to be diverted for such a cause. The situation cried out for a trust fund to be placed at the disposal of the SRSG with an appropriate enabling mandate that would allow the human and technical resources of the peace-keepers to be used to jump-start the repair of the devastated infrastructure in Rwanda. No specialized agency turf would have been encroached on and the baton would have been handed over to them as soon as they were ready to start their respective operations.

In this way, the peace-keepers would have made optimum use of funds spent on them, achieved the lasting gratitude of the Rwandan government and probably made the difference between the success and failure of the UN peace-keeping mission in Rwanda.

5. January – April 1995

Signs of tension
with UNAMIR

The Nairobi Summit

On 7 January 1995 the Nairobi Summit of the seven Great Lakes region states was called by President Daniel Arap Moi to discuss the regional situation. The Presidents of Burundi, Rwanda, Uganda, Tanzania and Zambia joined the host but, at the last minute, President Mobutu conveyed his regrets, sending his able and articulate Prime Minister, Kengo wa Dondo to represent Zaire. I was also invited to attend.

The Summit was held at the gracious Presidency in Nairobi where an extremely smart President's bodyguard greeted the guests who first gathered in the spacious lawns and were then ushered in for refreshments in the best post-colonial Commonwealth tradition. After a brief public opening with full delegations, the leaders met in camera with only Foreign Ministers assisting them. President Moi asked me to attend the closed-door session at which I was the only outsider. The discussions were conducted in English and interpreters sat behind the leaders of delegations who were French-speaking (Burundi and Zaire). The Rwandan President and Foreign Minister, being fluent in English, did not require interpretation.

Having recently visited Tanzania and Zaire, I expected broad agreement on inducing an early return of refugees by controlling intimidation, arresting known criminals and ensuring fair treatment for the returnees. I anticipated, however, that Rwanda would come under pressure on the issue of national reconciliation from at least five of the other leaders who would press for a general amnesty and negotiations with former government elements. I expected President Museveni to back Rwanda's firm opposition to this concept.

In the first round of discussions, there was quick agreement on encouraging the early return of refugees. Zaire then spearheaded a proposal calling on Rwanda to engage in a dialogue with the opposition in the interests of national reconciliation. Tanzania, Burundi,

91

Zambia and Kenya pursued a similar line, reasoning that the dialogue should take place with 'non-criminal' elements of the
opposition. Surely, they argued, not all members of the opposition
were tainted with criminality. Surprisingly, President Museveni also
joined in with the other five leaders in support of separating non-
criminal elements of the former government from those who were
'clean' and talking to them. President Bizimungu remained steadfast
and alone in vehemently opposing any dialogue with the opposition.
When pressed, he asked, 'Who are these moderates that you are
talking about? Can anybody give me the name of a person from the
former government who has acknowledged that genocide should be
condemned? Or who has shown regret and remorse over the genocide?' The discussion had become heated when I asked for, and
President Moi gave me, the floor.

I began by saying that I accepted the importance of national reconciliation in the healing process and in providing the essential
impetus for the voluntary return of refugees. Giving my experience of
the past six months, I said that the positive steps that the government had taken at the grassroots level needed to be recognized,
especially as they had not been given media coverage. I referred to
the return of IDPs in relative tranquillity, the Gako military training
process in which 2000 former RGF were being trained to rejoin the
national army, the return of middle- and junior-level civil servants
from exile, some of whom had walked back from Goma to rejoin their
old posts and, at a higher level, I pointed to Foreign Minister Dr
Anastase Gasana who had formerly served in the Habyarimana
Cabinet. I said that these steps at the middle and lower levels of the
pyramid of national reconciliation needed to be encouraged. The
overall healing process would take time and would need to await the
dispensation of justice.

After my intervention, the heat evaporated from the discussion
and the Chairman left it to the Foreign Ministers to work out the
communiqué which was adopted. The Nairobi communiqué was
important in that, being the first summit declaration after the
genocide, it became a trail-blazer for subsequent summits, such as
Cairo and Tunis.

After the formal meeting, the Zairean Prime Minister and the Tanzanian Foreign Minister sought me out separately and inquired
about the plan for separating and relocating refugee camps that we
had worked out in our joint commissions. I informed them that since
there were no backers for the plan from the international community, it was being shelved. They were clearly disappointed.

The Geneva Round Table

In mid-January, the first Round Table Conference on aid to Rwanda was scheduled in Geneva. There was much interest by donor countries in helping Rwanda, particularly after the media focus on the genocide and the refugee tragedy. As we approached the conference, donors were divided into two distinct schools of thought. The first felt that the flow of aid to Rwanda should be commensurate with its performance on the ground in meeting basic objectives of human rights, justice, fair treatment to returning refugees, and, above all, a meaningful approach towards national reconciliation. Aid should therefore be conditional on Rwanda's performance towards achieving these objectives.

The second view was that Rwanda needed aid immediately in order to have the capability of achieving these very goals. Without the wherewithal and the basic financial capability, the government could not hope to achieve the targets to which it had publicly committed itself. To make aid conditional on performance would mean denying the government the capacity to act.

At the Geneva Conference, Prime Minister Twagiramungu made a most enlightened and convincing speech in which he committed his government to achieving all the targets that the international community had set for it. As SRSG, I put my weight fully behind the second view and pleaded that donor countries should provide at least minimal aid immediately. Donor states could always turn off the tap at a later stage if Rwanda fell short of meeting its commitments. However, to make the aid conditional, *ab initio*, would be tantamount to ensuring that Rwanda did not have the capability to meet its objectives. This view was strongly supported by Jan Pronk, the Netherlands Minister for Development.

In the end, Twagiramungu and his team carried the day and a commitment of US$530 million was pledged. Six months later, a Geneva Review Conference was held in Kigali and the aid to Rwanda was almost doubled to 1.2 billion dollars – a significant sum for a country with a population of 7 million. The questions to be answered in the future were how quickly could this aid be disbursed in Rwanda and in what form would it be channelled by the donor community into the receiving state!

By October 1994, in every report to HQ and in every briefing to foreign visitors, I had underlined the need for the donor community and the UN to find a minimal sum of liquid cashflow for the government of Rwanda to enable the country to start breathing again. A government did exist in Rwanda, but it had no offices, no transport, no telephones and no cash to pay essential salaries. The international community expected the government to show results in many fields, including inducing refugees to return home voluntarily, but how could this be done if the civil servants could not be paid, the

crops remained unharvested and basic services were not functioning
through lack of cash. My frustration grew every day when I saw
millions of dollars of humanitarian aid being spent in the refugee
camps on jerrycans, blankets, medicines and baby food and not a
penny available to repair the power, water, telecommunications or
the services that would set the country on the move again. I was
embarrassed also at the significant financial outlays on UNAMIR
staff, their food, vacations, vehicles of every kind, communications,
air travel – not a cent of which could be diverted to improve the lot of
the Rwandan people because assessed funds for peace-keeping could
not be diverted for development use for which funding came from
voluntary contributions.

My inexperience of the UN system with its structured layers of
turf combatants, its assessed funding for peace-keeping and voluntary contributions for development, the methodology of releasing
funds even for emergency needs, added to my chagrin. By October,
my pleas for a small sum, i.e. around US$10 million to be placed in
the UN Secretary-General's Trust Fund had, except for the Netherlands, fallen on deaf ears. I therefore banked my hopes on the World
Bank releasing a sum for Rwanda to meet this basic requirement of
up-front cashflow aid. The World Bank already had a programme of
US$160 million with the former government and for it to siphon off
US$20 million for up-front aid to meet Rwanda's immediate require-
ments seemed reasonable. I spoke several times on the telephone to
Washington and New York and it seemed that the World Bank was
on course to provide this sum.

I was grievously disappointed, however, when an announcement
from the World Bank stated that a sum of US$20 million had been
placed at the disposal of four specialized agencies, UNHCR, UNICEF,
the WFP and WHO! These agencies were already well funded as could
be seen by their Rwanda-oriented programmes in the refugee camps.
Another US$20 million to their coffers would hardly make a differ-
ence to the emergency restructuring of Rwanda. The same sum
provided to the Secretary-General's Trust Fund or directly to the
Rwandan government could have worked wonders! However, it was
not to be, and what added salt to the wounds was the World Bank's
announcement that the Rwanda programme of World Bank aid
amounting to over US$160 million would only be activated when
Rwanda paid up US$9 million in interest due on it from the previous
government! To a government that had taken over a totally devastated country, with absolutely no resources, it sounded like wanting
to draw blood from a stone. When I remonstrated with a World Bank
official, he replied, 'After all we are a commercial bank and have to
adhere to our regulations.' Eventually, donor states clubbed together
and raised US$9 million to pay the World Bank so that the Rwanda
programme could start flowing again. A similar sum was extracted by

the African Development Bank before it reactivated its Rwanda programme.

So, as I left for home leave, I felt reasonably satisfied at the turn of events over the past six months, ending with the international community's support at the Geneva Round Table. There was overall security in Rwanda and signs of recovery in a totally devastated landscape. Even more satisfying was the co-operation between UNAMIR II and the Rwandan government which had manifested itself on several occasions, especially on important issues such as the takeover from Operation Turquoise and Operation Retour. This climate was to change for the worse in the months ahead.

The Bujumbura Action Plan

Immediately after my return from home leave in February 1995, I was directed by New York to accompany the UN High Commissioner for Refugees, Mme Sadako Ogata, to Zaire and to Rwanda. Mme Ogata's visit was aimed at addressing the central issue of a voluntary return of refugees to Rwanda. It took place against the backdrop of the cold shoulder that donor states had given to the proposal for the relocation of camps, for which neither personnel nor financing had been forthcoming. Instead, the ball had been thrown into UNHCR's court to seek 'a poor man's solution' to the issue. Added urgency had been provided by rumblings of discontent on the Zairean side: suggestions had been made publicly that, if the UN could not persuade the refugees to return voluntarily, the Zairean government would use force to close the camps. Rwanda, in turn, accused Zaire of condoning cross-border sabotage, intimidation and increased military activity in the camps. The former RGF forces were also continuously announcing military campaigns to recover territories lost during the war, the latest deadline being Christmas Day 1994, which had passed without incident. Accordingly, Rwanda had threatened to reach across into the camps in Zaire and resolve the issue militarily. These public threats and rising tension between Zaire and Rwanda had precipitated Mme Ogata's visit to the region.

Mme Ogata met Prime Minister Kengo wa Dondo in Kinshasa and President Mobutu in Gbadolete. Both leaders repeated that Zaire had suffered grievously from the presence of the refugees through damage to its economic, social and ecological resources. Even politically, as elections approached, the government had suffered a set-back as a result of the presence of Rwandan refugees. Zaire had already conveyed to the SRSG that it would co-operate with UN plans for the separation and relocation of refugee camps. It needed, however, financial and logistic support to perform this difficult task, but there was no lack of will on Zaire's part to urge the refugees to return home. Zaire would not, for the time being, force a closure of camps and would co-operate with international efforts for a voluntary return of refugees. However, Zaire felt that the main reason for refugees staying on in the camps was not intimidation, but the harsh, re-tributional treatment meted out to them by the Rwandan government. President Mobutu and Prime Minister Kengo therefore pressed Mme Ogata to persuade the Rwandan government to take a more accommodating approach towards national reconciliation.

In her calm and poised way, Mme Ogata explained that as the international community had not come forward with support for the earlier plan of relocation, she had been charged as High Commis-sioner for Refugees to activate an alternative plan to induce a voluntary return of refugees. In her plan, she needed Zaire's support to control intimidation in the camps and facilities to ensure a smooth passage for the refugees back to Rwanda. After some discussion, the Zaireans agreed to a specially trained 500-member elite force which would be paid the princely sum of US$8 per head per month. This force would be augmented by a small contingent of police officers recruited mainly from the Netherlands to oversee discipline in the camps.

In Rwanda, Mme Ogata was received by President Bizimungu but not by Vice-President Kagame, which she took as a deliberate slight. In my opinion, the omission was due to a protocol error which was not unusual in a fledgling, inexperienced government that hardly had access to telephones to conduct government business. The Rwandan leaders assured Mme Ogata of fair treatment for returning refugees and full support to humanitarian efforts to provide food, shelter and healthcare for them. Again, the Rwandan government emphasized the need for up-front, cashflow support to revive a destroyed infrastructure and government machinery.

From Rwanda, Mme Ogata proceeded to Bujumbura where the OAU and UNHCR had sponsored a regional conference on refugee-related issues. The UN and its agencies had supported the confer-ence which, apart from representatives of governments from the Great Lakes region, was attended by donor states, NGOs and UN agencies. The Bujumbura conference proved to be a most successful landmark meeting in which a detailed action plan was negotiated and agreed between the three principal groups: the country of origin (Rwanda), the countries of asylum (Zaire, Tanzania and Burundi) and the donor community. The Bujumbura Action Plan served as the agreed framework and a bedrock formula for refugee return.

At the time when Mme Ogata was visiting the region, a rather un-expected solution to the refugee problem loomed on the horizon. There seemed a distinct possibility of an eruption in the active volcano, Mount Nyiragongo. This possibility appeared imminent as the volcano had shown signs of heightened activity. Vulcanologists from the USA, Italy and Japan visited the site and at least two teams feared an eruption in March 1995. The third team – the Italians – felt that while Nyiragongo continued to show signs of anger, it was unlikely to lead to an explosion. By summer, the danger of an eruption passed and we reverted to considering more conventional means of inducing the voluntary return of refugees.

Tension between the Rwandan government and UNAMIR

On my return to Kigali from home leave, I sensed a downturn in the cordiality and co-operation that had characterized UNAMIR's relations with the Rwandan government. At the ground level, there were a number of grating incidents involving UNAMIR personnel, either with the RPA or with the civilian administration. Radio Rwanda began broadcasting highly critical comment on the conduct of UNAMIR with wild and unjustified accusations based on isolated incidents. For example, UNAMIR soldiers were accused of corrupting the morals of Rwandan girls, of spreading AIDS, of speeding and not stopping after accidents and of selling rations and currency in the black market. Rwandan officials who had taken over at the airport and in various ministries were deliberately provocative towards UNAMIR staff and there were frequent bureaucratic hold-ups that were clearly aimed at needling UNAMIR personnel. The weekly Friday working-group meetings between UNAMIR military and the RPA Chief of Staff were cancelled and even in conversation with officials, there was now an absence of warmth and, in its place, a cussed, plaintive approach.

This change in the atmosphere was sudden and deliberate. Given the fact that the government had completed a relatively successful six months and that UNAMIR, now at full strength, was doing everything possible within its mandate to assist the Rwandan government, the abrupt change of direction needed to be analysed and explained.

The most obvious explanation was UNAMIR's sheer size, its vast logistic capability and its omnipresence throughout the country compared with the Rwandan government's meagre, threadbare resources. The contrast was glaring and provocative. White UN vehicles of every description, from four-wheeler sedans to forklifts, from coasters to bulldozers, constituted almost 80 per cent of the traffic in Kigali. UNAMIR had helicopters and fixed-wing aircraft which twice daily brought in food, water, medicines and duty-free cargo. UNAMIR was the only tenant in town and the main paymaster. On the other hand, Rwandan ministers and civil servants barely had one car per ministry, offices with broken doors and windows, a skeleton staff who could not be paid their salary and bare residences with no furniture. The Chief of Protocol had no car and no telephone. The Prime Minister still occupied the suite we had provided on the fifth floor of the Meridian as his residence – with the hole in the wall covered by cardboard! His office had one table, one chair and one telephone. The window beside his desk was still broken! This contrast was itself a source of chagrin, but when it was seen that, over these six months, UNAMIR was spending almost half a million dollars a day on itself, but could not spend $1500 towards the repair of the infrastructure, the chagrin grew to open resentment and anger.

A second reason was the sensitive issue of sovereignty. UNAMIR's very presence, Vice-President Kagame argued, diminished the new government's sovereignty. He stated that the presence of 5500 formed troops and Milobs, with a vast logistic back-up, gave the false impression to the Rwandan people that UNAMIR, rather than the government, was running the country. Kagame added that, in fact, it was the government that had provided the security, the stability and the governance that had led to six months of peace. The Rwandan hierarchy, meaning the RPF High Command, were therefore insistent that UNAMIR's presence eroded Rwanda's sovereignty. They made the point that there was no peace to keep for UNAMIR's 5500 military contingent and as UNAMIR's mandate seemed to preclude it from directly assisting in Rwanda's recovery, there was no need for UNAMIR to continue at its present strength.

A third reason for the tension was that the first anniversary of the commencement of genocide was only two months ahead. The public was being prepared for a major catharsis in which UNAMIR served as a convenient whipping boy. Posters and demonstrators began to appear with slogans such as 'UNAMIR allowed genocide', 'The UN stood by while massacres took place', 'UNAMIR assassins'. I am convinced that this ugly mood would not have developed if UNAMIR could have had a minimal capacity to assist in the repair of Rwanda's devastated infrastructure.

Much later, General Tousignant provided a deeper and incisive rationalization of this growing hostility towards UNAMIR. He reasoned that, during and immediately after the civil war, it was UNAMIR that provided the security, the logistic support and the overall umbrella of security in the climate of danger and high tension that existed throughout the country. In the prefectures, all UN specialized agencies, NGOs, etc sought security with UNAMIR. They located themselves in or near our regional headquarters. They voluntarily co-ordinated their humanitarian activity with UNAMIR because of the danger to their security, and they often sought UNAMIR protection when they moved about in the countryside. Whenever problems, risks or danger arose, they invariably sought UNAMIR assistance to help them out. UNAMIR was thus the hub of all UN activity during the period of insecurity. By the turn of the year, security had improved to the point that there were no curfews, few road blocks and generally a relaxed atmosphere prevailed throughout the country. This led to the agencies and the NGOs gradually detaching themselves from UNAMIR and sprouting their own wings. Each agency now chose to pursue its independent agenda, negotiating assistance separately with the government rather than as part of an overall whole, under the guidance of the SRSG. Once the agencies began dispensing humanitarian and development aid under their own programmes, it not only eroded the overall authority of the SRSG, but made it apparent that UNAMIR had no funds to provide to Rwanda.

It was obvious that this anti-UNAMIR tension was being orchestrated by the hard-core RPF leadership and was being condoned by the top leadership. It was also leading to greater strain in the Cabinet between the RPF High Command and Prime Minister Twagiramungu. At meetings with the Prime Minister around that time he would dismiss his staff and speak to me *tête-à-tête*. He expressed his concern at the lack of consultation between the President and Vice-President on the one hand and his office on the other. Mr Twagiramungu confided to me that the RPF was running roughshod over the country, and paying scant attention to the government's promises to returning refugees and to the majority population. He felt sometimes that he could not continue in this fashion. I advised the Prime Minister to hang on and to seek change from within rather than from outside. He agreed but appeared increasingly dejected and despondent.

Two events at that time caused a shudder of alarm in the international community and seemed to widen the schism between the RPF leadership and the Prime Minister. The first was a speech delivered by Vice-President Kagame at the site of a mass grave in Gitarama. In the speech, highlighted by Radio Rwanda, Kagame was highly critical of the international community. He was disparaging in his comments about aid donors and in harsh terms stated 'it was a waste of time' to negotiate with any 'so-called moderates'. The speech seemed to serve as a guiding beacon to the hard-line RPF who took it as the Vice-President's seal of approval for their xenophobic, resentful attitude to the international community in general and UNAMIR in particular. As an immediate consequence, the already rancorous and critical campaign against UNAMIR went up several notches. Demonstrations were held outside the French and Belgian Embassies while UNAMIR became a target of increased vilification. I was therefore obliged to make a formal protest to the President and Vice-President and found them both regretful, almost embarrassed, at the treatment the UN and the international community had been receiving. Vice-President Kagame explained that his speech was made off the cuff. He said he had been at the graveside of a close family member who had been brutally murdered and he may have used 'undiplomatic' terminology when referring to the conduct of the former colonial powers. He appreciated UN support and the international aid that had subsequently been given and his speech should therefore not be misconstrued as critical of the international community. Despite Kagame's assurances, the hard-liners appeared to have been let off the leash and, in fact, much damage was done to Rwanda's cause by the frequent quoting from the Vice-President's speech.

The second incident that caused an international outcry was the asphyxiation of 24 'suspects' who had been herded into a small *cachot* – a temporary cell – overnight. Briefly, 24 suspects who were sent to Byumba Prison were refused entry because of overcrowding. The group, which included women and children, was therefore locked into the *cachot* by an RPA unit to await permanent prison allocation elsewhere. By morning, all 24 had died, their banging on the doors and cries of supplication obviously having been disregarded by the RPA guards. The news of the awful tragedy travelled quickly around the diplomatic missions and into the international media. RPA headquarters arrested and court-martialed the guards. However, it was the horror of death by suffocation that was so appalling. Equally horrifying was the attitude of inhuman callousness that was shown by the RPA guards. In a most telling comment by the Prime Minister who hung his head in shame over the incident, 'the cachot inmates did not dare break the skylight which would have given them oxygen to survive because they knew that the guards would suspect a breakout and kill them all'.

Both these events caused the donor community, which had been so supportive of Rwanda at the Geneva Round Table, to suspend its aid and to scrutinize again the direction that the government was taking towards its own people and towards the international community. I too was perplexed by the apparently deliberate campaign by the Rwandan hierarchy to vilify and gratuitously take up cudgels with the UN and the international community. February and March 1995 had therefore been difficult months, showing a reversal of the co-operation that had been manifested in the second half of 1994.

The first anniversary of the genocide

By March 1995, the schism between the Prime Minister and the RPF leadership had grown to the point where, in a Radio Rwanda interview on his return from a tour of the USA and Europe, the Prime Minister was openly critical of his own government as follows:

> Several countries are insisting on the issue of the lack of security. Wherever I visited in Europe and in the USA, it was not easy for me to explain the problem of internal insecurity. For the last four months, several criminal groups operating like the death squads known before have been carrying out killings – civilians as well as soldiers are implicated in the killings. We must put an end to the revenge killings, and the torture style of tying hands behind the back must stop for good in this country. We cannot any longer say that people are killing or seizing private property by

force out of anger, because of their family members who have been massacred. This has been going on for the last four months and it may go on endlessly. These criminal groups are sabotaging the government's action and we cannot tolerate that.

There are a lot of killings, and these have continued since July in all areas of the country. We cannot go on lying to the international community and Rwandan people, saying these are only isolated incidents. We cannot go on asking Rwandan refugees to return home when there is so much insecurity. We hear every day that here and there people were killed or robbed of their property and this has continued for the last four months.

It is not a matter of the government being incapable. People have been killed and the government's instructions have been ignored. We cannot accept the existence of two governments in the country, the government must otherwise recognize it and reconsider its own role and manner of operating. No two governments in the country, I repeat. Bandits have taken control over the country and this cannot be accepted. Insecurity is the major problem and if it is resolved, the other problems will be resolved as well.

We want security to be ensured for refugees to return home. If we give instructions that are not respected, we are not assuming our duties. Investors will not come either and reconciliation will not be possible if there is no security. We cannot tolerate revenge killings going on without the government reacting and the government's instructions being ignored.

I myself lost 32 members of my family. I cannot ask those still alive to take machetes and kill people in revenge.

It was against this background that we approached the anniversary of the genocide, which the government decided to commemorate at the top of Mount Ribero, a hill on the outskirts of Kigali. A martyrs' memorial was to be constructed there and the remains of prominent martyrs buried, ceremonially, at the top of the hill.

On 7 April, we first gathered at the old stadium where the leaders addressed the massed congregation. As a result of the smear campaign, the mood of the crowd against the UN and the international community was unfriendly. At the stadium, I took the President and Vice-President aside to inform them that negative references towards UNAMIR would only exacerbate the current atmosphere of tension and would be counter-productive for Rwanda. I told them in advance that the Secretary-General's message on the anniversary was particularly warm and supportive.

We then went in a convoy up the hill to Mount Ribero where we were greeted with placard-holding demonstrators: 'UNAMIR watched while we were killed', 'Where were you, UNAMIR, on 7 April 1994?' etc. We sat under a tent as VIPs and foreign guests, notably the Ugandan Vice-President, took their places. I was amused to note that, despite the public vilification of UNAMIR, it was the white UNAMIR trucks that transported the wooden coffins of the martyrs to the graveside for their ceremonial burial. I was informed by a Rwandan dignitary that originally, the central grave was earmarked for the martyred Hutu Prime Minister, Mme Agathe Uwilingiyimana, but the RPF hard-liners had, at the eleventh hour, changed the schedule and allotted the 'grave of honour' to a Tutsi unknown soldier. Such was the mentality of the hard-liners on both sides, who relegated to 'second-class martyrs' in the final order of priority even those who had sacrificed their lives for their cause!

The ceremony was tense for us, but both President Bizimungu and Vice-President Kagame made a point of differentiating between the UN's 'let-down' in April 1994 and UNAMIR II's co-operative, supportive effort since then. These remarks lowered the tension and when I spoke, conveying the Secretary-General's message and also my own views on Rwanda, the speech was well received. I hoped that with the commemoration behind us, the relationship between the government and UNAMIR could get back on to a co-operative track. Now, however, another crisis loomed ahead, the renewal of UNAMIR's mandate which was ending on 6 June.

Immediately after the anniversary, the momentum of the 'hate UNAMIR' campaign saw an overflow into excess. Radio Rwanda began to broadcast vastly exaggerated comments which seemed to give the green light for all and sundry to regard UNAMIR as an acceptable target for abuse, theft or hijacking. A spate of robberies took place during this period, followed by hijackings of our vehicles by youths wearing RPA uniforms. Three of these hijackings took place near our headquarters with the hijackers pointing pistols at the drivers' heads. We noticed that the co-operation between UNAMIR military personnel and the RPA in the provinces was less cordial, and in Gisenyi a demonstration against UNAMIR ended up with the demonstrators smashing windscreens while the RPA watched. The worst incident, however, took place on 13 April when a demonstration outside UNAMIR headquarters was led by the Prefect of Kigali, Major Rose Kibuye, a serving officer of the RPA. She heaped vitriolic criticism against UNAMIR, accusing our drivers of callously running over pedestrians and our soldiers of black-marketing and corrupting Rwandan girls. Major Kibuye ended her harangue by calling on Rwandan citizens to throw stones at UNAMIR vehicles if they saw Rwandan girls being driven in them. Ironically, most of the local staff employed by UNAMIR were Rwandan women who were dropped home after work by UNAMIR vehicles as there was no public transport. If they worked overtime, a kind Milob or office vehicle would take the workers home.

I lodged a formal protest with the Foreign Office and with President Bizimungu, informing him of the incidents. I mentioned particularly Major Rose's comments, which were carried on Radio Rwanda. I told President Bizimungu that the campaign appeared to have the benign sanction of the government. The President – who had recently returned from a foreign visit in a UN plane placed at his disposal – was clearly embarrassed and told me that Major Rose would be asked to make a clarification of her remarks on the radio. She never did.

At the time, Vice-President Kagame, driving his own car, met with an accident, colliding with a local minibus. He was shaken and had a whiplash injury to his neck. He left for treatment in Germany and on return met me with an expression of regret at the anti-UNAMIR campaign, saying, 'I know UNAMIR has had a rough week.' The succeeding weeks saw Rwandan government–UNAMIR relations hit rock bottom.

6. April – June 1995

The Rwandan government's retribution

Kibeho

The tragedy of Kibeho, where between 1500 and 2000 IDPs were killed in a mass breakout from a hilltop siege, was a major blot on the government of Rwanda's reputation. Ironically, the operation was nearly a remarkable success for the government. The Kibeho syndrome therefore needs to be placed in perspective.

By August 1994, over a million IDPs had taken refuge in camps located in the HPZ, protected by Operation Turquoise. After Turquoise's departure on 22 August, the UN-sponsored Operation Retour saw over 700,000 IDPs return voluntarily to their communes, but the number of returnees began to show a drop towards the end of February 1995. Thus, by March, the RPF was again straining at the leash to forcibly close down the remaining IDP camps. The total number of these IDPs was approximately 250,000. They were now located in nine camps in the Gikongoro prefectures, the camps in the Cyangugu and Kibuye prefectures having melted down voluntarily.

The RPF's reasoning to forcibly close the remaining IDP camps was their contention that they consisted mainly of hard-core sympathizers of the former government. The RPF argued that the innocent had gone home and only the saboteurs and genocide sympathizers were left in the camps. The RPF also believed that the camps were harbouring militia and Interahamwe 'guerrillas' who were not only spreading disinformation against the government, but were linking up with their counterparts in the refugee camps of Zaire and Burundi. The RPF contended that it had demonstrated its bona fides by co-operating with the UN in Operation Retour, but there was no likelihood of further progress and it was now time for the RPA to take more forceful action to control guerrilla activity and to assert the government's full sovereignty over its territory.

Faced with this ultimatum, the UN agencies put together an intensified action plan to persuade the remnants of the IDPs to go home. The action plan was elaborate and impressive. It comprised an information programme, visits by ministers to camps, look–see tours by camp representatives to their communes, briefings by those who had left the camps and settled in their communes and assurances of healthcare, transport and basic requirements, all aimed at inducing what were obviously the most recalcitrant IDPs to return home.

Basically, the UN's effort was aimed at convincing the Rwandan government to agree to one last effort to persuade the IDPs to return voluntarily rather than resort to a forcible closure. The action plan was discussed with various ministers, notably the Minister of Rehabilitation, Dr Jacques Bihozagara, and the Minister of the Interior, Seth Sendashonga. Both ministers showed an interest and even made proposals to refine the plan. The elements of the plan that were acceptable to the government were the information campaign and the preparations in the 13 communes to which the majority of the IDPs were expected to return. Special arrangements for food, shelter, healthcare and transport were to be made in these communes through co-operation between the UN, the NGOs and the Rwandan authorities. Milobs and human rights observers were to be posted to the communes to ensure fair and humane treatment. The main point that had not been agreed was the arrest procedure for the 'criminals' in the camps. The UN and its agencies proposed that arrests should only be made after due process of law and after registration with the ICRC and human rights observers. This was not entirely acceptable to the RPA. The arrest procedure, and also the timing of the joint operation were therefore the subject of continued discussion. On 23 March, I met President Bizimungu and requested him not to proceed with the forcible closure of the camps and to support the action plan that we had almost finalized. He agreed to consider the plan.

These discussions on the action plan continued during the first half of April with the finalized version being formally conveyed to the government in a letter addressed by me to the President on 6 April. I expected a response before the government took a final decision on the issue of the camps. However, on the morning of Tuesday 18 April, General Tousignant reported that the RPA had encircled all nine camps near Gikongoro and had fired in the air to demonstrate that the camps were being closed. Of the nine camps, the following four were significant: Kibeho (100,000), Ndaza (50,000), Kamana (25,000) and Munini (10,000). The remaining five camps were small with populations of less than 6000 each. At 5.00 am, a brigade-strength contingent of the RPA surrounded the nine camps and, at first light, fired shots in the air and announced on megaphones the government's decision to close them. Seemingly, the RPA's patience had run out.

The first setback to the RPA manoeuvre took place at Kibeho, which was the largest camp and spread over five hillocks. In the panic to run for safety to the main hillock, where there was a church, a medical centre and a structure in which the Zambian regiment was stationed, a stampede took place and ten small children were trampled to death. Thus, within half an hour of the RPA's action, the hillocks at Kibeho had emptied and around 80,000 IDPs had collected on the main hill, encircled by the RPA. The remainder had made a run for it and scattered towards the nearby forest.

At 9.00 am, the RPA Chief of Staff, Colonel Sam Kaka, telephoned General Tousignant and informed him that the IDP camps in the Gikongoro prefecture were being closed down. He said that the RPA had fired in the air only to demonstrate that they meant business. No force had actually been used against the IDPs. Colonel Kaka requested UNAMIR's assistance in transporting them back to their communes and in providing humanitarian relief. Colonel Kaka then invited a UNAMIR representative to join him on a visit to Kibeho to see the situation at first hand, and requested a helicopter. The visit was quickly arranged and by 10.00 am, Colonel Sam Kaka, accompanied by the Deputy Force Commander, Brigadier-General Anyidoho, were on their way to the Kibeho hilltop where the milling crowd of about 80,000 was tightly encircled by the RPA. The Zambian company consisting of about 135 personnel was also inside the circle, occupying one of the small buildings adjacent to the church.

Meanwhile, news of the RPA's action had spread like wildfire and we were already being questioned by CNN, the BBC and others about the Rwandan government's action in forcibly closing the IDP camps. 'Were you consulted?', 'How many casualties?', 'Will the UN condone this action by the government?' they asked. The embassies, the UN agencies and the NGOs were equally taken by surprise, especially as they knew that the latest action plan had been conveyed to the Rwandan government and was under active discussion. Understandably, there was consternation all round at the RPA's precipitate action.

By 2.00 pm, Brigadier-General Anyidoho was back at UNAMIR headquarters and reported the following account of his helicopter trip to Kibeho. He confirmed that, at first light, the RPA had surrounded the Kibeho camps and fired shots in the air. The same action had been synchronized in the other eight IDP camps. Only in Kibeho had there been panic and a stampede. In the remaining camps the IDPs had agreed to fold their tents and to return home as soon as transport and escort was provided. In Kibeho, however, everyone had run towards the church situated on the main hill where the Zambian company was billeted. Probably, the Kibeho IDPs felt they would be more secure near the building. In the stampede, some women had been injured and ten children trampled to death. Anyidoho reported that there had been no injuries due to the firing and the IDPs had been allowed to take essential items, e.g. clothes, pots and pans with them. The few tents that were burnt caught fire due to overturned stoves.

On arrival at Kibeho, Colonel Sam Kaka addressed the 80,000 IDPs gathered on the hill. He said that the government had decided to close the camps, but no one would be harmed if they decided to co-operate and go home peacefully. He knew there were some 'criminals' hiding in the camps. They would be arrested, registered with the ICRC and the UN Human Rights Field Office and given a fair trial. The innocent need have no fear. They would be escorted to their communes in vehicles, given food, water and healthcare. As soon as arrangements had been worked out with the UN, the IDPs would be able to go home. For the present, everyone should stay calm and co-operate. At the end of the speech, Colonel Kaka asked all those who wished to go home to raise their hands. Brigadier-General Anyidoho related that about 95 per cent of the people gathered raised their hands and said they would go home. As a result of Colonel Kaka's speech, there was a visible easing of tension.

Anyidoho had returned to Kigali with a request from the Rwandan government for UN support to assist the IDPs to return home. This request placed me in a dilemma. First, the government had betrayed our trust by acting unilaterally to close the camps when we were actively engaged in negotiations with it to launch the revised action plan. Secondly, the very act of forcibly closing the camps was against international humanitarian norms and its perpetrators did not deserve our co-operation. The humanitarian agencies felt particularly aggrieved at the Rwandan government's action.

On the other hand, we were faced with a real humanitarian problem on the ground. Rightly or wrongly, the government had decided to close the camps. So far, it had used force only to convey a message and had taken care not to point a gun at human beings. The government had co-operated with the UN for the past nine months, but had probably come to the conclusion that the residue of the IDPs were hard-core and would therefore not voluntarily leave the camps. Its decision was aimed at ending the anomaly. The RPA, in order to retain an element of surprise, could not have held prior consultations with UNAMIR or UNHCR for fear of leaks. In fact, I found out that most members of the Cabinet, including the Prime Minister, were not aware of the timing of the RPA action. My dilemma now was that 80,000 desperate IDPs needed to be transported home from the top of that hill in Kibeho. Only UNAMIR and the agencies had the capability of providing the transport and the humanitarian care to assist in this operation.

After consultations with Tousignant and Anyidoho and after weighing both sets of arguments, I decided that UNAMIR and the agencies should make the best of a bad job by giving their full co-operation to resolving the humanitarian problem that we were now facing. Accordingly, Anyidoho was sent back to Kibeho and then to Butare to convey this decision and to seek agency and NGO co-operation in the evacuation of the IDPs from the hilltop. UNAMIR decided to send all its spare vehicles, 24 in number, and also its engineers and logistic support to Kibeho in order to start the evacuation. However, by far the largest number of vehicles (buses, trucks, etc) were available with UNHCR and the IOM (International Organization for Migration).

In the afternoon, I was informed by Randolph Kent, head of UNREO, that the agencies were reluctant to go along with my decision to co-operate with the government. In Butare, where he met the heads of the UN agencies and NGOs, Brigadier-General Anyidoho argued our case for over six hours but was unsuccessful in persuading the agencies to co-operate with UNAMIR. In fact, this was the first important occasion where the agencies had declined to fall in line with a decision made by the SRSG. The agencies, particularly UNHCR, stated that they needed instructions from their headquarters.

That evening, on learning that the agencies were not inclined to follow my decision, I telephoned UNHCR headquarters in Geneva and spoke to Deputy High Commissioner Walzer, whom I had known as the UNHCR representative in Islamabad. I gave Walzer my reasons for co-operating with the evacuation and sought his organization's support. Walzer said he would call me back the following morning. He did so and said that UNHCR would follow my lead, provided I conveyed in writing that I was responsible for the decision on political grounds. I faxed the certificate immediately and Walzer, in turn, sent instructions to his local representative. This process delayed UNHCR/IOM support by a critical 48 hours and it was our bad luck that for the next two days it also poured with rain, a deluge the like of which I did not see again in my two years in Rwanda. The result was that our vehicles got bogged down in the mud and could not proceed on the dirt-track roads to Kibeho.

By the evening of Thursday 20 April, three days had passed since the stampede on top of the hill in Kibeho where the situation had deteriorated sharply, turning the open-air camp into a cauldron of appalling misery. Our Zambian unit had been augmented by another Zambian company and an Australian medical unit and they reported that 80,000 people continued to be squeezed in a tight circle by the RPA on top of the hill. At night, the hard-core political elements (the militia and Interahamwe) would threaten and intimidate the families who had shown an inclination to go home. Some of these 'doubters' would be tortured and even hacked to death, so that by morning, no one was prepared to leave voluntarily. The result was that 80,000 human beings stood shoulder to shoulder, with barely any food and water, as the local RPA commander only allowed pre-cooked food (biscuits) and a limited ration of water to pass through into the circle. The RPA also prevented the humanitarian agencies from entering the circle. The appalling consequence of this siege was that the IDPs were hungry, thirsty and exhausted. They urinated and defecated where they stood as there was no room to move. At night, they were subject to murderous intimidation by the Interahamwe. To make their misery totally intolerable heavy rains came, preventing all vehicular traffic from approaching the camp. The RPA also insisted that cooked food and humanitarian aid should be available at the exit point and in the 13 communes to which the IDPs were expected to return, but not inside the camp. The RPA allowed exit only in escorted vehicles and only after careful screening. The net result was that the outflow of the IDPs from the Kibeho hilltop was slow and desultory.

Our Zambian and Australian units reported that a humanitarian crisis was imminent due to the appalling hygiene conditions on top of the hill, and to the savage intimidation at night. What made the situation unbearable was that even though some IDPs – about 20,000 – had been evacuated, the RPA had not allowed the resultant space to be used by those who remained, but had, instead, closed and tightened the circle so that a sense of suffocating hubris was being felt by the people left on the hill. The Rwandan people are perhaps the most long-suffering of all, accepting the most horrendous hardships without showing any sign of protest, but even for them the conditions in Kibeho were reaching breaking-point as dysentery, hunger, thirst and the stench of human waste surrounded them for the fourth day, while they stood under pouring rain. The Zambian regiment reported horrifying stories, shrieks of pain at night as the Interahamwe set about killing and maiming those who dared co-operate with the government.

There is a videotape taken by Lieutenant Kent Page, a young Canadian public relations officer, from inside this cauldron of despair. He had gone into the Zambian/Australian field HQ in his four-wheeler to conduct some journalists. No sooner had his car arrived inside the camp than it was surrounded by a pleading, beseeching, crazed mass of humanity, who wanted food, water or simply sanctuary because they could not get out of the hilltop prison. Inside, they were being killed and tortured by the Interahamwe. The tapes showed a boy of about 16 with a machete gash across his forehead, desperately trying to enter the vehicle. Kent Page and his companions were trapped for four hours in their jeep, unable even to open their window-panes except for an inch to be able to breathe. Eventually, the Zambian regiment saved them by clearing a path for the four-wheeler to exit. It is to the immense credit of the Zambian regiment that in the lion's den, they conducted themselves with great restraint and responsibility, arresting 17 murdering intimidators and handing them over to the civilian prefect of Gikongoro.

The RPA's justification for tightening the circle around the 60,000 people in the Kibeho camp was that they said they contained a large element of criminals who had participated in the genocide. These criminals had to be plucked out of the cauldron and arrested.

Accordingly, the egress from the camp could only take place after a careful screening process had been carried out. Meanwhile, the IDPs had to be fed and provided with healthcare by the agencies and NGOs who, after their initial stand-off with UNAMIR, had come on board after two crucial days of hesitation.

Inside the camp, the Zambian contingent and the Australian medical unit were performing a heroic task. First, they maintained an equable relationship with the RPA, enabling the UN agencies and NGOs to eventually enter the camp with food, relief and medical facilities. They also took on the responsibility of preventing the RPA from forcibly arresting people inside the camp which would have created a violent blow-out. They then took into their building the small children who had either been separated from their parents or had been handed over in order to prevent their being intimidated by the Interahamwe. These children were cared for throughout by the Zambian regiment. The Australians, the ICRC, MSF, WHO and UNICEF were also performing a superb role in bringing medical care to the IDPs.

By the fourth day, Friday 21 April, I decided to meet Vice-President Kagame who received me in his new spacious Defence Ministry Office. It is significant that Kagame had just returned from a week's visit to Germany where he had been receiving medical treatment for an injury sustained while driving his own car. I related to him the reports of an imminent crisis and told him that I would go to Kibeho after my meeting with him. He instructed a senior official in the Refugee Ministry, Christine Umutoni, to accompany me, along with our Liaison Officer, Major Frank Kamanze.

At 10.00 am, I took a helicopter for Kibeho accompanied by General Tousignant, Ms Umutoni and Major Kamanze. During a three-hour visit, I became convinced that a crisis was imminent. For four days 80,000 people had been tightly encircled in the open, with little food, no sanitation, no space and pouring rain, while suffering the brutal assaults of the Interahamwe from within and certain to be shot by the RPA if they broke out. Already, dysentery had broken out leading to 13 deaths and I was informed by the WHO and MSF that unless conditions improved, cholera was certain to follow. As we toured this awful, horrendous camp, we came across the 13 dead bodies of the dysentery victims lying in a heap. The RPA had refused to bury them and it took some hard bargaining before the Zambians were allowed to do so. I was convinced that unless the government acted immediately to ease and redress the situation, a crisis would take place in the next 24 hours.

Back at headquarters, I sent an urgent message to General Kagame as I could not reach him on the telephone, informing him of an impending catastrophe played out in full view of the media. I gave him a description of the conditions and made the following suggestions. First, that the tight cordon by the RPA should be loosened to allow space. Secondly, that instead of insisting on screening and transportation by vehicle under RPA escort, people should be allowed to walk home after peremptory screening, as vehicles were not able to reach Kibeho due to the rain. This was necessary to ease the tension on top of the hill. A quick melt-down on the hill would give the remainder hope. Thirdly, I requested greater access by humanitarian organizations to prevent cholera and disease spreading. Fourthly, I pleaded for greater restraint by the RPA in arresting criminals. Since they knew the identity of most of the criminals they could be arrested later, even if they decided to walk away. I made it clear that unless these measures were taken, a disaster was certain to take place.

My message clearly had an impact because the following morning, General Kagame rang me at home, before breakfast, to inform me that he agreed in principle with my suggestions. He said he would be sending Colonel Sam Kaka to discuss implementation in detail. I welcomed the Vice-President's support and on reaching the office, I was informed that the Chief of Staff would arrive at 10.00 am. I waited till 10.40 am and then, as I had an appointment at the Integrated Operation Centre to brief the agencies, NGOs, etc on my visit to Kibeho, I left. I was informed at the Centre that Colonel Kaka had been unavoidably delayed and had arrived five minutes after I left. He apologized and said he would return at noon. I arrived back at my office to receive Colonel Kaka who informed me that he had instructions from the Vice-President to co-ordinate the measures that I had proposed. At the meeting, I was accompanied by General Tousignant and we began to work out detailed, co-operative action for the evacuation of Kibeho.

It was evident to me that General Kagame and the military head-quarters had not been given an accurate picture of the conditions in Kibeho by the local RPA commander. As soon as the general learnt of the real situation and of the imminent crisis, he had decided to take corrective action. Possibly Christine Umutoni may also have given her independent report. Kaka's visit to my office was clearly an attempt to change course from the direction that the RPA's local commander had taken and to retrieve a fast-deteriorating situation.

While Kaka, Tousignant and I were discussing the action to be taken in my office, we were interrupted by General Tousignant's staff officer, the excellent Colonel Arp, who informed us that there had been an attempted break-out from the camp. Shots had been fired and people had died. There were reports of firing from all around the camp and the Zambians were reporting panic and mayhem. On learning this news, Sam Kaka understandably excused himself and rushed back to his headquarters. The corrective measures were too late.

At 2.30 pm we were informed that the RPA had succeeded in establishing order and that the circle had been repaired, but many casualties had taken place, some in front of journalists who happened to be visiting Kibeho.

The lull did not last long. By 5.00 pm another breach in the circle was reported, followed by several others all around the camp. The dam had burst and a swarm of IDPs was now running helter-skelter from the hill with the RPA firing on the fleeing mass with rifles and machine guns. The worst possible scenario had taken place.

At headquarters, we were inundated with telephone calls from the media, asking for our comments on casualties. We were receiving regular reports in the operations room where General Tousignant and I gathered till late in the night. At 10.00 pm the journalists' party returned from Kibeho, shaken and distraught. One of our radio journalists was crying hysterically, repeating simply 'They killed them in cold blood' over and over again. By nightfall, the guns were silent. About 2000 IDPs had stayed back in the medical compound in Kibeho, the rest had fled – some to the communes, some for the refugee camps in Zaire and Burundi, while others, probably the hard-core militia, scattered to hide in the forests, aiming to reach sanctuary with known sympathizers.

By evening, reports from Kibeho conveyed by the NGOs and our own units indicated a death list ranging between 4000 and 8000. The RPA had closed off half the camp and the preliminary estimates were about 4000 dead on the side of the camp to which UNAMIR, the agencies and NGOs were restricted. There was an assumption that an equivalent number had died in the other half. At nightfall, one of the Australian senior officers, accompanied by the British Provost-Marshal, Colonel Cuthbert Brown, walked through the debris on the hill and reported an estimate of around 4000 killed. This estimate was the preliminary figure that circulated among the journalists gathered at Amahoro headquarters.

By nightfall, it was evident that Kibeho had been a disaster. The world media, the international community and the NGOs were up in arms and I felt in my bones that the achievements of the new government – and there were many – would be washed away by this single incident. Early next morning, General Tousignant took a helicopter flight to Kibeho. There, he went over the same ground with the Provost-Marshal that was covered the night before and as a result of a carefully taken count, in broad daylight, he revised the estimate of the dead to 'between 1500 and 2000'. At night, the figure had seemed higher because the debris had included mangled clothes and abandoned sacks, pots and pans, which appeared in the dark like dead bodies. Moreover, many IDPs had obviously feigned death at night, but had later skulked away when the firing stopped. The Provost-Marshal and the Zambians agreed that the revised figure was nearest to reality and we issued it as our formal estimate and did not change it thereafter.

Some of the press who had, the night before, sent out estimates of the dead at over 8000, were angry with UNAMIR's figures, mainly because they were so much lower than theirs. These journalists criticized UNAMIR for trying to appease the government by reducing the count. In fact, the government was furious with UNAMIR for giving its figure and the grating relationship that had developed between UNAMIR and the RPA in March/April, was now heading towards rock bottom.

Clearly, the final break-out was due to human endurance having been pushed to extreme limits. The first signs had occurred the day before when some IDPs attempted to snatch a rifle from one of the RPA soldiers. There was shooting and three IDPs were killed. The precise chronology of the break-out on 22 April was as follows: a first attempt occurred at 12.10 pm, but the RPA had it under control by 2.00 pm. Casualties had taken place and there was a tension-filled lull inside the circle. Then at 5.45 pm the mass break-out took place. It caused consternation and panic among the RPA, many of whom were young, untrained and inexperienced. Eye witnesses stated – and some of these scenes were caught on video – that RPA soldiers began firing indiscriminately. They trained their guns on the fleeing IDPs. The Zambians reported some firing from within the camp, obviously from militia who had guns hidden in the camps. The RPA claimed that snipers had taken up position on the roof of the Zambian unit's barracks and that machine-gun fire was aimed at them. As a result, they retaliated with more machine-gun fire. Clearly not only had the panic and crisis led to the RPA losing their nerve but, probably, memories of the recent genocide had also led to some of the younger elements losing all reserve and discipline. One eye witness told me how a middle-aged woman sought shelter in a latrine and an RPA soldier followed her in and shot her in the back.

That night, our Zambian and Australian units who had been ordered by the RPA to remain in their quarters, were aware of hectic activity all around the camp. Floodlights were switched on, a number of heavy vehicles had driven up and there were signs of digging throughout the night. Some of our soldiers managed to peep across into the forbidden zone. It was evident that the RPA was engaged in a clean-up operation. Dead bodies were being collected and driven away. Shallow graves were being dug and a general damage limitation operation was taking place.

Next day, President Bizimungu visited the camp. He was evidently briefed by the local RPA commander (who was later punished for his role in the Kibeho tragedy) and his colleagues. They first informed the President that there had only been about 300 casualties, most of them in the stampede and at the hands of the Interahamwe! They also indicated that UNAMIR (meaning the Zambians) had given wrong advice to the people in the camps and had even fired at the RPA. All these false accusations fitted neatly into the 'smear

UNAMIR' campaign that had been waged since February. As a result, the President was in a fury when he met the local UNAMIR officer – a Zambian captain – and publicly demanded why they had lied to the media by giving such a high death-count when only 300 people had been killed, mostly in the stampede and by the intimidators. The Zambian captain stood his ground, at the graveside, and politely but firmly told the President that he had personally counted 1500 dead bodies on 22 April. The Zambian officer was jostled by the RPA officers for his impudence while the President moved on in high dudgeon.

Because the accusation had been made, we checked with the Zambians if, in fact, they had fired shots in self-defence. UN regulations require the meticulous recording and accounting for of every round of ammunition that is fired. The registers were checked and matched with the ammunition available and it was confirmed, without the shadow of a doubt, that not a single bullet was fired by the Zambians. The Zambians also became unpopular with the RPA because some Zambian soldiers spoke a dialect which made it relatively easy for them to understand Kinyarwanda. Two Zambian officers were therefore able to talk freely to the IDPs in their own language! The RPA took this as some form of conspiracy by UNAMIR against the Rwandan government. In fact, when UNAMIR's phase-down was agreed, the Rwandan government requested that the Zambian regiment should be one of the first to be phased out.

Over the next two days, the Kibeho cloud mushroomed across the globe and cast a negative shadow over the Rwandan establishment's reputation as a civilized, humane government. The Secretary-General made a statement and decided to send a Special Envoy, Mr Aldo Ajello, to Rwanda. Donor countries suspended aid programmes and a shudder could be felt going down the collective spine of the UN, its agencies and the NGOs operating in Rwanda. In my meetings with Rwandan leaders, I counselled an immediate damage limitation exercise. After all, the RPF's strongest public relations card was that it admitted errors. I advised that an international inquiry commission be appointed immediately.

The President and the hard-line RPF leaders were, however, on a xenophobic, anti-UN warpath. On 25 April, the entire diplomatic corps was summoned to Kibeho by order of the President and an extraordinary drama was played out on the hilltop in front of the entire Cabinet, the diplomatic corps, the NGOs and the RPA High Command. It started with a 7.00 am telephone call to me from Major Kamanze stating that the President desired the diplomatic corps, the UN agencies, the NGOs, the international press and the entire Cabinet to be present at Kibeho camp at 9.30 am. I anticipated an awkward encounter, as Major Kamanze told me that the President demanded the presence of the Zambian captain with whom he had publicly contested figures of the death toll last Sunday. Radio

Rwanda had also announced that bodies would be exhumed to prove that media and UN figures were highly exaggerated and to confirm the government estimate of 300. I expected the President to use the diplomatic corps as witnesses supporting the government's contention.

At Kibeho hilltop, addressing all of us, the President made the following announcement:

a) An independent international inquiry commission would be set up on the Kibeho tragedy. He requested the following to participate in the Commission: the USA, Canada, the UK, France, Germany, the Netherlands, Belgium, the OAU and the UN (UNAMIR). He added that Rwandan government representatives would also participate.

b) The commission should start work within one week (i.e. from 3 May). He requested financial and administrative support for the commission and requested that each member should sponsor its own delegate.

c) The terms of reference for the commission would be the examination of the following:

— the reasons which had led the government to decide the closure of the IDP camps

— whether prior consultations with UNAMIR had taken place

— whether actions had been taken on the basis of ethnicity

— the reasons for the Kibeho tragedy, apportioning responsibility to the Rwandan army (RPF), UNAMIR, the agencies or the Interahamwe supporters

— the number of deaths and their causes.

Having publicly announced the government's decision, the President stated that he was ready to verify the death toll, 'on the spot', through personal visits to the mass graves to count the actual number of dead bodies. He then publicly demanded the presence of the Zambian captain. In response, I was obliged to state that he had been rotated. I added that the UNAMIR Provost-Marshal, Colonel Cuthbert Brown, who was present throughout the tragedy, would be able to point out the shallow graves. Satisfied with my suggestion, the President and his entire entourage, followed by the media and diplomats, marched off to the mass graves to exhume the bodies. This process took about three hours with gruesome scenes of the graves being opened up in full view. Eventually, we returned to the press tent where the President requested the Foreign Minister to provide the 'results of the investigation'. The Foreign Minister then announced that the graves had been opened and that a total of 338

bodies had been counted! The President then handed the microphone to me.

This was an extremely awkward and embarrassing moment as the
President was virtually expecting an endorsement of his figures
through the implied acquiescence of the SRSG and the diplomatic
community. I first welcomed the President's announcement of an
independent international inquiry commission. I said the commission
would help to establish the objective reality. I expressed the hope
that governments would await the commission's report before making final policy decisions. I expressed the UN and the international
community's readiness to co-operate with the commission.

I then stated that the commission's terms of reference to calculate
the number of deaths and the manner in which people had been
killed would require forensic expertise, and also recourse to eye-
witness accounts of those present, including journalists. On the
critical issue of the death count, I stated that the commission should
also take note of why UNAMIR and the agencies had been blocked off
from part of the hill. As the commission was specifically charged with
pronouncing on this important issue, it would be inappropriate to
pre-judge its decision by establishing figures based on a casual
count from the graves. I therefore urged that the issue of the death
count be left to the commission.

The critical moment passed, the issue was diffused and all eyes
focused on the deliberations of the International Commission of
Inquiry on Kibeho. It was quickly appointed and comprised the
following:

— Colonel-Major Abdel Aziz, Tunisian military expert (OAU representative) (President)

— Mr Bernard Dussault, diplomat (Canada) (Vice-President)

— Mr Ernst Wesselius, prosecutor (Netherlands) (Rapporteur)

— Mr Marc Brisset-Foucault, prosecutor (France)

— Mr Koen de Feyter, Professor of International Law (Belgium)

— Mr Karl Flittner, diplomat (Germany)

— Mr Ataul Karim, diplomat (UN organizations)

— Dr Ashraf Khan, forensic pathologist (UK)

— Mr Maurice Nyberg, lawyer (USA)

— Ms Christine Umutoni, lawyer (Rwanda).

The Commission met over a period of two months. The following are
the summary conclusions of the Commission's report:

1)   In the opinion of the Independent International Commission of In-
     quiry, the tragedy of Kibeho neither resulted from a planned action by

Rwandan authorities to kill a certain group of people, nor was it an accident that could not have been prevented.

2) The Commission recognizes the legitimate interests of the Rwandan government and of the international community to have the displaced persons camps closed as quickly as possible, both for reasons of national security and in order to remove an important obstacle to the country's efforts to recover from the devastating effects of last year's genocide.

3) The Commission recognizes the efforts made by the UN Special Representative, UNAMIR, the government of Rwanda and other organizations to keep the situation at Kibeho under control.

4) The Commission regrets that the UN agencies and NGOs were not able to contribute more efficiently to the speedy evacuation of the IDPs from the camp.

5) There is sufficient reliable evidence to establish that, during the events at Kibeho camp between the 18th and the 23rd April 1995, unarmed IDPs were subjected to arbitrary deprivation of life and serious bodily harm in violation of human rights and humanitarian law committed by RPA military personnel.

6) There is sufficient reliable evidence to establish that, during the events at Kibeho camp between the 18th and the 23rd April 1995, unarmed IDPs were subjected to serious human rights abuses, including arbitrary deprivation of life and serious bodily harm, committed by armed elements among the IDPs themselves.[1]

Even after the immediate crisis had passed, a bizarre sequel to the Kibeho break-out took place in the medical centre compound on top of the hill. Here, in a large courtyard with about ten rooms on its periphery, around 1500 IDPs stubbornly refused to leave the hilltop building. The RPA surrounded this group and initial attempts by the UN agencies, NGOs and the Rwandan government itself to persuade these people to go home were unsuccessful. They all seemed brainwashed into believing that they would be killed by the RPA the moment they left the compound.

Conditions inside the medical compound were ghastly. Amidst the milling crowd of 1500 IDPs, people were dying either of disease or from machete wounds inflicted by the murderous intimidators. In a week, UNHCR counted 42 dead, their bodies gradually decaying in the compound. There was no sanitation and human excrement lay everywhere. Within the courtyard, women cooked for their families on makeshift wood-stoves. Several days after the crisis, and in order to allay fears, the RPA encirclement was withdrawn to a safe distance so that only UN blue berets could be seen around the medical centre. The inmates were promised food, water, escort by UNAMIR, UNHCR,

---

[1] Kibeho Commission report contained in Secretary-General's letter to Security Council, Document no. S/1995/411, dated 23 May 1995.

the ICRC and MSF, but to no avail. They adamantly refused to budge from their horrendous conditions in the compound.

On 28 April, the heads of the diplomatic mission, UNAMIR and the agencies, in full co-operation with the Rwandan government, decided to make a supreme effort to persuade the inmates to leave the compound. About nine ambassadors gathered at the medical centre and spoke to the crowd through megaphones, urging them to relent. I also lent my voice on the megaphone, assuring inmates of fair treatment. The distinguished German Ambassador, Mr August Hummell, was prominent in imploring the women and children to leave, but though one could see doubt in the eyes of the women, they seemed to be under the hypnotic, intimidatory vice of their leaders.

When we went inside the rooms, we saw the horrendous sight of many women and children lying lifeless against the walls, hungry and dehydrated. Some men were using dead bodies as their pillows to lean against. In the courtyard full of debris, I nearly stumbled over the dead body of a child. Further on, the corpse of an old women lay rotting amongst the rubble. In a final effort to reassure the inmates, the Belgian, German and French Ambassadors along with the Deputy Force Commander Brigadier-General Anyidoho and the Provost-Marshal, Colonel Cuthbert Brown, accompanied inmate representatives to a nearby commune where they saw for themselves that former Kibeho IDPs had not been slaughtered, but were resettled and making a new life for themselves. Although on that day only a few inmates left, over the following week the medical centre emptied voluntarily with, of course, a large number of arrests of alleged criminals and saboteurs from among them.

Looking back on Kibeho, it seems to mirror the Rwandan tragedy, in a microcosm. In my mind, the initial decision to close the camps was the result of frustration with the international community for not comprehending that the hard-core that was left in the IDP camps was not willing to leave voluntarily. No amount of inducements or incentives that the UN was working on could, in the Rwandan government's view, resolve this problem. It was not only a no-go area within its own territory but a hotbed of saboteurs and guerrillas which the Rwandan government needed to control. The eventual decision to move in was the first time that the Rwandan government had acted without consulting UNAMIR. It showed a desire to 'go it alone' and a lack of confidence in the UN and the international community.

I share the conclusion of the Commission that the operation was conceived to be implemented with as little violence as possible. This was evident from the initial command decision not to fire at the IDPs and to protect life and property as best as possible. The address by Chief of Staff Sam Kaka on the Kibeho hilltop reflected government policy. Finally, the manner in which Vice-President Kagame reacted to my red-light concern over the Kibeho camp reflected a policy from the top that aimed at avoiding violence.

Where Kibeho spiralled out of control was in the local RPA commander's decision to keep a tight circle around the IDPs, to deny them food, proper sanitation and medical care and not to allow a liberal walk-home policy that would have led to a thinning-out of the crowd on the hilltop and a progressive easing of the appalling conditions. The IDPs were therefore pushed to the extremes of human endurance. Eventually, when the dam burst on the fifth day, some RPA soldiers lost control and went berserk. Thereafter, the RPA tried a cover-up, and the damage limitation exercise under the glare of media publicity was neither effective nor plausible.

The irony is that the remaining eight IDP camps were closed down without tension or any adverse fall-out. If Kibeho had been handled with greater sensitivity, the government could have been vindicated in taking the step for a forcible closure. The difference was that Kagame's corrective measures came too late.

During this momentous week, Hedi Annabi, head of the UN Department of Peace-Keeping Operations' Africa programme, chose to visit Rwanda. He was with us at the Kibeho hilltop where the President challenged UNAMIR on the body count of the dead. He accompanied the UN Secretary-General's Special Envoy, Aldo Ajello, to his meetings with Rwandan leaders and sat in on our weekly negotiations on UNAMIR's future mandate. A wise, experienced and highly motivated official, Hedi Annabi was able to witness, at first hand, the burning cauldron of issues with which the UN was confronted at the time. His visit helped to provide perspective to the UN's efforts in Rwanda and to allay unfounded doubts about UN intentions that Rwandan leaders had gleaned from corridor gossip in UN circles.

Prisons

In October 1994, I had reported serious overcrowding in Rwanda's 11 prisons. These were designed to take a maximum of 9000 inmates, but by April 1995 the prison population had grown to 40,000 with a weekly intake of about 1000 and no compensating releases, so that Rwandan prisons now presented an image of unbelievable horror.

The ICRC, human rights observers and our own Milobs were reporting overcrowding of such proportions that it made the Black Hole of Calcutta appear like the opening day of the Harrods sale. Earlier, when I had taken a helicopter ride over Kigali Prison, I had been struck by the sheer density of the prison population which seemed like a human beehive on a deserted landscape. Kigali was, however, a luxury compared to Gitarama Prison where the prisoner density was four persons per square metre: roughly four people living in the space of a normal bathtub. There was no room to sit or lie down, only to stand and doze while leaning against another prisoner. Day after day, week after week, month after month these prisoners, most of whom were suspected of genocide and who had been put in prison without due process of law, would simply stand and pass the time. Many became gangrenous in their legs due to the lack of circulation. Doctors reported limbs decaying and falling off. In sheer frustration, some prisoners began biting the ears or the flesh of the prisoner next to them.

The prison conditions became so grave, such a scar on the treatment of humanity, that on 23 March 1995, I formally requested the President to form a prison commission in order to alleviate the appalling overcrowding. The plight of the prisoners was expected to grow worse as there were no signs of a judicial system becoming operative in the near future. I promised the President the UN's full co-operation in seeking an improvement in the prison conditions. I made the point that, if the media focused on prison conditions, this single blot on Rwanda's copybook could erase, in one stroke, all the positive achievements of the Rwandan government since its installation.

President Bizimungu took due note and soon after my meeting, he asked me to accompany him to N'Sinda, a prison about 50 kilometres east of Kigali. N'Sinda was one of the better prisons, but it was still one of the more grisly sights of my stay in Rwanda. The prisoners were packed knee to knee and back to back in their cells so that while they could sit, they could not lie down. As we entered the compound, a terrible stench of stale, unwashed bodies came from the cells. I noticed how resigned and calm these prisoners were, suffering the appalling conditions without manifest anger in their demeanour or hatred in their body language. The President spoke to each group through the bars in Kinyarwanda, promising them a fair deal and improved conditions, which brought a cheer and a clap. He then asked me to say a few words, which I did, assuring them that their conditions would improve and repeating the President's commitment for a fair trial.

We then moved to the women's section which also held some children, obviously the offspring of the accused. I was struck by the ordinariness of the women prisoners. They seemed like simple farmers' wives caught in a horrendous situation of mistaken identity. The women were more assertive than the men and said to the President, 'Why do you keep us here without trial? We have been brought here only because some people wanted us out of the way to take our farms and property. Why don't you call the accusers here? You will see yourself that we have been falsely accused.' The President was clearly moved by their apparent sincerity. He promised early justice. It made me wonder how many of the 40,000 in prison were innocent, accused by neighbours or relatives wanting to settle scores or simply to gain access to property. Two nuns were serving sentences in Gitarama Prison. When asked the reason for their incarceration, they said, 'We do not know. We were never charged. It is perhaps God's will that we serve people in these dreadful conditions. We will continue to serve God's children.'

The prison issue burst into the open after the visit to Rwanda of the German Foreign Minister, Klaus Kinkel, in June 1995. He was appalled by the horrific conditions he saw and sent an immediate message to the Secretary-General. He made it clear to the Rwandan leadership that Germany's significant aid package of over US$100 million would be reviewed if prison conditions were not improved.

Accordingly, the Prison Commission that I had proposed to President Bizimungu in March was announced in July 1995, to be headed by Claude Dusaidy, the RPF's former representative in New York and now the Vice-President's political adviser. The Prison Commission associated UNAMIR, the agencies and the ICRC with its deliberations and within a short while produced an interim report with an action plan. In short, the immediate – first track – requirement was to provide special facilities for women and children; improve health, medical and sanitation facilities; find new temporary detention centres, like large warehouses or bus depots, which could be converted into temporary prisons; and expand existing prisons to create more space. The second track was the building of new prisons, a long-term measure for which donor countries were reluctant to commit funds. They argued that building more prisons would mean more prisoners and, in any case, the tax-payer would not agree to channelling development funds for such purposes.

With these constraints, the UN family and the ICRC began its assistance programme to improve prison conditions on the first track. UNAMIR engineers and logisticians set to work and helped expand several prisons by helping to build boundary walls, watch towers, floodlights and sanitation units. UNICEF funded a special centre for children at Gitagata and the ICRC and the agencies set about improving medical and health facilities. The President formally opened an expanded N'Sinda Prison on 5 October. By the end of October, the situation in Rwandan prisons was marginally improved. The ICRC reported that incidents of gangrene had virtually ended and that, even though there was still appalling overcrowding, the treatment of the prisoners by the prison authorities was correct and disciplined in that they received their food on time, were able to meet their relatives, received medical treatment when necessary and had access to basic sanitation. However, the prison nightmare continued because there was no outlet, due to the lack of a judicial process. In April 1996 alone, over 70,000 were herded into the prisons of Rwanda.[1]

---

[1] At its height in 1998, the prison population in Rwanda was reported to have reached 110,000.

Negotiations for a new mandate

After Kibeho, the relationship between the Rwandan government and UNAMIR had reached its lowest point. Around that time, Vice-President Kagame raised the issue of UNAMIR's forthcoming mandate which was to be renewed on 9 June. In a nutshell, the Rwandan position was that, first, UNAMIR's peace-keeping presence in such large numbers was no longer necessary as there was no peace to keep and the Rwandan government was responsible for security in the country. Secondly, UNAMIR's overbearing presence with its vast resources undermined the sovereign authority of the government. People wrongly believed that UNAMIR was governing the country. And thirdly, UNAMIR's mandate was not directed towards assisting Rwanda and therefore such a large peace-keeping presence was pointless. In fact, the funds spent on maintaining a force in Rwanda could be diverted towards rebuilding Rwanda's shattered infrastructure.

Accordingly, the Rwandan government called for a drastic reduction of UNAMIR troops and for a change of mandate that would remove UNAMIR's authority for the maintenance of internal security, which the Rwandan government considered to be its exclusive domain. Thus, Rwanda's stand on UNAMIR's new mandate represented a significant departure from its earlier policy of co-operation.

At UN headquarters, there was a measure of understanding for Rwanda's point of view, but the demand for a drastic reduction of troops was seen as too radical. It was argued that the UN formed-troop presence across the country was contributing significantly to the preservation of security. The blue berets acted as a beacon of reassurance to the harassed population and were an important factor in persuading refugees to return home. While UNAMIR was not responsible for security, its presence ensured that no excesses could take place by over-zealous RPA soldiers.

As regards assistance to Rwanda, although development support was not, in fact, part of UNAMIR's mandate, its resources were being used to assist Rwanda towards recovery. Our vehicles were transporting refugees to their homes, our bulldozers were levelling land for prison extensions, our engineers were helping rebuild bridges, our logisticians were distributing agricultural seeds and implements, our aircraft were flying Rwandan leaders to neighbouring capitals, our doctors were attending to Rwandan patients throughout the country, our radio was informing all concerned about humanitarian assistance, transit camps and arrangements for the reception of refugees. Lastly, UNAMIR's presence provided a reassuring backstop to the agencies and NGOs to perform their functions in an atmosphere of security. The agencies frequently located their offices in our compound, used our excellent communications and went out on joint patrols with our Milobs.

I myself shared headquarters' view that while a gradual reduction of UNAMIR military presence should be effected, UNAMIR should, for the next six months, retain a sufficient presence in Rwanda to provide a sense of reassurance to returning refugees. It was the presence of blue berets in the prefectures that would make the marginal difference to a refugee between returning or staying in the camp. Kagame had a counter-argument to this point. He said that, in the final analysis, the refugee would return home because of the Rwandan government's policies and not because of UN blue berets. Therefore, the sooner the blue berets left the better, because they projected a false sense of security!

As a result of Rwanda's request for a revised mandate, a joint commission was set up to review the existing mandate and to recommend a revised one to the Security Council. This joint commission had on the Rwandan side, Emmanuel Gasana (no relation of the Foreign Minister), a highly experienced and articulate diplomat, and Colonel Frank Mugambage who was the RPA spokesman, a Member of Parliament and an adviser in the Ministry of Defence. (Several months later, Colonel Mugambage replaced Emmanuel Gasana as adviser to the President.)

The broad outlines of Rwanda's position had already been articulated to me by Vice-President Kagame in my meeting with him on 14 March. In the joint commission meetings, Gasana underlined the sovereignty issue, stating repeatedly that the government was now master of its own house and had sole responsibility to decide its destiny. So insistent were the Rwandans on this issue that I gained the impression that the RPF hierarchy believed that the Security Council would impose a mandate against the government's wishes. Some Rwandan ministers even believed UN corridor loose talk that the Security Council would revert Rwanda to Trust Territory status!

In response, I emphasized the fact that UNAMIR's presence in Rwanda was based on a Chapter VI mandate and that the government had a sovereign right to decide whether and in what form it chose to accept a UN presence on its territory. I assured my interlocutors that no formula would be imposed on Rwanda and therefore it was desirable to work out a mandate for a UN presence that would be acceptable all round. Once the Rwandan side felt reassured of respect for their sovereign rights, discussions moved to the narrower issues of UNAMIR's revised mandate and the reduction of its military component.

The Rwandans also maintained that security was the government's responsibility, certainly as far as Rwandan citizens were concerned and even with regard to the UN agencies, NGOs and humanitarian relief operations. They grudgingly accepted that UNAMIR was required to protect the ICTR – but not the human rights observers – and its own headquarters. They argued that there was no need for formed troops in the prefectures and only a 600-

member contingent was required for Kigali. Unarmed Milobs could remain in the prefectures. Surprisingly, the Rwandan delegation called for the removal of Civpol which had made such an important contribution to the training of the gendarmerie and was now poised to perform a similar role in training the civilian police.

After the weekly joint commission meetings, I would brief the donor country diplomatic missions and local UN agency heads. As the discussions progressed, the member states and UN agency heads began to express themselves bilaterally to the Rwandan government. For instance Judge Goldstone and Mr Ayala Lasso made it clear that UNAMIR protection was necessary if the ICTR and the Human Rights Field Operation in Rwanda (HRFOR) were to carry out their responsibilities. The development and humanitarian agencies were also against a drastic cut in UNAMIR's strength. As regards member states, all donor countries favoured the retention of a significant UNAMIR presence, mainly with a view to sustaining the improved security climate in the country and to inducing refugees to return home. The Secretary-General of the OAU, Dr Salim Ahmed Salim was also a forceful and articulate supporter of this viewpoint.

From my point of view, the most important factor in the new mandate was the need for UNAMIR to assume a peace-building role in addition to its peace-keeping mandate. Even though my efforts to launch the Rwanda Emergency Normalization Plan had been met with indifference, I felt that the new mandate could provide UNAMIR with a framework within which we could usefully employ our unique logistic and technical capability on the ground to repair the infrastructure and revive governance in a country that still lay shattered from the devastating effects of the civil war and genocide. In my opinion, only in this way would UNAMIR's continued presence in Rwanda find acceptance with the government. I therefore renewed my efforts for UNAMIR to assume a peace-building role, both with headquarters and in my briefing of donor country ambassadors in Kigali.

Between March and May 1995, I sent several telegrams to headquarters analysing the real rather than the stated reasons for the Rwandan government's disenchantment with UNAMIR. I indicated that in peace-time the Rwandan government viewed UNAMIR as a supervisory, monitoring agency, bringing no material benefit to the country. Unlike the agencies, it did not channel funds, it did not help in the economic or social uplift of the country, and did not provide material help like building barracks for the military or supplying vehicles and telecommunications to the security forces. It did not even repair the bridges, roads and buildings that it had used. I emphasized that a peace-building role should become the primary theme of our new mandate. This role, in my view, should be entrusted to the overall charge of the SRSG.

Eventually, my recommendations were reflected – albeit somewhat mildly – in the Secretary-General's report to the Security Council no. S/1995/457 of 4 June 1995:

> During these consultations, my Special Representative discussed with the Government a new mandate comprising tasks which, in my judgement, should be performed by UNAMIR during the next six months. These tasks would continue to be carried out with full respect for the Government's sovereign authority. They would entail shifting the focus of UNAMIR's mandate from a peace-keeping to a confidence-building role.

Regrettably, the Security Council did not respond to the Secretary-General's recommendation and the Council's decision on the new mandate included no mention of a peace-building role for UNAMIR.

Eventually, the differences boiled down to the issue of whether or not UNAMIR would retain company-strength formed-troop presence (i.e. 200 troops) in five of the more difficult sectors in addition to a battalion at the headquarters in Kigali. It was against this background that I had my final meeting with the Vice-President on 2 June before proceeding to New York where Emmanuel Gasana was to have his final round of discussions. I give below a summary of my meeting with General Kagame.

a) Kagame said that it should be clearly understood that UNAMIR was to perform a monitoring role and had nothing to do with 'security or protection'. I replied that we had deliberately removed references to protection and security from the new mandate.

b) Kagame clarified that this monitoring role could be done by armed persons 'in tanks' or by unarmed Military Observers, so long as it remained confined to monitoring.

c) He had no problem with the stationing of company-strength 'armed monitors' (i.e. formed troops) in six provinces. He asked me how large was a company to which I replied 200. He said in his book a company was 100. He agreed, however, to allow six companies at 200 strength in the provinces, i.e. a total of 1200.

d) Turning to headquarters strength, I said that there had been an understanding of a battalion plus the four logistic back-up companies. Kagame disagreed and stated that 600 was the maximum he could agree for the capital. He added that even the protection and security of foreigners was his government's responsibility, but in view of 'international opinion' he was agreeing to UNAMIR's monitoring presence. I argued that 600 soldiers plus the logistic companies would seem reasonable, but Kagame was adamant. He said that his bottom line was a total of 1800 in Rwanda. We could add to the Kigali contingent by drawing from the provinces, but the overall total should not exceed 1800.

e) Kagame was not against the existing Civpol contingent continuing until bilateral arrangements were in place. He said the existing contingent of 65 Civpol could be added to the figure of 1800.

f) Kagame twice underscored that Rwanda would 'willingly' co-operate with UNAMIR on the basis of an 1800 force. He clearly implied that the current 'UNAMIR-bashing' campaign would be replaced by a welcoming approach sponsored by the government.

It was evident that Kagame had accepted the concept of UNAMIR formed-troop presence in the provinces in return for a 60 per cent reduction in UNAMIR's overall strength. He insisted, however, that UNAMIR would not perform a security but a monitoring role. I had already clarified that the government alone would be responsible for the security of its nationals. UNAMIR's security role related narrowly to its own contingent and to the ICTR. Kagame also agreed to the retention of Civpol and Milobs.

From the outset of the discussions on the mandate, I had been informed by headquarters that my proposal for UNAMIR to play a peace-building role was not acceptable because assessed peace-keeping funds could not be channelled for essentially development purposes. I was disappointed because we clearly had the capacity to play a part in this revival process by linking up our logistic support, vehicles, engineers and communications experts with the development agencies and NGOs. Regrettably, there was to be no enabling clause in the mandate for this purpose, even though in Somalia and Cambodia peace-keepers had dug tube wells, repaired roads, run hospitals, etc as part of their respective mandates. To this day, I cannot grasp why such a peace-building mandate could not have been given to UNAMIR by adding, for instance, the following clause:

> In order to encourage the voluntary return of refugees and in addition to its peace-keeping responsibilities, UNAMIR would assist where possible in the repair and rehabilitation of Rwanda's infrastructure.

Given General Kagame's approval for the overall framework of the new mandate, agreement was reached at New York after some eleventh hour haggling over numbers. It was agreed that the number of formed troops would initially scale down to 2400 and to 1800 by the end of the six-month mandate.

A comparison of the operative parts of the two mandates is given in Figure 1 opposite.

The negotiations on the mandate also brought to the fore the marked difference in approach between the Tutsi and Hutu members of the Cabinet. Whereas the Tutsi elements sought a drastic reduction and a significant change in UNAMIR's mandate, the Prime Minister and his moderate Hutu colleagues considered UNAMIR's presence essential in ensuring security in Rwanda and acting as a safety magnet for the refugees. They felt that UNAMIR should remain

Secretary Council Resolution no. 965, dated 30 June 1994, approving UNAMIR mandate from 9 December 1994 to 9 June 1995

Contribute to the security and protection of displaced persons, refugees and civilians at risk in Rwanda, including through the establishment and maintenance where feasible, of secure humanitarian areas

Provide security and support for the distribution of relief supplies and humanitarian relief operations

Exercise its good offices to help achieve national reconciliation within the frame of reference of the Arusha Peace Agreement

Decides to expand the mandate of the mission to include the following additional responsibilities within the limits of the resources available to it

Contribute to the security in Rwanda of personnel of the International Tribunal of Rwanda and human rights officers, including full-time protection for the Prosecutor's Office, as well as security details for missions outside Kigali

Assist in the establishment and training of a new, integrated, national police force

Security Council Resolution no. 997, dated 9 June 1995, approving UNAMIR mandate from 9 June 1995 to 9 December 1995

Exercise its good offices to help achieve national reconciliation within the frame of reference of the Arusha Peace Agreement

Assist the government of Rwanda in facilitating the voluntary and safe return of refugees and their reintegration in their home communities, and, to that end, to support the government of Rwanda in its ongoing efforts to promote a climate of confidence and trust through the performance of monitoring tasks throughout the country with military and police observers

Support the provision of humanitarian aid, and of assistance and expertise in engineering, logistics, medical care and de-mining

Assist in training of a national police force

Contribute to the security in Rwanda of personnel and premises of United Nations agencies, of the International Tribunal of Rwanda, including protection for the Prosecutor's Office, as well as those of human rights officers, and to contribute also to the security of humanitarian agencies in case of need

Figure 1

in significant strength in Rwanda until the bulk of the refugees returned. The Prime Minister considered that only a token reduction in numbers was required. His views and those of like-minded Hutu moderates reflected the divide in attitudes towards UNAMIR throughout the country. Basically, the Tutsis saw UNAMIR as an intrusive, watchdog presence which undermined the government's sovereignty and brought no significant assistance to Rwanda. They wanted UNAMIR to phase out. The Hutus regarded UNAMIR as an insurance against Tutsi excesses and wanted UNAMIR to stay. I had no illusions that the former point of view would represent the government's final policy.

So ended the rather bitter negotiations on the mandate. Seemingly, the Rwandans had started their campaign in February with the deliberate raising of the tempo against UNAMIR and the constant reminders of the UN's failure to save Rwanda from genocide in April 1994. The call for a new mandate had exacerbated the divisions within Rwanda and the issue of the reduction in UNAMIR's troop strength was obviously a source of controversy across the country. The divergence of approach could be felt from the Cabinet down to the grassroots level in the communes where the Hutu majority saw UNAMIR as guardians against excess while the Tutsi regarded UNAMIR's presence as irksome and intrusive.

Immediately after the new mandate was agreed, the mood in Rwanda changed visibly. The RPF and the government were back in the groove of smiling co-operation. All misunderstandings were to be put behind and a new era of mutual confidence was actively promoted. It was surprising how quickly the atmosphere changed. The hijackings and robberies against UN personnel virtually stopped. There was co-operation at all levels, requests for humanitarian aid came pouring in from the government and the stand-off of previous months gave way to a friendly, helpful attitude. The Vice-President stated that all minor problems – and there were several – would be resolved through official discussions between UNAMIR and the government. The change in atmosphere reflected itself in Kigali: people went out to restaurants and night clubs, there was improved social contact and sports championships were held with football, volleyball and athletics competitions between UNAMIR and the RPF.

7. July – September 1995

The UN Secretary-General's visit and its aftermath

Exactly a year had passed since the new government had taken over the reins of power when it was announced that Mr Boutros Boutros-Ghali would schedule the first ever visit by a UN Secretary-General to Rwanda on 13/14 July. It was an appropriate time to assess the main issues that faced Rwanda. In a report I sent to the Secretary-General, I summarized the main issues under the headings of refugee return; justice; reconciliation; international aid; and sabotage, militarization and infiltration from refugee camps.

Refugee return

Central to peace and stability was the need for a voluntary and safe return of refugees from neighbouring countries. To achieve this objective, not only must the mainly Hutu refugees be promised justice and security, but these promises must also be implemented on the ground. The Nairobi Summit Declaration, the Bujumbura Action Plan and the Tripartite Agreements signed between UNHCR, Rwanda and the neighbouring countries (Zaire, Tanzania and Burundi) provided the basic guidelines for future action. These agreements needed to be revived and implemented. I recommended that the Secretary-General urge all three parties to fulfil their respective commitments in a synchronized effort to achieve refugee return.

Justice

I recommended that the ICTR, which was scheduled to begin functioning in the second half of 1995, should be supported to fulfil its designated role. At the same time, the Rwandan government should be persuaded to start its own system of transparent justice so that the 70,000 alleged criminals herded into inadequate prisons were duly processed. Meanwhile, the conditions in the prisons must be improved on an emergency basis.

Reconciliation

I felt that reconciliation needed to be seen at several levels, starting at the grassroots, where ordinary citizens could begin to pick up their daily lives in the communes and towns without fear of retribution and in an atmosphere of fair play and security. Former civil servants, businessmen and army personnel might then be encouraged to return in dignity and security, and eventually political elements that were not tainted by criminal charges might be encouraged to return to the political fold. Reconciliation should not be seen as synonymous with impunity or with immunity from criminal responsibility. At the same time, the government should consider publicizing a definitive list of people suspected of having participated in the genocide. Determined efforts should be carried out by the government to promote harmony and peaceful co-existence among all ethnic groups. No one group should be made to feel excluded or persecuted. The principle of power-sharing, which underpinned the Arusha Accords, should be reaffirmed and some contacts should be initiated, first discreetly, with those Hutu political leaders in exile who were *not* implicated in the genocide.

International aid

I advised that the Secretary-General should assure the Rwandan leaders that the UN and its agencies would make every effort to achieve meaningful disbursement of aid pledges. It was essential that Rwanda and the international community maintain the momentum of this operation. Rwanda's co-operative attitude towards human rights, justice and reconciliation would be an important factor for maintaining this impetus.

Sabotage, militarization and infiltration from refugee camps

I referred to Rwanda's concern at the increased militarization, sabotage and infiltration from the refugee camps, which had caused increased tension within Rwanda. The Secretary-General should inform Rwandan leaders of the Security Council's concern at this dangerous development and refer them to the report of his Special Envoy which recommended measures to reduce this tension.

The Secretary-General's visit to Rwanda was an important landmark in Rwanda's history. In scheduling the visit, Mr Boutros Boutros-Ghali underlined the importance he attached to Rwanda and to its recent tragedy. He also expected the visit to clear a number of misunderstandings that Rwanda's leadership held about the UN in general and the Secretary-General in particular. I was eager therefore that the Rwandan leadership and Rwandan public opinion should see the Secretary-General's role in its correct perspective. Accordingly, his 18-hour programme was drawn up so that, apart from talks with leaders, there was also space to allow the Rwandan intelligentsia to interact, at first hand, with Mr Boutros-Ghali. I therefore insisted that he should address a special session of the National Assembly.

The Tutsi-dominated RPF had formed a subjective assessment of the Secretary-General as a francophone African who inclined towards France on international issues. This assessment was based on reports from the RPF's own operators in New York. France's support for the Habyarimana government was seen by the RPF as influencing Mr Boutros-Ghali's personal attitude to events in Rwanda. The fact that the Secretary-General had proposed an increase in the UN peace-keeping force in Rwanda which was reversed by the Security Council was countered by the RPF by pointing to his decision to appoint a francophone African – Cameroonian Foreign Minister Booh-Booh – as his first Special Representative to Rwanda and also by the fact all three experts in his genocide commission were drawn from francophone African countries. I was aware therefore that in visiting Rwanda, Mr Boutros Ghali was stepping into the lion's den, as he was seen by the RPF-dominated government as prejudiced against their country.

I met the Secretary-General in advance at Kampala Airport where he was whisked away for a two-hour meeting with President Museveni. He emerged from the meeting delighted at having persuaded the Ugandan President to play a leading role in seeking national reconciliation between the Rwandan leadership and 'non-criminal' members allied to the former government. The formula agreed between President Museveni and the Secretary-General was that the Ugandan President would, in consultation with the Rwandan leadership, select 10–20 representatives from the former government and invite them to Uganda. The Rwandan government would also send an appropriate delegation to Kampala to start political discussions.

Knowing the government's negative views on such efforts at reconciliation, I felt that the Rwandan leadership was not likely to warm to the suggestion and that only if President Museveni gave the idea his full backing would the proposal carry weight in Rwanda. During the plane journey from Kampali to Kigali I expressed the view that the greater chances of success in the process of national reconciliation was through efforts at the grassroots upwards rather than from the top of the pyramid downwards. For example IDPs and refugees returning home and settling down without pressure or fear, Hutus returning to their jobs from camps in Zaire or Tanzania, RGF soldiers rejoining the national army, were all part of a grassroots reconciliation. Already a number of senior officials of the former government were being reassigned posts as prefects, judges, *burgomestres*, and so on. Major Habyarimana, former member of the RGF and signatory of the Kigeme splinter group, was a Member of Parliament representing the RPA. The gendarmerie was headed by a former brigadier of the RGF. Dr Anastase Gasana, the Minister of Foreign Affairs, held the same post in the Habyarimana government. These were examples of a process of national reconciliation at the lower and middle levels which needed to be encouraged. Moreover, I felt that reconciliation with political elements of the former government would have to await the start-up of the justice system, both national and international.

Mr Boutros-Ghali did not agree. He felt that unless there was definitive and early movement towards reconciliation between the leadership of both sides, the refugees would remain rooted in their camps. Only if they saw elements of their own leadership co-operating with the government in Rwanda would real movement take place on refugee return and in favour of national reconciliation across the board. National reconciliation needed the catalyst of former government members being brought in to join the national fold. The Secretary-General laid great store in having persuaded President Museveni to support this proposal for a round-table meeting. His reasoning was rational and persuasive, but I feared it would run up against the rock of the RPF's intransigence, as at Nairobi.

The Secretary-General arrived in Kigali at 4.00 pm on 13 July and was received by the Prime Minister, the Cabinet, members of the diplomatic corps and agency representatives. He then held a meeting with the Prime Minister. This was followed by an address to the National Assembly which had been called specially to receive him.

I give below extracts of the Secretary-General's address and also the question and answer session that followed:

> But let us return to the elements of satisfaction. We see that we are on the road to reconstruction and Rwanda is trying to put the tragedy behind it. Unfortunately, much remains to be done. First of all there is an urgent need to work to achieve the objectives that were set during the Arusha Accords. I wish to stress in particular, and this will be the subject of our discussion, the importance, the necessity of the entire Rwandan nation's being able to participate fully and democratically in the management of the country's affairs. Policies of exclusion would have consequences that you have experienced and we have experienced with you. What is more, policies of exclusion would make it exceedingly difficult for the international community to assist, co-operate and collaborate with your country and other African countries.

The second very important idea to which we are committed concerns the protection of human rights. I am well aware that human rights have been violated in the most atrocious manner and that genocide has occurred. I wish to remind you that I was the first to use the word genocide in the international assemblies in order to mobilize and sensitize international public opinion, in order to secure increased international assistance for your country, whether political, military, financial or technical. I did not succeed. I encountered far greater difficulties than in other situations which were not so serious but which called for assistance. It is therefore important to find a solution and in particular, a solution to the problems of refugees. In this connection, the United Nations is bound by certain international norms, one of which forbids us from compelling refugees to return to their country. We therefore have no way of forcing them to return. This is a first obstacle.

A second obstacle is the fear that you find in refugee camps, whether in Bukavu or Goma or on the Tanzanian border. In view of this fear, it is your duty – because these are your brothers and I am not trying to preach – it is your duty and I would say that it is in your interest to engage in a dialogue with these refugees. Some people are guilty and they must be punished. We have established an International Tribunal to assist you and you will have your own National Tribunals. But it is important to engage in a dialogue with the great mass of refugees. Only through dialogue can they be prompted to return to their country, to their village and to participate in political life, in rebuilding your country. As long as they remain in refugee camps, the reconstruction will be incomplete and what is more serious, international assistance will also be incomplete. And we will have difficulty in securing this assistance.

I think that I had an extremely frank discussion with the Prime Minister, in the course of which I explained to him the difficulties that I am having today, as Secretary-General of the United Nations, obtaining assistance, whether from donor countries or from non-government organizations. You will ask why that should be. Given the multiplicity of conflicts, the international community's assistance, interest and attention is being directed to countries where the situation is improving. I am the first to have acknowledged that progress is indisputably being made in the reconstruction. But in the area of the return of refugees, which is related to human rights problems, there has not been any progress. I do not know what the solution is, and it is certainly not up to the United Nations to find a solution, because that is an internal problem of Rwanda. It is up to the Rwandans to find a solution to their own problems. The sooner you find a solution, the more effective the international assistance, co-operation and support you will obtain from the international community. The longer you take, the greater the conflicts and difficulties we will be faced with in the future.

And what worries me most – and I am talking to you as a brother, I am talking to you as an African – what worries me the most is that we are facing a new donor fatigue. Donor states have other priorities. Their constituents are dissatisfied. Their constituents are saying, 'We have our own refugees in our own countries, we have our own sick, we have our own poor; why should we bother with others?' Obviously the role of the United Nations is to promote international solidarity. The role of the Organization of African Unity is to promote African solidarity, and that of the Group of

77 is to draw the attention of the Group of Seven and to say to them, 'Do something about the countries of the third world, do something about the developing countries.' But we are finding – and we will continue to find – it increasingly difficult to get that support, that collaboration from the international community.

Everyone thought that since the Second World War was over there would be no more genocide, but there has been another genocide. We must therefore find solutions. Return to peace must be a prerequisite for the reconstruction of Rwanda. Unless you find a way to integrate the refugees and have them return, you will not have any real reconstruction. If ever they begin to return, if ever you do succeed in taking steps to restore confidence, to show that you want justice, not vengeance – I know you do want justice, you are in favour of justice, not in favour of vengeance – then, at that time, you will be able to build a new peace. It will take many years to forget this genocide, to forget this fratricidal war during which many thousands of women, children and men were killed in the most horrible manner.

And we need reconciliation; reconciliation must not be confined to words, it must be reflected in deeds. We are being watched by 185 states, by thousands of non-governmental organizations, each of which has its own opinion and its own requirements. I face these problems every day; I receive requests from international organizations, criticisms from international organizations. Public opinion has become a new factor in the media revolution which brings us to what is happening all over the world. We are therefore compelled to deal with this problem.

As to the United Nations forces, I wish to tell you that if it were up to the Security Council or to the international community, there would be calls for the United Nations forces to leave right away. You can see what has happened in the former Yugoslavia, in Somalia. I am fighting right now to be able to keep the United Nations forces in the former Yugoslavia. Every day, I am pressured by Member States who say, 'Enough is enough, we must withdraw; if they want to fight, let them go on fighting; if they want to go on preparing future conflicts, let them do so; we will no longer intervene; we will no longer send our men to deal with the problems of other states. These are independent States, let them take charge of their sovereignty; let them sort things out themselves.

I say again, therefore, that it is important that we speak to the international community, that we explain to it that we want to find a solution, and not a provisional solution. You have seen some provisional solutions and you are well aware that they merely lead to further confrontations. We want a real solution, one which is based on dialogue, on the spirit of fraternity which should exist in a spirit of reconciliation, of moderation. I would even say that we must try to forgive, even though that is difficult. We must try to forget. I agree that we must not forget the criminals, but it is essential above all that we not punish an entire people, because if you punish an entire people, you punish yourselves. You are part of that people, it is your country, and the international community will be less interested in you.

I wanted to tell you that the United Nations and particularly the Secretary-General of the United Nations who has spent much of his life dealing with African problems – I started almost 40 years ago with my first journey in 1944 before the independence of Sudan, and I later came to know all the African countries and have visited them dozens of times – I feel that it is my duty to help the African continent. And I am grateful to the international community for having elected me Secretary-General so that I can be of more help to the African continent. I must confess to you, in all honesty: I have often failed, and the African continent is not helping me to help it.

The Secretary-General replies to questions from two deputies and two ministers:

Question: Our people were massacred in the presence of very well-armed United Nations forces. Instead of helping the population in distress, the United Nations force withdrew. At the time when the patriotic forces were courageously fighting against the force of evil – I am referring to the Government forces – and when they were going to drive it from the country, the United Nations established a zone to save the murderers. My question is the following, Your Excellency: our people today no longer trust the United Nations forces. How are you going to help us in order to restore their trust, which you need?

Reply: I believe that only the Rwandan people can restore that trust for themselves. The United Nations can help you. Nevertheless, you have to help yourselves and God will help you. You have to find solutions. It is for you to develop ways to achieve reconciliation. We are prepared to help you, but we cannot replace you. This is one of the United Nations policies: it helps peoples, it helps the protagonists in a conflict. But the protagonists themselves must find solutions. We are ready to help them. So far as trust is concerned, the Rwandan people themselves must dress their wounds and find ways to initiate a dialogue in order to begin to take measures to create trust. And, on that basis, you'll be able to build peace, I would even say, to institutionalize peace. This is what we call, in our United Nations jargon, 'peace-building'. So it is not only a question of even bringing the refugees back. It is a question of arriving at another stage and preparing for a further, more important, stage of peace-building.

Two countries experienced three terrible wars: France and Germany. In 1870, 1914 and 1939, those countries suffered millions of deaths, but they were able to build a unit. They had two great men: Adenauer and De Gaulle. If they were able to find a solution, if Spain after a fratricidal war was also able to find a solution, if Nigeria was also able to bring about a solution, if others have found a solution, you must find one and it will be your solution. It is for you to find the way; it is for you to begin the dialogue and create mutual trust. We are here to help you but we cannot replace you. This is my message: help us so that we can help you because I am encountering difficulties in helping you. If you do not help me, I shall not succeed in helping you. You must find the solution.

Question: You dwelt on the question of dialogue. And I am sure, both the United Nations and the international community in general know that Rwanda has opened its gates to Rwandans outside its borders, unconditionally. But you insist that there should be dialogue. My question is this: must we have dialogue with those who committed genocide? Is that your advice?

It has been reported time and time again that people who committed genocide in this country have been armed and are continued to be armed outside this country. This government has inherited an arms embargo and that arms embargo is being maintained by the United Nations, the same United Nations that has had consistent reports of armed people who committed genocide. Is that logical, Your Excellency?

The question of reconciliation. In Rwanda we think and believe that reconciliation is a process that needs a number of prerequisites. The first prerequisite is justice; the second prerequisite is that there must be a level of consent of whoever committed crimes. Even those against whom a crime was committed must have a kind of relationship with those who committed it. How does the United Nations foresee a reconciliation without those necessary prerequisites? That is some advice I would like the Secretary-General of the United Nations to give this country.

Answer. Concerning the first question, certainly I did not advocate dialogue with those who committed genocide or those who were the instigators of genocide. They have to be condemned. This is why we have the International Tribunal. But there is a difference between those who were behind the operations and the average men who may have made a lot of mistakes. So this is the first difference.

The second one, I completely agree. This is why we adopted a Resolution of the Security Council to send observers on the border to stop the infiltration of arms coming to certain elements belonging to the former government. We are aware of this, but again we cannot do this unless there is an agreement of the Member States. The Security Council has sent a special envoy who was received by your Government; he went without delay around the neighbouring countries and all of them refused the presence of observers. They said the observers would intervene in their internal affairs, and this is the problem of the government of Kigali.

It must find a solution to bring back the refugees and it will not be at our expense. It is enough that we are paying the price of having a million refugees with all the complications, and I have received letters asking to intervene to get rid of those refugees. So we have tried, but again the problem is that, according to the rule, and I have mentioned this already, we have no permission and our system does not allow the use of force to compel the refugees to return. It must be based on their own political will.

Finally about the embargo, I have no objection to the lifting of the embargo. It is not my decision, it is the decision of the Security Council. But I am afraid that the day you lift the embargo, you will have complications: the international community will be saying, 'they are buying arms; they are using our assistance to buy arms, so let us stop our assistance.' So if you are sure lifting the embargo will have no impact on the international community, I am the first one to say lift the embargo. We had the same problem in Bosnia, but again you have to understand this is not my decision. This is the decision of the donor countries and unless the donor countries are ready to adopt a new resolution, we will not be able to change their mind.

Question: Mr President, Your Excellency Mr Secretary-General, I think that your diagnosis is correct when you say that the problem of Rwanda is essentially the problem of the refugees from within the country. But it is perhaps less correct to maintain, as you do, that it is a basically Rwandan problem. This is the same as if you said that Rwanda refused to repatriate its refugees. Unless you had reports containing information to this effect, Rwanda declared its intention to receive the Rwandans who are situated outside the country. The problem that we have always raised is the fact that those refugees are being organized by those who committed genocide. And we ask the United Nations to take steps to separate this other part of the population from those who carried out the genocide. I think therefore that part of the international community should help us to bring about this separation. What is the United Nations doing to promote this separation?

There is another matter: the prisons. You seem to say that there will be peace in Rwanda only if there is justice and not vengeance. There is a sort of unfounded accusation in what you said, at least in the way that you presented it. In the current situation, there are indeed many prisoners; but if there was vengeance, there would not be any prisoners. We are waiting for justice and we want this justice to be dispensed. I think that we are aware of the fact that indeed the future of Rwanda will be based on sound justice. And we want to have it. But I think that your statement levels accusations that we would sooner advocate vengeance. I assure you that this is not the case and if the reports that you received indicated this I think that they should be reviewed or, at least, those reports should prove what they assert.

Answer. Mr Deputy, I am not accusing anyone and I am not making any unfounded accusations. I am trying to help you; you are isolated here; you do not know what the attitude of international public opinion is. My objective is to help you and to tell you how the international community perceives the situation. This does not in any way mean that I share their point of view. On the contrary, I am trying to help you by telling you I have tried to achieve what you want; I called upon 46 States to obtain forces in order to clear the refugee camps and eliminate the negative elements there, who, as you know, are arming themselves and preparing for further confrontations. I haven't succeeded. It doesn't depend on me. It is interesting to know why I did not succeed: it is because the international community did not accept this approach, and this is the problem. It is in your interest to try and convince the international community. The fact that 46 States refused to intervene or send troops shows that they do not support my analysis of the situation.

My analysis is the same as yours. I support it 100 per cent, but I am only one individual. The international community has another view of the situation. Your role as Members of Parliament therefore is to correct that view or perception. The information that I am giving to you is correct. It is not at all from our reports. I am telling you what I receive as the reactions of non-governmental organizations. I am telling you what I receive as a response of Member States of the international community. Take a specific case: 46 said no. But that indicates something. I wish to tell you specifically that I fully support your analysis of the situation and your three questions. I agree with you. But my hands are empty. I am 'an honest broker'; I serve as a catalyst trying to gain the support of the international community; I do not have any money. I am the one who requests States, who tells them that a special fund should be set up to help Rwanda, that we need the money necessary for such an operation. The international community responded differently.

The only thing that I am going to tell you – and this is my message – is that you should take account of the international community. Because today, it is playing an increasingly important role and we must call upon it in order to get co-operation, support, assistance, particularly technical assistance, and so forth. Be careful! You do not know what the international community is thinking, what Governments are thinking. I am telling you now so that you will bear it in mind and try to find a solution to this problem. You do need the international community. All States need the international community. We are witnessing a further globalization of international events in which an important role is to be played more and more by the international community, be it through non-governmental organizations, trade unions, Members of Parliament, the press, CNN, the television, newspaper commentators, articles, and so forth. They form the image held by the international community. It is not only a question of an image, but also of results. I am fighting for you, but I have more and more difficulty in getting assistance for you. I have been fighting to obtain soldiers, but it is more and more difficult for me to obtain them; I have not succeeded. Do you think that when you experienced genocide, I was not fighting in order to obtain soldiers, to keep the soldiers in place? I did not succeed because I am unable to tell States 'You must stay.' They are the ones who decide. It is important to consider the international community. Today, no one is alone any longer. And the position of the international community is as I indicated to you.

I thank you as a former Member of Parliament. I wish you good luck and I want to tell you that you have at least a friend who desires to help you. I spoke to you so frankly because I consider myself a brother of the Rwandan people. I could have said very nice words to you and you would have left this meeting remarking, 'What a nice man he is, the Secretary-General. He told us, "Well done, you are making progress; you found a solution to your problems; I am going to help you; everything is marvelous."' I felt that you were very wise and important enough for me to speak to you frankly. Maybe this shocked you, but it is because I consider myself a brother and a friend. I have fought for you for two years and shall continue to do so. But help me. This is my message. I need your help if you want me to win the fight that I am waging for you. I was asked to go to the former Yugoslavia at this time. I refused. I came here to express my support to you and to tell you how much I want to help you. But I ask you to help me and this is what I told your Prime Minister, and you, Members of Parliament. This is what I shall also say to the Rwandan people if I have the opportunity to meet them. It is your task to find a solution. What you may have thought was an unfounded accusation is not. I merely told you what the international community's image of Rwanda is.

The Secretary-General's remarks produced an animated, almost provocative response. His references, particularly to policies of mutual exclusion, to dialogue with refugees, to the international community's disappointment with the Rwandan government and a virtual equating of the two combatant groups led to visible resentment. However, his concluding remarks and his frankness almost carried the day. The session had certainly been cathartic.

After a banquet hosted by the President which brought a long day to an end at 11.00 pm, I thought the Secretary-General would retire. On the contrary, he returned to his room and began a series of telephone calls to Bosnia, Moscow, New York and Haiti that took several hours to complete.

Next morning he was ready at 7.00 am to visit UNAMIR head-quarters where he was given a guard of honour and enthusiastically received by the civilian and military staff. He also met the heads of mission and the UN agencies who had been invited to the function. He addressed the staff, visited the Deputy Prosecutor of the ICTR's office and then took a helicopter ride to Nyarbuye, the grim site of one of the worst massacres. There, having toured the site, he addressed the crowd of survivors and then flew over N'Sinda Prison which was being expanded with UNAMIR's help. He was then jointly received by President Bizimungu and Vice-President Kagame at President's House. The meeting took place without aides and lasted over two hours.

The Secretary-General briefed us afterwards and said that he had made a strong plea for reconciliation which the Rwandan leaders had not accepted. Nevertheless, a great deal of ground had been covered in their frank exchanges. He felt that the discussions had been highly beneficial and left me with instructions to follow up on the Museveni initiative. I am sure he felt that Rwanda's leadership would not turn down the Ugandan President's advice. In my heart, I remained sceptical as I had seen President Museveni and President Bizimungu taking up opposite positions on the same issue at the Nairobi Summit in January 1995.

The Secretary-General was already late for his departure ceremonies, but as we arrived at the VIP lounge, I was perturbed to see that a demonstration had been mounted. It transpired later that the demonstration had been hastily organized by some extremist RPA officers serving at the airport. The demonstrators sang and danced the usual routine criticism of the UN, but were not too prominent. The Secretary-General chose not to notice them, but their presence left a bitter taste in the mouth. The Prime Minister was angry and embarrassed and so were some other moderate members of the Cabinet, particularly as the Secretary-General had shown courage and sincerity in giving his advice, even if it was not palatable to some members of the government. To raise a demonstration at the time of farewell against one of the most important personalities on the world scene seemed to all well-wishers of Rwanda to be asinine and wholly counter-productive.

The Secretary-General's parting remark to me at the airport was, 'I had to shake the Rwandan leadership into appreciating that, as a small country, they need the goodwill of the international community to overcome their problems. They need to do much more to earn this goodwill. I gave this advice as a friend and well-wisher.' The comment was sincere and entirely rational, but it missed the mark in understanding the Tutsi psyche.

The Tutsis of Rwanda realize that in the global or even the African context, they are a minute dot on the landscape. Nevertheless, they believe that their achievements have been due entirely to their own efforts with no assistance from the international community. They feel that the international community spurned them when they were chased out of their homeland. They argue that the world turned a blind eye to the atrocities that were perpetrated against them and gave no heed to the warnings of genocide that they specifically conveyed to the UNAMIR leadership. Instead, the planners of genocide were supported with arms and finance while the remainder of the international community looked the other way. Furthermore, when the genocide actually began, the international community turned and fled, allowing the killers free rein to massacre a million people. The Tutsis maintain that it was not the United Nations that brought an end to these massacres, but their own patriotic army which received no help from abroad. Even after the massacres had been halted, the international community poured in vast sums of aid to the refugees who had sympathized if not actually perpetrated the crimes, while no effort was made to stop these killers gaining full control of the refugees camps. In contrast, the survivors of genocide received a raw deal.

These are, of course, exaggerated and specious arguments, but they have sunk deep into the psyche of the Rwandan leadership. For them, international goodwill is at best a convenience, a bonus. It counts for little in influencing their attitudes, which are governed by their subjective experience of history.

So ended the eventful 18-hour visit of the Secretary-General whose energy, grasp and focus during a high-intensity programme was remarkable.[1] Subsequently, I twice reminded the Ugandan Foreign Minister about the 10–20 names that President Museveni was to suggest for the reconciliation talks, but there was no response from Kampala.

Zaire–Rawanda relations
Forced repatriation of Rwandan refugees

Central to the prospect of peace and stability in the region was the fate of Zaire–Rwanda relations. Historically, relations had been complex and fraught with tension. Before the colonial conquest, the Rwandan kingdom extended into parts of Zaire and a fair number of

---

[1] After retiring as UN Secretary-General, Mr Boutros-Ghali assumed the assignment of Secretary-General of the francophone commonwealth, based in Paris.

Tutsis had settled in pockets of Eastern Zaire, notably in the Masisi region. Given the latest influx of Hutu refugees, Rwanda–Zaire relations were tense and volatile. After the RPF's military victory, Zaire was expected to adopt a hostile attitude to the RPF-dominated government in Rwanda, particularly as, during the civil war, the RPF was highly critical of Zaire's role in support of the RGF. Late President Habyarimana was held in high esteem by President Mobutu and the two had close personal relations. Zaire had sent its troops in support of the Habyarimana government when the RPF made its first incursion into Rwanda in 1990. Ethnically, also, the Hutus had closer links with East Zairean tribes. Finally, Zaire was francophone while the dominant elite in Rwanda was now anglophone.

However, in July 1994 President Bizimungu made a special gesture to Zaire by scheduling his first meeting as President with President Mobutu, who was holidaying at the time in Mauritius. The meeting was surprisingly friendly and successful. President Mobutu did not hide his sympathy for the late President Habyarimana and his family, but made it clear that he wanted to deal with Rwanda on a state-to-state basis. He assured the Rwandan President that Zairean territory would not be used to destabilize Rwanda; that the RGF would be disarmed and confined to barracks, and that hate radio broadcasts would be stopped. A tripartite meeting with UNHCR was arranged and President Bizimungu returned to Rwanda highly satisfied with his talks.

However, with the passing weeks, this cordiality began to slip back into mutual acrimony as the refugees in Zaire began to adopt a highly political profile against the Rwandan government. Radio Mille Collines reappeared in Eastern Zaire on a different wavelength, broadcasting its usual hate message from mobile vans. Mme Habyarimana who, together with her brothers, was seen as a strong supporter of extremist Hutus, was frequently received by President Mobutu and raised eyebrows by accompanying him to China on an official visit. When the tripartite meeting took place in Goma, Seth Sendashonga, the Rwandan representative, told me that the Zairean delegation had the audacity to drive up to the meeting in Rwandan government vehicles bearing Rwandan number plates!

The former Rwandan leadership seemed to have free rein in the camps and the RGF and militia began military training and to engage in cross-border raids into Rwanda. These developments were seen by Rwanda to have Zaire's tacit approval. Rwanda thus began to implicate Zaire indirectly in its accusations of intimidation in the camps. There were veiled threats from Rwanda that if Zaire (and UNHCR) could not impose discipline in the refugee camps, Rwandan forces might be obliged to reach across the border and 'sort out the killers themselves'. At this time, Vice-President Kagame made a speech which had reverberations throughout the world in which he claimed the right of hot pursuit against saboteurs operating from Zaire. He told me that it would take his forces only a few days to 'clean-up' the intimidators in the camps. The speech was given wide publicity in Zaire and when I subsequently visited Kinshasa and Gbadolete, Zairean leaders regarded the Vice-President's remarks as examples of hostile intent.

Thus, Rwanda–Zaire relations began to slide downwards in the second half of 1994 and early 1995. A low watermark came with the report by a British TV journalist, Brian Johnson-Thomas, who leaked information that he had collected for a TV programme, cataloguing Zairean government complicity in transporting military supplies to the refugee camps and in military training and Zaire's support for reviving the RGF. Johnson-Thomas quoted air cargo flights to Goma full of military supplies from Bulgaria, Israel, the Seychelles and South Africa. He pinpointed caches where arms were being stored and supplied names of the intermediaries and air companies who had arranged these military supplies. The outline of the TV documentary was described in the following hand-out:

RETRAINING AND REARMING OF THE FORMER RGF AND INTERAHAMWE MILITIAS IN ZAIRE AND TANZANIA

The supply by Israel of at least two hundred tonnes of munitions via Goma Airport, these flights included about 40 tonnes of Egyptian grenades captured by the IDF in the 73 war, along with Uzzi machine pistols and Chinese manufactured 7:62 mm rounds: The use of a British airline, Peak Aviation, as the company responsible for these flights: The fact that the flights themselves were actually made by Ghana and Nigeria registered aircraft: The use of fictitious flight documents was commonplace – for example, on at least one occasion the authorities at Cairo Airport were told that Ghanaian Boeing 707 freighter 9GEBK was carrying aid supplies to N'Djamena in Chad when it was actually carrying 33 tonnes of munitions, including heavy mortar rounds:

More importantly, my research for the next film shows that: At least eight flights carrying arms for the Interahamwe and former RGF have arrived at Goma Airport between November '94 and February '95: The weapons on these flights came from the Bulgarian state factory at Plovdiv and the majority of these flights were made by six Russian Ilyushin transport aircraft. Observed munitions landed include AKM assault rifles and 60mm portable mortars: These aircraft – on part of their return journey – carried some of the approximately 1000 RGF and Interahamwe now under training in the Central African Republic: Former members of the then Rwandan government and militia leaders in both Zaire and Tanzania are giving a date of 15 July this year for an attempt to invade Rwanda: This is to follow a destabilization campaign due to begin April of this year: Their stated objective is not to recapture the whole of Rwanda in one sweep but to seize 'a couple of thousand square kilometres' in the Gisenyi–Rhuengeri region; recognition by a 'major European power' will then follow, thus providing both legal war material supplies and putting pressure to negotiate on the RPA: The Interahmwe/RGF have established a series of arms caches in the frontier region, about five to seven kilometres inside Zaire along much of the length of the Parc National des Volcans: I was able to gain access to one of these dumps which included French M-60 medium machine guns, AK-47 assault rifles, fragmentation grenades and land mines in boxes with US markings and South African 7:62mm ammunition: Please note that some of this came with them out of Rwanda last year and ties in with known sales to the then Rwandan Government Forces.

Finally, it is clear that a fair quantity of the weapons seized by the Zaire Armed Forces last July have been returned to the militias. My guess – for what it is worth – is that they were obtained by bribery rather than as an act of policy by Mobutu Sese Seko et al.

BJT Kigali 7 March 1995

Soon afterwards, Human Rights Watch repeated similar accusations of Zairean complicity in supporting the former government with arms, training and funds. Tremors of concern began to develop on this issue and the UN Security Council decided to appoint an Inquiry Commission to look into the accusations which Zaire had formally denied.[1] The six-member Commission was headed by Ambassador Mahmoud Kassem of Egypt and included representatives from Canada, the Netherlands, Germany, Pakistan and Zimbabwe.

Zaire, for its part, underplayed the intimidation factor and accused Rwanda of a harsh, vengeful attitude towards returning refugees as the main reason for their reluctance to leave the camps. The Zaireans quoted incidents such as Kibeho, the appalling conditions in Rwandan prisons, the arbitrary arrests by the RPA, especially in the border areas and the absence of any form of justice as examples of Rwanda's harsh treatment of Hutu returnees. Prime Minister Kengo wa Dondo wrote a plaintive letter to the Secretary-General calling for a UN Inquiry Commission to look into the accusations of Zaire's complicity in the militarization in the camps.

These acrimonious arguments were publicly aired between the two governments, tempered occasionally by high-level exchanges which usually ended up paying lip service to the implementation of Tripartite Agreements and the Bujumbura Action Plan. At these meetings, Zaire would also reaffirm its promise of returning Rwandan material that was in their possession. In this way, relations would be held back from breaking-point though, in due course, the diatribes would start again. Sometimes, even these high-level exchanges did not succeed as when, after careful scheduling through the UN, Foreign Minister Anastase Gasana went in a UNAMIR plane to Gbadolete as the President's Special Envoy, only to be informed at the airport that President Mobutu had left an hour earlier for Portugal!

A crisis in Rwanda–Zaire relations developed on 16 August 1995, when the Security Council decided to lift the embargo on arms supplies to Rwanda. The Rwandan government had argued that the

---

[1] Security Council Resolution no. 1013, dated 7 September 1995, establishing International Commission of Inquiry.

embargo had been imposed during the civil war, but now that a civilian government had taken over, the embargo was redundant and unfairly penalizing the government for its legitimate defence needs. Rwanda also pointed to reports of military supplies to the former RGF in Zaire as another reason for lifting the embargo. Stung by the decision of the Security Council, Zaire registered a formal protest and made it known that if the international community did not seriously address the refugee issue, Zaire would use force to vacate the camps.

To everyone's surprise, Zaire began to make good its threat on 19 August, when its armed forces forcibly closed some camps in Goma and Bukavu. The Zairean forces surrounded the camps, fired shots in the air and then commandeered UNHCR vehicles, forcing the refugees to be carried across the border into Rwanda. In a four-day blitz, about 14,000 refugees were forced across the border – 8000 from Goma into Gisenyi and 6000 from Bukavu to Cyangugu.

The decision for the forced return of refugees created an international outcry as *refoulement* (the forced repatriation of refugees) is contrary to refugee and humanitarian conventions and is tantamount to an international misdemeanour. The Secretary-General and the High Commissioner for Refugees remonstrated publicly with Zaire and were supported by a chorus of international disapproval. As a result, Zaire was obliged to halt the forcible repatriation after the fourth day.

Some observers felt that it was the international pressure that halted Zaire in its tracks, others that the initial decision was taken by Prime Minister Kengo and was later countermanded by President Mobutu. Another explanation is that Zaire ran out of petrol to carry the refugees to the border! The Rwandans felt that the Zairean government had assumed that a large influx of refugees would create political turmoil in Rwanda, but, when they found that the refugees were being settled expeditiously, they stopped.

Although Zaire's action took the international community by surprise, the reception, treatment and onward despatch of the refugees on Rwandan soil saw a remarkably successful operation in which the Rwandan government, UNAMIR, the specialized UN agencies and the NGOs co-ordinated their actions brilliantly. On arrival, the refugees were received at the border and escorted immediately to the well-stocked transit camps. In order to avoid a tense build-up at the border, the RPA decided not to screen the refugees at the frontier, but did so on arrival in a less fractious atmosphere at the transit camps where food, water, medicare and shelter were available. The RPA screening was conducted before human rights observers and UNAMIR Milobs. Once screened, the refugees were accommodated reasonably comfortably in tents in the transit camps. They were provided fuel to cook and pit latrines for sanitary purposes. In the transit camps, the Rwandan civil administration divided the refugees into groups according to the communes to which they were moving. UNHCR and the IOM then took the refugees under RPA escort to the communes, where the administration was informed in advance of their arrival. The whole operation was conducted with remarkable efficiency and co-operation. Not a single incident took place and the entire load of 14,000 refugees was conducted back to their communes within four days. Less than 1 per cent of the refugees were detained for further questioning by the RPA.

When I visited a transit centre near Gisenyi and spoke to the families who were forced back, I found them relaxed and not particularly apprehensive. They were simple rural folk who told me that they had not returned earlier because they were not sure of the treatment they would receive on their return. Now that their minds had been made up for them, they were glad to be home and eager to return to their communes. They were pleasantly surprised at the treatment they had received at the hands of the government and the UN. I noticed that the family groups consisted mainly of women, children and elders, but included also a fair number of young men between the ages of 15 and 35.

The importance of this highly successful operation lay in the fact that the Rwandan government's track record had been tested and found positive. Agreements, speeches and resolutions are essentially declarations of intent. The real test lies in their implementation. In this case, the Rwandan government had treated the 14,000 refugees humanely and efficiently. Few arrests had been made and the refugees had been quickly settled in their communes. The Rwandan government's co-operation with UNAMIR and the agencies had also been exemplary.

When the High Commissioner for Refugees, Mme Ogata, arrived in Rwanda, interrupting her vacation in Japan, she was able to see Rwanda's performance on the ground in implementing its commitments. She left Rwanda highly satisfied with the treatment of the refugees, as was evident from the following communiqué that was issued after her meeting with President Bizimungu on 6 September:

> The Government reiterates its unflinching determination to do everything possible to enable the safe return of all the Rwandanese refugees, in the letter and spirit of the Bujumbura declaration. No efforts will be spared to ensure that every Rwandanese enjoys equal right to citizenship and protection by the government. The return of all the Rwandanese is without preconditions and this right is inalienable whatever the circumstances.

> It is on this basis that when Rwandan nationals in Zaire were expelled under humiliating conditions, the government employed great effort despite our immense limitations to ensure that all those expelled were safely and conveniently settled into their homes. The number of persons that crossed at Cyangugu and Gisenyi were 7268 and 5079 respectively. Of the total number of 12,347 persons expelled from Zaire, only 42 persons were separated from the rest at the border post of Cyangugu, while the number for Gisenyi was 205 persons. The separation was a safety pre-

caution as 123 of those separated were soldiers of the former army and they have after screening been taken to Gako Military Training Centre for a reintegration program. Among those separated were 55 criminals that were in jail in Goma and the rest were suspected criminals of genocide. The total number of persons (69) being held for suspected involvement in genocide constitute about 0.6 per cent of all those expelled.

Within 4 days all the returnees had been settled in their properties, with the support of UNHCR, UNAMIR and other members of the international community. These organizations have followed the returnees into their areas and are working with the government to help these persons to start a new life.

I fully accept that refugees should return home voluntarily and should not be forced into returning. Nevertheless, I am convinced that, at least in Rwanda, a third reason for refugees not wishing to return home – intimidation in the camps and fear of vindictive treatment on return being the other two – is that the refugees enjoyed a higher standard of living in the camps than they could expect at home. In the camps they were assured meals, milk for their children, clothes, medicare, drinking-water, schools, etc. The camps in Zaire and Tanzania had cinemas, night clubs, churches, clubs and many facilities that a normal rural family would not find at home. They also had security. Therefore, despite the apparent squalor, there was an in-built reluctance to leave the camp, especially as return represented a leap in the dark. In these circumstances, an element of pressure was, in my view, necessary for the refugees to be induced to return home. I know that this is not strictly going by the book, but a number of senior UNHCR officials held the same opinion.

President Bizimungu also appeared to share this view as he remarked to me, off the record, 'I am against forced repatriation. But you have all seen how we have treated these 14,000 returnees. There has been no coercion, no arbitrary arrest. They have all been settled in their communes without a problem. Sometimes, I feel that now that the Zaireans have taken this step, they should go through and complete the exercise. You will see that we will settle all the other refugees in the same manner. Of course, the hard-core criminals will not return.'

Meanwhile, UNHCR, UNAMIR and the agencies had prepared themselves to receive a vast number of refugees, not only from Zaire but also from Tanzania and Burundi, in case the message of a successful forced repatriation caught on. We reckoned that 8000 to 10,000 refugees per day could have been handled by UNHCR over a period of two to three months. But once Zaire stopped its forced repatriation, the torrent of returning refugees turned to a trickle and later virtually dried up.

The Prime Minister's departure from the Cabinet

In August 1995, two major events in Rwanda saw a red warning light turned on for refugees intending to return voluntarily. The first was Prime Minister Faustin Twagiramungu's decision to leave the Cabinet. He was followed by the Interior Minister, Seth Sendashonga, and three other ministers: Alphonse-Marie Nkubito, Minister of Justice, a champion of human rights, the Information Minister, Mr Jean-Baptiste Nkuliyingoma, and the female Transport Minister, Mme Imaculee Inyumba, who was the only Tutsi among the five ministers to leave.

As indicated earlier, differences between the Prime Minister and the RPF leadership had grown to the extent that there had been a public stand-off. Kibeho and the difference over the mandate had brought out the increasing chasm between the Vice-President and the Prime Minister. It was rumoured also that Seth Sendashonga, the dynamic Interior Minister who would often speak critically of some RPF measures, was being threatened by the RPF High Command. Within the MDR (Mouvement Démocratique Républicain), the Prime Minister's moderate party, divisions were emerging. The Foreign Minister, Dr Anastase Gasana, was viewed as a loyalist to the government and was encouraged to stand against the Prime Minister for the leadership of the MDR. This led to his expulsion from the party which, in fact, meant that the MDR became fragmented into factions.

The case of Seth Sendashonga was even more complex as he had been a leading figure in the RPF. By cutting him down to size, the RPF was running the risk of undermining one of its pillars – that it was a party across the ethnic divide as it included Hutu leaders in the party notably, Pasteur Bizimungu (now President) Colonel Alexis Kanyarengwe (Vice-Prime Minister) and Seth Sendashonga.

The differences between the Prime Minister and the Vice-President again became public as a result of statements given to the press by the Prime Minister while travelling abroad to Canada and Belgium. The thrust of his complaint continued to be that there was a government within a government which made all the crucial decisions. He maintained there was no consultation before these decisions were made and that his advice was given short shrift. Moreover, the RPF's repressive policies were causing insecurity within Rwanda, creating friction with neighbours and with important donor countries (France and Belgium) and preventing refugees from returning. RPF policies also provided a handle for the opposition to criticize the government.

The Vice-President was critical of the Prime Minister for acting more like the leader of the Opposition than a Prime Minister. He resented the Prime Minister airing his views publicly and felt that responsible action required that contentious issues be raised confidentially at Cabinet meetings. He felt that the Prime Minister should work for consensus from within rather than stand outside the circle and criticize publicly.

At a meeting of the Cabinet on Friday 25 August, Interior Minister Sendashonga made a highly critical intervention against the RPA, accusing it of creating an atmosphere of tension and insecurity in the country. He quoted arbitrary arrests, the prisons and an oppressive attitude towards the majority community that, in his view, were reversing the process of reconciliation in the country. Vice-President Kagame took strong exception to the Interior Minister's remarks and challenged him to prove his case. When Prime Minister Twagiramungu, who had not taken part in the earlier exchanges, inclined himself in favour of the Interior Minister, Kagame was incensed and walked out of the Cabinet meeting.

Twagiramungu told me later that although angry exchanges had taken place in the meeting, he did not anticipate a crisis. He himself had not initiated the discussion nor had he taken a prominent part in the debate and he therefore expected that the tension between Kagame and Sendashonga would soon be resolved, especially as the Interior Minister was a member of the RPF. However, over the following weekend, he learnt that the President and Vice-President had interceded with all the political parties represented in Parliament with a view to passing a censure motion against the Prime Minister. He therefore decided to pre-empt the move and sent in his resignation to the President at 12 noon on Monday 28 August. The Information Minister, who was a member of the Prime Minister's MDR party, announced the news on Radio Rwanda at 2.00 pm, one hour ahead of the National Assembly meeting in which the President called for and obtained the 'dismissal' of the Prime Minister. The 65-member Parliament endorsed the President's decision with 59 members voting in favour and six abstaining. Four of the abstainers were members of the MDR.

For a short while, a childish controversy raged as to whether the Prime Minister had resigned or had been dismissed by the President. The important point, however, was that Faustin Twagiramungu and Seth Sendashonga had left the Cabinet, sending tremors across Rwanda and into the international community. The donor community again began asking themselves if RPF-dominated Rwanda was, in fact, taking the moderate course that it had earlier set itself. Twagiramungu was a highly respected figure, the only name that was in the Arusha Accords as the agreed interim Prime Minister. He was seen as a moderate, urbane, sophisticated and sensible figure. Sendashonga's departure was perhaps an even greater blow to Rwanda's image because he was a leading member of the RPF. He had been the most dynamic minister of all in the Cabinet and was an open, frank and highly effective personality.

I met the Prime Minister on 5 September, two days before he left Rwanda. He told me that he did not feel in danger for his life from the government, despite his open differences with Kagame, but he feared the Tutsi extremists. The reason for the heavy guard outside his house was to protect him from such people. Twagiramungu made a special point of thanking the Secretary-General for the frankness with which he addressed the Rwandan leaders at the National Assembly during his visit to Rwanda. He added that the Secretary-General's bluntness had shaken the leadership out of its self-induced euphoria. He was also profoundly grateful to UNAMIR which had saved his life in April 1994 and was appreciative of UNAMIR's supportive role since then, adding that Rwanda would not have achieved its current level of security without the help of UNAMIR. Twagiramungu told me that he would stay relatively low key while living abroad and still hoped to play a constructive role for Rwanda whenever conditions permitted in the future.

Rwanda's leadership moved quickly to repair the damage of the Cabinet breach and the five dismissed members of the Cabinet were replaced. Mr Pierre-Celestin Rwigyema, the former Minister of Primary Education, became Prime Minister. Like Twagiramungu, he was a Hutu and a member of the MDR. Colonel Alexis Kanyarengwe, the Vice-Prime Minister, chairman of the RPF and in many ways the forgotten man of the last Cabinet, was given the Interior Ministry portfolio. The Justice Ministry was given to a highly capable woman, Mme Marthe Mukumaretsa, who was as intelligent as she was vivacious. Overall, the former complexion of the Cabinet was retained, with 13 Hutus and nine Tutsi, and with two women. The new Prime Minister was an affable, open and manifestly decent man who did not have Twagiramungu's international stature, but would clearly fit in as a team man, performing the role of co-ordinator.

While shock waves from the crises were being felt abroad and especially in the neighbouring countries where the government's opponents felt they had been totally vindicated, my reading of the situation was that though the boat had been rocked, the government would ride out the storm and stay on course. I therefore advised Judge Goldstone and Mme Ogata, who had visits scheduled to Rwanda, not to alter their plans. Mr Twagiramungu's departure for Belgium was preceded by a reception at which the President invited former ministers and thanked them for their contribution. The function gave a welcome impression of a civilized parting of ways.

For a brief period after they left, Twagiramungu and Sendashonga kept a low profile, but by December Twagiramungu had fired a critical broadside against the RPF, accusing it of perpetrating a reign of terror and killing 300,000 Hutus after assuming power. Twagiramungu virtually confirmed the Gersony accusations which he had so vehemently contradicted in September 1994.

Sendashonga went further. In Nairobi, he not only issued highly critical statements against the RPF, but also launched a party and a manifesto that accused Rwandan leaders of corruption and malpractice. Subsequently, there was an assassination attempt on him in Nairobi which the Kenyan government maintained had been carried out by Rwandan agents operating from its embassy. He was injured by a bullet fired at close range but recovered.[1]

The Kanama incident

The second incident that provided cannon fodder to the opponents of the Rwandan government and sent shivers of apprehension down the spine of donor countries was the killings by the RPA of 104 civilians in a commune called Kanama. Before describing the incident, its immediate background needs to be placed in perspective.

The growing cross-border sabotage and de-stabilization activities emanating from the Zairean camps had resulted in the build-up of a tense, overbearing presence of the RPA in the border areas adjacent to Zaire. The saboteurs came across Lake Kivu or through the forest in small groups, armed with mines and guns, and targeted public utilities. Some families that had returned from Zairean camps were punished for their 'disloyalty'. This activity started a vicious circle since it led to the RPA suspecting every Hutu of being a collaborator in providing sanctuary to the saboteurs. Many innocent people were picked up and put in prison on the slightest suspicion. The news of these arbitrary arrests and the RPF's overbearing attitude created tension and panic in the Hutu community which, in turn, stopped intending returnees from leaving the camps. Moreover, the news of arbitrary arrests and increasing horror in the prisons was carried to the donor countries by human rights observers and the NGOs, leading to the holding-back of aid commitment. Frustrated and antagonized, the Rwandan government's attitude towards the international community became more xenophobic.

It was against this backdrop that on 12 September in Kanama – a commune 14 kilometres east of Gikongoro – an RPF patrol headed by a particularly able young officer was scouring the countryside in search of collaborators, suspected to be in hiding and supporting the guerrilla squads that were known to be operating in the region. The RPF patrol car was stopped at a road block and, when the four-wheeler slowed down, a group of guerrillas jumped out of a bush and targeted the young RPF captain, shooting him and two of his colleagues dead. The assassins then made off in the direction of Kanama.

As soon as the news spread to the local RPF base, a company was despatched to chase and locate the assassins. They surrounded the small Kanama commune overnight and at 5.00 am began a ruthless shoot-out in which women, elders and children were targeted. 104 people were shot dead and when the news broke in Kigali and

---

[1] Seth Sendashonga was subsequently assassinated in Nairobi on 16 May 1998.

subsequently across the international radio waves, the government and especially the RPF was called upon to explain how this could happen. The news of the killings was first reported by Milobs and broadcast by Radio UNAMIR.

Initially, the local RPA stated that their patrol had been fired upon and that when they returned fire, some people had been killed in the cross-fire. However, the evidence of cold-blooded revenge killings was too great to sustain this argument. It was clear from the nature of the wounds that many of the killings were executions and the picture that built up was of the local RPA unit losing all control when informed of the assassination of one of their brightest officers and wreaking revenge on the villagers who had been suspected of harbouring the guerrillas.

As in the past, Vice-President Kagame moved quickly. He ordered an initial inquiry followed by a court martial that found several RPA officers guilty, and a damage limitation exercise was mounted. Nevertheless, the Kanama incident, revived the doubts and fears that Kibeho had engendered and provided ballast to the opponents of the regime in their assertion that the government was equally guilty of mass killings. Kanama seemed to vindicate the claims of Twagiramungu and Sendashonga, representing a nadir in the government's efforts to sustain a viable human rights image.

Justice

The issue of justice was vital for the people of Rwanda because the psychological rehabilitation of a traumatized nation cannot begin without the dispensation of transparent justice. There were several levels at which the clamour for justice was apparent. At the pinnacle was the demand for the banishment of the 'culture of impunity' which had seen civil wars, massacres and eventually genocide overtake the people of Rwanda. At another level, a national judicial system needed to address the appalling suffering of the prison population in Rwanda, now estimated at 80,000. Thirdly, justice was also needed to adjudicate on the competing claims of refugees who, on return, found their lands and properties occupied by others. This clamour for justice was not limited to the people of Rwanda but stretched across to the outside world which had witnessed on its television screens the horrors of genocide, the suffering of the survivors and the appalling distress of the prisoners and refugees. Thus, the international media, human rights organizations, foreign governments and even public opinion abroad joined the people of Rwanda in calling for immediate and transparent justice. This thirst for justice led to the emergence of two parallel judicial systems; the national system of justice, which needed to be revived after it had been completely decimated in the civil war, and the international, in the shape of the International Criminal Tribunal for Rwanda (ICTR).

Internally, the justice system had sunk without trace. In July 1994, not a single judge or magistrate was available. They had either fled or been killed. The same was true of the registrars, prosecutors, clerks and judicial cadres that sustain a judicial system. There were no gendarmes, no communal police and no jail warders, with the result that the RPA had to perform all these basic law and order functions. The courts had been looted bare and there were no records left. Clearly, the revival of the national judicial system presented itself as a Himalayan task for the new government.

Since the planners and instigators of genocide – the big fish – left Rwanda with the defeat of the former government, the internal judicial net was cast over the minor collaborators – the small fish – who had not joined the Interahamwe and militia in the refugee camps. At its height, the number of arrests of these collaborators and sympathizers was around 1000 a week. Most of the arrests were made as a result of accusations by neighbours or eye witnesses. Often, the accused not only pleaded innocence, but claimed an ulterior motive like proprietorial acquisition or settling old scores as the reason for the accusation. Despite directions from its senior echelons for the RPA to be fair and non-retributional in their arrests, it was evident that, at the lower level, the RPA indulged in arbitrary, sometimes vengeful arrests. Our Milobs reported that the pattern of arrests differed from prefecture to prefecture, depending on the attitude of the local RPA commander. Those that were fair insisted on the government policy of four witnesses before making an arrest. In other prefectures, people were arrested for 'not stopping their neighbours committing crimes'.

As the jails filled to bursting-point with prisoners who had not passed through any judicial process, international demands for a judicial system to begin functioning became more intense. On a number of occasions, Hutu suspects were chased into our compounds and sought asylum from pursuing RPA soldiers. Tension would usually follow when the RPA were prevented from entering UNAMIR compounds and we would be accused of 'sheltering criminals'. We therefore worked out a procedure with the government through which any such asylum seekers were first interviewed by the ICRC and/or human rights observers and then handed over to a civilian official of the government. At one point, the ICRC conducted a survey of such prisoners that had been registered with them and found that all except one were accounted for and were being correctly treated while awaiting trial.

In order to process the vast number of people accused of humanitarian crimes, the government instituted a grassroots level of primary justice which aimed at weeding out the innocent from the prima facie suspects. This 'triage' system was to be applied across the communes and the triage tribunals consisted, usually, of a civilian official (a *burgomestre* or a deputy prefect), an RPA official and a respected member of the community. The idea was a good one, but the system barely functioned, as triage tribunals met infrequently, perhaps once a week. The government pleaded that officials in the triage tribunals had their normal, urgent responsibilities to carry out and lack of logistic support and facilities prevented them from visiting scenes of the crime and personally interviewing witnesses.

The task of restructuring the entire judicial system fell to the Minister of Justice, Jerome Nkubito, a man of immense courage who had been a fearless fighter for human rights, especially during the genocide. Nkubito had neither funds nor personnel to rebuild the system and his efforts to induce judges, magistrates, prosecutors and judicial cadres to return showed scant results. Training new cadres was a long-drawn-out process which, though necessary, did not meet the demand for immediate justice. Framing new laws to deal with genocide and related crimes was also a well-nigh impossible task, as the National Assembly was divided between the hardcore Tutsi who called for draconian laws and the moderate Hutu who sought laws that would encourage reconciliation and the early return of refugees. Besides genocide, the laws needed to deal with conflicting claims to property by different waves of refugees. Above all, the teeming, overcrowded, gangrene-infested prisons cried out for immediate recourse to primary justice.

The international community was particularly sympathetic towards Rwanda's effort to revive its internal judicial system. Funds were quickly earmarked by donor countries and Nkubito's request for foreign judicial cadres – mainly African judges and magistrates – to help jump-start the internal judicial system was accepted and processed expeditiously. So keen were the UN agencies to be seen helping in the restructuring of Rwanda's judiciary that there was an unseemly tug of war between the UNDP and the Human Rights Commission, each vying for the right to train the judiciary. In my opinion, the issue should have been decided by the funds that the UNDP had for training the judiciary being made available to the HRC to actually run the training programme. Of course, I had not reckoned with turf wars!

By summer 1995, more than a year after the government of national unity had taken control, there was no judicial system in sight. The prisons were being stuffed with an intake of around 1000 a week and were a living nightmare. The triage system existed on paper but barely functioned for the lack of funds and equipment. The genocide laws and the newly structured Supreme Court proposed by the Justice Minister were rejected by the National Assembly and the effort to induce judicial cadres to return had not been a success, especially after Kibeho. It was not surprising therefore that in September when a Cabinet crisis took place, Nkubito was replaced by his deputy, Mme Marthe Mukumaretsa, a tough cookie who was as bright as a fresh-cut diamond.

Mme Mukumaretsa quickly reviewed and revised practically all Nkubito's policies. She felt that her predecessor had taken no practical steps to revive the judicial system. She withdrew the proposals for new laws that were before the National Assembly and informed the UN and donor country ambassadors that the foreign judicial cadres were not needed. Further delay in reviving the judicial system became inevitable while she cleaned the stables with her new broom and started afresh.

The international community was particularly angered by Mme Mukumaretsa's refusal to accept foreign technical assistance. In fact, some African magistrates had already been selected and their tickets issued. The UNDP and the donors argued that there was no shortage of funding for the judicial system and the arrival of some foreign judicial cadres would provide a fillip to reviving Rwanda's judicial system. They rightly pointed to the internal and international clamour for the judicial process to begin, which was by autumn 1995 reaching a crescendo.

Mme Mukumaretsa remained adamant. She did not discount utilizing foreign judicial cadres at a later stage, but for them to arrive now – in September – would, she argued, be counter-productive. There was no system into which the foreign cadres could be fitted, no accommodation, no courts, no judicial administration and no transport. They would simply become a burden on the government with no capability to contribute. Moreover, she was not sure that she accepted, in principle, that non-Rwandans should sit in judgement over Rwandans. She told donor countries that money allocated to financing foreign judges and magistrates would be better spent in training Rwandan judicial cadres. More delay was inevitable, but it was better to take a considered decision rather than hurtle hastily down a dark alley. Mme Mukumaretsa's tough stand was not popular with the donor community, some of whom saw further delay as a deliberate attempt to postpone the judicial process. On balance, I was inclined to accept her difficulties. While it is true that a year had passed and no judiciary was in place, she had inherited a ministry that, in practical measures, had only scratched the surface of the problem. Pragmatic steps had to be taken and, given the importance of the task, they needed to be carefully evaluated before being adopted. I therefore found myself in a minority defending her trenchant stand with my diplomatic colleagues.

Eventually, more than two and a half years after the new government was formed and long after UNAMIR had bid farewell, the first signs of a revival of the internal judicial system became apparent. Perhaps it had taken too long. Perhaps Nkubito's idealistic musings had lost the government a year, but the judicial process was too important to be put together without careful consideration, given the depth of feeling and the complexity of the task in dealing with the aftermath of genocide.

The external system of justice was also slow in taking shape, leading to even sharper international criticism than the delay in the revival of Rwanda's internal judiciary. I recall, in November 1995, President Carter, so gentle and soft-spoken, referring to the fact that not a single indictment had been made by the International Criminal Tribunal as 'disgusting'. The reason for this sharp comment was surely due to the horror with which the world had watched the images of genocide on television, seemingly unable to stop the most gruesome, murderous rampage in living memory. Naturally there was a deep sense of outrage at the world's inability to prevent the genocide and an equally sharp desire to bring the criminals to book as quickly as possible.

After the Commission of Experts published its report in October 1994, the Security Council had passed its Resolution no. 997 in March 1995, setting up the International Criminal Tribunal for Rwanda. Judge Richard Goldstone of South Africa, who was already the Chief Prosecutor for the Criminal Tribunal on Yugoslavia, was appointed the Chief Prosecutor for Rwanda. Another decision was to site the Deputy Prosecutor's office in Kigali and to locate the court in Arusha, Tanzania. Judge Honore Rakotomanana of Madagascar was appointed Deputy Prosecutor and by May 1995 the Deputy Prosecutor's office had begun its activities, at half cock, because budgetary and selection problems prevented the Deputy Prosecutor's Office from being at full strength. The six judges to the ICTR were appointed on 25 May 1995, with Judge Leiti Kama of Senegal being elected Chairman.

The ICTR issued its first indictment on 12 December 1995 and held its first formal session in Arusha on 8 January 1996. The tribunal had only two chambers and its officials estimated that not more than 10–15 cases a year could be processed. By March 1996, the tribunal's special prison in Arusha, which conformed to basic Western requirements, was not ready to receive more than a few prisoners. By May 1996, three accused had been transferred by Zambia to the tribunal's prison in Arusha.

The delay in the tribunal's starting of its functions became the subject of strong criticism, particularly by the Western media. Editorials and leading articles castigated the UN system for the delay. For Rwandans too, the wheels of the International Tribunal were turning much too slowly to assuage their quest for justice, their chagrin heightened by the fact that the big fish, like the owner of Radio Mille Collines, were living scot-free in neighbouring and Western capitals.

Where, in my opinion, the Rwandan leadership felt justifiably aggrieved was in the indifference shown by member states and particularly Rwanda's neighbours in apprehending the known, high-profile leaders who had masterminded the genocide. Security Council Resolution no. 978 placed a moral, if not legal, responsibility on member states to take such steps, but most countries extricated themselves from this responsibility, either by claiming that they first needed to pass enabling domestic legislation, which took time, or, as in Zaire's case, by contending that they had enough on their hands in receiving over a million refugees and it was not for them but for the UN to distinguish which were criminals and which the ordinary refugees. These, mainly African, countries were then sent a formal list of 443 alleged criminals by the government of Rwanda with a request to apprehend and extradite them. None of the neighbouring countries responded positively. In fact, the Kenyan President went so far as to state that he would reject requests even from the ICTR for the arrest of alleged criminals. This statement was later retracted by the Kenyan government when it was pointed out that the ICTR had been established under Chapter VII and that its recommendations were mandatory. Some countries, like Belgium, Canada and Switzerland began arresting some of the high-profile personalities whose alleged involvement in the genocide had been widely publicized. Nevertheless, by the time UNAMIR folded its tent in Rwanda, exactly two years after the genocide was unleashed, only four arrests had been made in Western countries under domestic laws and 19 in African countries. It represented a beginning, but a painfully slow one that was unlikely to assuage the outrage that the victims continued to feel at the freedom with which the masterminds sauntered through their lives in expensive hotels. This indifference towards the perpetrators of one of the worst crimes of the century must remain a scar on the conscience of the international community.

Viewed dispassionately and taking into account the entire undertaking of creating an international tribunal – nominating its judges, budgeting for its expenditure, drafting rules of procedures, gathering evidence to indict the accused, persuading the countries where the accused are located to arrest and extradite them, preparing the prisons to retain the prisoners according to established norms – a certain lapse of time seems inevitable. For instance, the election of the 11 judges had to be carried out through the UN General Assembly (UNGA) where consultations with governments, reference to committees, minimum time for a selection process, geographical distribution and a final endorsement by the assembly took its time. Nevertheless, while some delay in putting the ICTR in place was inevitable, a lack of urgency and a bureaucratic approach to administrative problems was apparent. A more cohesive and urgent approach between the tribunal headquarters in The Hague, the UN's legal department and the Deputy Prosecutor's office in Kigali could have shortened the gestation period for the ICTR.

From the outset, the Rwandans had argued in favour of locating the tribunal in Kigali and appointing some Rwandan judges. They also wanted capital punishment. On these issues, I disagreed with my Rwandan interlocutors. A tribunal located in Rwanda would have been besieged by frenzied crowds calling for the blood of the major criminals. A fair trial would never be seen to have taken place, as the defendants could justifiably claim that the judges were swayed by the local atmosphere. Secondly, in the cauldron of hate and revenge, defence lawyers and witnesses would be at risk, as indeed would the defendants themselves who would be at the mercy of the RPA. For the same reason, transparent justice would never be available if Rwandan judges served on the tribunal. I felt Rwanda's requests were more emotional than rational and once the reasons for siting the tribunal in Arusha and for not accepting Rwandan judges and capital punishment were explained to the Rwandan leaders, they were accepted in good faith. In fact, it suited Rwanda that the two systems, internal and external, ran on parallel lines, each covering the same crimes, but with different sets of criminals and with differing sets of procedures and punishment. Of course, the irony of this arrangement is that the big fish will be able to watch television in their international standard, specially built cells in Arusha while the small fish will probably either be hanged publicly or left to rot in the rat-infested hell-holes of prisons like Gitarama!

The fact that differences in approach towards the ICTR were amicably smoothed over was due primarily to the extraordinary qualities of the Chief Prosecutor, Judge Richard Goldstone. Setting the tone from his first visit to Kigali in December 1994, Judge Goldstone exuded integrity, commitment and urgency in his task. He was frank and highly persuasive in his discussions with the Rwandan government who clearly held him in the highest esteem. Judge Goldstone was assisted from his headquarters in The Hague by a group of motivated staff, notably Catherine Cisse, a legal expert whose grace and luminous personality was matched by her brilliant intellect.

Mention of intellect and grace leads me immediately to Elizabeth Lindenmeyer, our 'control' at the DPKO in New York. Elizabeth is French and totally bilingual. She had seen peace-keeping action in Somalia and assumed charge of Rwanda soon after I arrived in Kigali. Elizabeth brought to bear a most thorough, rational, unhurried and sensitive approach to our problems. She was never flustered, always sharply focused, full of good cheer and highly dynamic in her approach. In fact, I was deeply impressed by the teamwork that existed in the DPKO from the most junior secretary upwards to Kofi Annan: everyone seemed to be backing up colleagues and keeping each other fully informed, always cheerfully and with a welcoming smile.

On her long-awaited visit to Rwanda in winter 1995, Elizabeth stayed at the Belgian Village in one of the small guest suites that we kept in case hotels were booked up, as they often were. The entire aspect of the Belgian Village was peaceful and calming, with its swimming pool, tennis court and rolling gardens. Elizabeth was enchanted with the Village, perhaps a little amused to see Colonel Abdel Aziz's monkey doing his tricks outside her room. Soon after her arrival, she walked up to my chalet for a cup of tea, passing my pet black goat nibbling away at the plants in the garden. After tea and now ready to turn in after a long, exhausting journey, Elizabeth went back to her room and got ready for a nice hot shower. She opened the bathroom door and found my goat devouring her toilet bag! These were some of the less daunting hazards that we lived through in Rwanda.

8. September – November 1995

Attempts to reconcile Tutsi and Hutu

The Gako military training camp

On the critical issue of national reconciliation, divergent opinions were held on the best approach towards a solution. I was firmly of the view that national reconciliation of the refugees should be allowed to assert itself gradually from the grassroots upwards. At HQ in New York, an alternate view was prevalent, namely that the focus should be primarily on high-level negotiations between the former RGF and the RPF. At the same time, some of Rwanda's neighbours believed in an immediate general amnesty while, within Rwanda itself, a deep schism on the issue had led to the resignation of the Prime Minister along with other moderate Hutu Cabinet stalwarts. Thus, every institution, every diplomat, every individual had a different approach to the problem. There was general consensus, however, that the Gako military training process was the most significant factor in favour of national reconciliation in Rwanda.

This process aimed to reassimilate a significant element of the former RGF into the national army. Gako is a commune in the Kibungo prefecture, about 85 kilometres south east of Kigali where the RPF had opened a military training and re-education centre. Around 2500 soldiers from the former RGF were being trained there. Most of these volunteers had stayed on in Rwanda after the departure of Operation Turquoise. Others had trickled back from their camps in Goma and Bukavu. The training and re-education was taking place in a large compound where some stark military barracks housed the trainees.

When the Gako training centre was started, UNAMIR was requested by the RPA to assist in providing basic facilities at the centre. Since national reconciliation was an integral part of our mandate and the Gako process was so manifestly a key factor in that direction, General Tousignant and I were able to provide a generator, vehicles and basic logistic and engineering facilities to the centre.

I first visited Gako in October 1994 when it had 2500 personnel, of whom about 80 were officers. I was received by the Tutsi RPA major in charge of the camp and was shown around the barracks with their elementary facilities. The training period was to take six months per batch of 1000. The first group was to be inducted in the national army by March 1995 and the second by September. When I asked the RPA major how the Gako trainees were responding to their re-education programme, he replied that they needed to be motivated psychologically towards a national cause. Most of them were short of such commitment. The soldiers being retrained told me that they had registered at specially opened recruitment centres in the HPZ. They felt more of their former colleagues would rejoin if they were assured of an amnesty. I then addressed the 80 officers gathered in the lecture hall. Two of these officers were Brigadier-Generals Gatsinzi and Rutasira of the Kigeme Group and seven colonels. I was struck by the fact that the RPA commander left me alone with the 80 officers during the question and answer session, clearly indicating that the officers were free to express themselves. The officers then asked me questions which were obviously not rehearsed and which revealed some basic doubts that officers in their situation would normally be expected to hold. For instance, I was asked, 'How can the UN ensure that the Arusha process is adhered to in letter and spirit?', and 'What role can the UN play to ensure that innocent people who did not participate or sympathize with the genocide are not persecuted?'. I left Gako impressed by the objectives and by the manner in which the government had set about achieving them.

On 24 November, at a meeting with General Kagame, I expressed my appreciation of what I had seen in Gako. I then suggested that an effort should be made to attract more former RGF personnel to rejoin the national army by establishing contact with them in the Zairean refugee camps. I told Kagame that I had already discussed this possibility with Zairean ministers who had welcomed the idea, particularly as they felt that seeing some of the RGF return to Rwanda would provide an incentive to other refugees to return home. Kagame agreed that a continuing flow of former RGF would be welcome. The military returnees would be filtered through the Gako process and re-absorbed into the national army. Kagame only requested that, before the optees crossed over, their names and credentials should be given to the Rwandan government for prior clearance 'so that there is no problem when they arrive,' he added. Kagame clearly wanted to protect himself against planted saboteurs being infiltrated into Rwanda. It was not surprising that in informal discussions with RPF leaders, a distinction was made between the RGF on the one hand and the Presidential Guard, the militia and the Interahamwe on the other. In terms of guilt for humanitarian crimes, the RGF was considered less guilty.

Later, in March 1995, a sad and poignant episode took place relating to the Gako process, which every visitor to the training centre recognized as a significant factor in the effort towards national reconciliation. I received a call from the RPA Chief of Staff, Colonel Sam Kaka, in which he stated that the Gako retraining process had proceeded successfully and the government was now ready to accept a larger contingent of RGF optees from Zairean camps. Through intelligence reports and informal contact, the RPF had been informed that a larger number of former RGF soldiers wanted to cross back and rejoin the national army. However, the RPA's dilemma was that it had no facilities to provide to these optees. They basically needed barracks, as the least they could provide was a roof over the heads of soldiers who, during the Habyarimana government, had been given privileged status and who wanted to return with their families. Colonel Kaka asked whether the UN could help provide these barracks as no one knew better than UNAMIR the devastation to the housing in Rwanda and the fact that the RPA was in no position to provide these facilities.[1]

I felt the Chief of Staff's request was not only valid, but would have a significant bearing in encouraging national reconciliation. Of course, I had no funds in my own budget to respond to this legitimate request, so I quickly went round, with the usual cap in hand, to the specialized agencies to inquire if they could help provide funds for the building of these barracks. There was sympathy and understanding from the UNDP, Habitat, UNICEF and UNHCR but clearly building barracks for the military was not part of their mandate. I then turned to the bilateral donors, but they too declined, stating that their tax-payers would not countenance the spending of aid on the construction of military barracks!

Thus my efforts, and those of the Rwandan government, to induce more military personnel to return and join the Gako process received a severe set-back. I am sure that the Rwandan government saw the lack of a positive response to the legitimate request as yet another example of UNAMIR's inability to implement, on the ground, what was a vital part of UNAMIR's mandate. In fact, President Kagame clearly said so in a public speech. It represented another let-down in helping Rwanda pick itself up from disaster. Even as late as August 1995, when Zaire began a short period of forced return of refugees, some RGF in military uniforms attempted to cross back into Rwanda at the Bukavu–Cyangugu border. They were prevented from doing so by Zairean guards who told them to return to their camps in Bukavu.

On 9 September 1995, the second batch of Gako re-trainees was integrated into the national army. The ceremony took place at the Butare Stadium in the presence of the President, the Vice-President,

---

[1] Colonel Kaka died of an illness in 1997.

the Rwandan Cabinet and the diplomatic corps. 1200 Gako trainees – all former RGF officers and soldiers – were formally inducted into the national army, making a total of 2400 since the beginning of the Gako induction process. At the ceremony itself, the senior RGF officer, Major Balthazar Ndegeyinka, was promoted to the rank of Lieutenant-Colonel. He was given a Tutsi second-in-command and the new regiment marched past to military music played by a Rwanda military band which, incidentally, had been trained by our excellent Ghana band. In his speech, Vice-President Kagame pointedly referred to his government's disappointment that the international community had not come forward with assistance to a project that aimed to promote national reconciliation and to safeguard security. Colonel Ndegeyinka was later interviewed on Radio UNAMIR and stated that he had thought hard for several months in Goma before deciding to rejoin the army. He said he was satisfied with the training programme.

The Gako regiment was assigned to a vital and sensitive area east of Kibuye. This was a Hutu stronghold which had received a large number of returnees from IDP and refugee camps. UNAMIR Milobs operating in the region were firmly of the view that the presence of the Gako Hutu regiment had greatly helped to calm the situation and that there had been a significant downturn of incidents in the area. Seemingly, the Gako experiment had paid dividends, not only in encouraging the prospect of national reconciliation but also in calming the fears of the Hutu community on the ground.

To provide balance to the Gako syndrome, I must record the views of the late Seth Sendashonga, contained in the manifesto that he released from Nairobi after his departure from Kigali. Sendashonga contended that the Gako process was a sham and an eyewash. He argued that the Gako-trained regiments were not given any real authority and that its officers were constantly supervised by the RPA and not allotted sensitive tasks. He believed that the Gako trained personnel were already deeply disillusioned and would revert back to their colleagues in Goma if given an opportunity. Sendashonga thus dismissed the Gako process as window-dressing by the Tutsi-dominated government of Rwanda.

The deployment of UNAMIR formed troops

By October 1995, half-way through our six-month mandate, relations between UNAMIR and the Rwandan government had settled into an amicable, co-operative groove again. This was partly due to the fact that UNAMIR had been downsized to less than half its former strength – a fact that many RFP hard-liners did not believe would be allowed to happen – and now that UNAMIR was scaling down further and its complete phase-out was in sight; there was a general lowering of tension. Moreover, Rwanda's naive expectation that the money saved on the downsizing could, somehow, be converted to Rwanda's treasury had also been recognized as unrealistic. There was disappointment, even anguish, at UNAMIR's inability to help Rwanda directly, but there was also a realization that UNAMIR military personnel were bending over backwards to help, within their limited means, to repair and revive the devastated infrastructure. After the fresh mandate, the local RPA commanders and prefects were noticeably more relaxed and co-operative with our formed troops that were stationed outside Kigali.

Our formed troop battalions were located in five critical sectors. As already stated, the Indians were in the capital and performing their task with commendable efficiency. In Cyangugu, the Ethiopians had performed a remarkable bridge-building role in an area that was of high tension as it was opposite Bukavu and the target of guerrilla attacks from across the frontier. The Ethiopians were somewhat unorthodox, very much a people's army, not the smartest on parade, but extraordinarily adept at gaining the goodwill of the people. The Ethiopian soldiers, apart from performing their normal duties, would go out into the fields and help the farmers sow their crops and tend the vegetable patches. It was evident that the Ethiopians had seen real war and were able to make use of their experience by relating meaningfully to the population.

The Ghanaians succeeded in another way. The Ghana army is trained for peace-keeping and their units arrive thoroughly prepared for a peace-keeping role. Their commitment to peace-keeping is extraordinary in its human dimension and also in its organization. Their discipline is superb and visiting their units was always a joy because of their brilliant drill, their impeccable manners and the smiling warmth of their officers. I noticed also that women soldiers were part of their units and would stand shoulder to shoulder on the parade ground with the men. This enabled the Ghanaians to bridge the gender gap more effectively than other units which were exclusively male. After their truly heroic role during the genocide, they were later assigned a relatively easy task in Kibungo. And of course there was always the wonderful Ghana band.

The Rwandan government wanted UNAMIR to phase out as quickly as possible, the only exception being the Ethiopians and the Ghana band whom they requested should be allowed to stay till the last. Ghana agreed but Ethiopia could not spare its battalion.

Canada was represented in UNAMIR by two outstanding force commanders, a highly professional headquarters staff, a communi cations unit and a logistic unit. At a time when a number of contingents were withdrawn from Rwanda, the Canadians unflinchingly lived through the atrocities that are now part of Rwanda's history. Canada, of course, prides itself on its peace-keeping role. It has been in the forefront of troop-providing countries in several UN peace-keeping operations and though the Canadian government is subject to the same pressures with regard to soldier casualties as the USA and Western Europe, it has unswervingly committed its peace-keepers to UN peace-keeping. Canada also has the advantage of being bilingual, in French and English.

Britain and Australia were also enthusiastic participants in UNAMIR, but for relatively short periods. The British logistic unit performed a superb role as a kind of dynamo, providing the electric current for the entire UNAMIR system. The Australians sent a medical unit whose enthusiasm was unbounded. They willingly worked 24 hours a day, inoculating, vaccinating, treating patients in the remotest communes and maintaining an excellent hospital in Kigali. Both British and Australian units relished the opportunity of putting their training and expertise to effect in a real theatre of operations rather than the simulated drill on which they learnt their trade.

I have already referred to the performance of the Indian Gurkhas and the Zambians who covered themselves with honour at Kibeho. The Nigerians and Malawians were also highly professional in their performance. The Malawi contingent producing a squash-playing major who put paid to my long-cherished ambition of becoming a national squash champion. I thought I had a good chance, late in life, in Rwanda where there was one squash court and a pervasive French culture that thought squash was some kind of fruit juice.

Once while driving through Kibungo, we stopped unannounced at a Nigerian company unit. The Nigerian company commander, a lieutenant, greeted us and gave us an impromptu briefing which left all of us deeply impressed at the composure and quality of Nigeria's young officers. The Nigerian army can pride itself on the performance of its peace-keepers in Rwanda.

The Tunisian battalion was assigned to the Gisenyi–Ruhengeri region. The Tunisians were also a highly professional unit, adding their special North African flavour to the mosaic of different cultural hues represented in UNAMIR. Having served as a diplomat in Tunisia, I spent a lot of time with officers and soldiers reminiscing about Tunisia over a cup of mint tea. Every Sunday, Colonel Abdel Aziz, the Tunisian force commander, would send me Tunisian delicacies of burreuk, couscous and casse-croutes which I consumed with relish. The colonel was a gentle, kindly officer who replaced Brigadier-General Anyidoho as Deputy Force Commander when he completed his outstanding tenure in Rwanda.

I recall particularly the little monkey that he once brought back from Gisenyi and which became a sort of mascot at the Belgian Village. The monkey lived in the Tunisian officers' chalet, but would visit all the other inhabitants of the Village. He was a particularly friendly monkey whom I would pass on my way down to the tennis courts. He would watch the tennis and then move over to the volleyball game being played by the Gurkhas. This monkey was famous, however, for the price for which it was bought. Colonel Abdel Aziz told me that when in Gisenyi, he had been approached by a Rwandan lad who offered to sell the monkey for US$5000, claiming it to be a rare species. There was a lot of bargaining between Colonel Abdel Aziz and the lad who eventually accepted $4 for the sale! When the colonel returned to Tunis the monkey left with him, but unfortunately it died in quarantine.

While on the subject of the Tunisian contingent, I must mention the brilliant contribution made by Colonel Chabbir, the Tunisian second-in-command who was assigned to UNAMIR headquarters. No challenge was too great for Colonel Chabbir and the word 'no' simply did not exist in his vocabulary. If a job had to be done, however impossible it might seem, Chabbir volunteered to do it and never failed. Chabbir was an outstanding officer, totally dedicated, selfless and modest. I would be surprised if he is not, one day, the Commander-in-Chief of the Tunisian army.

Finally, the Franco-African battalion (Fran-batt) that was inherited from Operation Turquoise was a mixture of troops from Senegal, Chad, Mali and Guinea. This battalion was assigned the most difficult prefecture, Kibuye, where they had already served and gained the trust of the local population. The Fran-batt performed their role with great credit particularly as the RPA had always treated them with suspicion and had never really extended a hand of cooperation to them.

In praising the units that were part of UNAMIR formed troops (as distinct from our Military Observers who came from every part of the globe, ranging from Fiji to Uruguay and from Russia to Pakistan), I must also record some of the problems and difficulties that arose during their assignment in Rwanda. These were caused mainly by soldiers mixing with the vulnerable female population. There were also incidents of black marketing in goods and currency, and also of rash driving. Once a typically swaggering Aussie unwittingly overtook the President's solemn cavalcade, causing a furore and an accusation of UNAMIR's 'lack of respect' for Rwanda's leadership. These incidents, however, were rare and the only act that the superb Ghana regiment regretted was when, in a friendly football match with the RPA, the Ghanaian full-back kicked the referee! The offender was sent back in disgrace on the next flight.

Milob conferences

In accordance with our 6 June 1995 mandate, UNAMIR had retained 340 Military Observers as part of its military contingent. These Milobs were assigned various duties at headquarters and were also posted to the ten Rwandan prefectures. In the difficult zones, where

UNAMIR had assigned formed troops, the Milobs operated in harness with them. Otherwise, they operated on their own, co-ordinating closely with agency field representatives. Generally, UNAMIR military personnel enjoyed good relations with the local RPA and civilian administration because of the various facilities, such as medical and logistic help, that they could provide. The Milobs were particularly welcome as they were unarmed and did not represent to the RPA the 'derogation of sovereignty' or 'overpowering presence' sensitivity of UNAMIR formed troops.

Milobs were therefore uniquely well placed to gain the confidence of the local administration and people. They were easily the best informed outsiders in Rwanda and had their ear to the ground at all times. Thus, in order to keep myself informed and to feel the real pulse of the country, I decided to hold regular conferences of Milobs at which presentations would be made on specific themes followed by discussions. I found these Milob conferences to be extremely informative and I would invariably share their conclusions with agency and NGO heads and also with heads of diplomatic missions. As an example, the following conclusions were reached at the Milob conference held in October 1995.

> Except in Kibuye, where the Prefect is regarded as hostile, co-operation between UNAMIR and the Rwandan administration has continued to improve. In most prefectures, the RPA has excellent relations with our formed troops and Milobs. The local population see UNAMIR as an insurance against the RPA's overbearing attitude. Requests for co-operation at the local level are growing with, regrettably, limited capability on our part to respond to them.

> It is evident that in the prefectures adjoining Zaire, there are increasing attempts at infiltration and economic sabotage by the former RGF, militia and Interahamwe. This, in turn, leads to a large RPA presence, often suspicious of the local population's supportive role towards the infiltrators. Arbitrary arrests, harsh treatment and human rights violations are, therefore, more prevalent in this border zone than elsewhere. In Kibuye, the RPA has acted particularly ruthlessly against the Hutu population. It must be noted that there are no UNAMIR formed troops in this Sector.

> The former RGF's sabotage campaign is on the increase. Land mines, eco-sabotage assassinations, etc have led to RPA cordon and search operations. Skirmishes are taking place regularly but there is no danger yet of a full scale invasion. Ijwi island seems to be the main base for RGF infiltration.

> The RPA has not won over the hearts and minds of the local Hutu population, particularly in the Sectors adjoining Lake Kivu, Butare and Gitarama. The RPA, though not popular and often overbearing, is disciplined and generally correct. It has been established that soldiers have not been paid in the last six months. This fact may contribute to their restlessness and tension, specially when faced with assistance being provided to returnees by the NGOs and international community.

The Justice System is not functioning on the ground. The Triage Commission exists on paper with no output. The prisons are still appallingly overcrowded. The medical facilities serving the prisons are better which means fewer deaths and more amputations.

In spite of tensions, there is room for refugee resettlement in Kibuye. However, the poor road conditions make it difficult, especially during the present rainy season, for transport to move. Approximately 700,000 people left from Kibungo Sector although some have returned. Kibungo Prefecture can take in 400,000 refugees. Most other prefectures are now over-flowing with refugees but some, e.g. Ruhengeri and Butare, can still absorb more.

Returning refugees have, in the main, been well treated, absorbed and processed efficiently. Rwanda and the UN agencies/NGOs are ready to process a much larger in-flow of refugees. Transit camps that could accommodate 15,000 each are ready in several locations near the Zaire border. Transit camps processing refugees from Tanzania are also well equipped. The difficulty would be in the absorptive capacity in the communes which do not have adequate housing, jobs, agricultural material, etc. In addition, the Rwandan Government needs to intensify its information campaign in the refugee camps.

Vast numbers of cattle continue to enter Rwanda through the Gatuna border-post from Uganda and also from Tanzania. This cattle is gathered in the Akagera Park, endangering whole ecosystems of marshes and veld not suitable for either grazing or cultivation. However, culturally the Tutsi have been pre-eminently pastoralists and cattle is a symbol of their wealth. On the other hand, the installation of a slaughterhouse would help the economy and effect some culling of these herds.

Radio UNAMIR can now be heard clearly everywhere and especially in the camps. The main issue is how to make people aware of Radio UNAMIR for which a publicity campaign is necessary. The distribution of free FM radios would help.

The Mugabo disappearance

An incident that left me with a deep sense of anguish and concern was the disappearance of one of our interpreters, Augustin Mugabo, who worked for Radio UNAMIR. Mugabo was Radio UNAMIR's principal interpreter and was responsible for translating speeches, bulletins, etc from Kinyarwanda into French/English. After the furore created by General Kagame's speech of 28 February at Gitarama, RPA intelligence officers had questioned Mugabo about his translation of the speech, accusing him of giving it an incorrect and unwarranted interpretation. In fact, the speech had first been heard on Radio Rwanda and Mugabo had made an honest translation. Nevertheless, the RPA accused him of giving it a malicious twist in the interpretation.

Several months later, Mugabo took paid leave and told his family that he would be visiting relatives in Uganda. After leaving his house, he was not seen again. At first, we felt that Mugabo would be found in a prison or a *cachot* accused of complicity in the genocide. This was the case with about 14 UN local employees who were in prison awaiting trial. However, there was no trace of him. I took up the issue with all the ministers concerned, and also with RPA intelligence and security. Eventually, I raised the matter at the bilateral meetings on the mandate with the Rwandan delegation. The only response was that they would try to locate Mugabo.

I fear that Mugabo was punished for his association with Radio UNAMIR, which the hard-liners in the RPA had always opposed, especially after the incident of the translation of Kagame's speech. This incident, more than any other, brought home the terror that ordinary innocent folk in Rwanda lived with when they sought employment with UN agencies or with diplomatic missions. For me, it was a scar on the image of the government and a cause of profound anguish as I feel his association with Radio UNAMIR was the reason for his almost certain death. Of course, I have no proof, but the circumstances of Mugabo's disappearance sends a shiver down my spine every time I think of him and of his family, who were deprived of their breadwinner. I know that Mugabo was doing an honest job and was innocent of any wrong-doing.

The Iwawa Island incident

On 11 November, the Rwandan government gleefully announced that the RPA had routed a guerrilla operation that had been surreptitiously mounted by the RGF militia from Iwawa, a small island in the Rwandan half of Lake Kivu. As described in Chapter 4, the RGF's campaign to raise a military force with a view to waging a guerrilla war had been gaining strength. Already reports of militarization in the camps, increasing attempts at cross-border sabotage and the consequent heightening of security by the RPA had led to the appointment of the International Commission of Inquiry (ICI) headed by Ambassador Mahmoud Kassem. For its part, Rwanda had mounted a counter insurgency effort and had sought assistance from UNAMIR to purchase amphibian craft which could intercept guerrillas crossing the lake in darkness. Of course, the UN was not able to provide the amphibian craft and eventually the RPA acquired a couple of boats with high-speed motors which they converted into a counter-insurgency amphibian unit. In the first week of November, RPA intelligence reported a build-up of RGF guerrillas on Iwawa. At 5.00 am on 11 November, an RPA military unit attacked the island with its two amphibious boats. Catching the guerrillas by surprise, they routed the 400-strong guerrilla force that was on the island. Their leader immediately abandoned his men and fled in a small rowing-boat. About 100 guerrillas drowned as they attempted to swim for

Zaire in panic. Another 47 guerrillas were killed and 45 captured and taken prisoner. The RPA also captured arms that the guerrillas had intended to use.

By sheer co-incidence, the ICI's visit to Rwanda took place shortly after the Iwawa operation. The Rwandan government, after briefing members of the Commission, conducted them to Iwawa Island to see evidence of militarization and sabotage at first hand. The Commission noted that some of the arms and ammunition captured at Iwawa were old and of Belgian manufacture, while other ammunition was brand new, having been delivered recently – probably through the international arms bazaar. For instance, there were Italian mines that had not even been opened from their wrappings. The Commission was also able to meet some of the prisoners who had been taken at Iwawa and were informed of the training and indoctrination that had been given to them before they were sent on their guerrilla expedition.

The Iwawa Island incident represented an important moral victory for the government as it provided proof of complicity in the militarization and training of guerrillas in the refugee camps. It also exacerbated the already tense relations between Rwanda and Zaire as the Rwandan government and radio accused Zaire of complicity in the militarization and delivery of arms to the guerrillas. Zaire vehemently denied the charge. It was apparent that Zaire was noticeably cool and unco-operative with the Commission of Inquiry when it visited Zaire.

The report of the Commission – rejected by Zaire – makes for interesting reading.[1] The report states, inter alia, that Colonel Bagasora, a leading figure accused of genocide, twice visited the Seychelles and bought a consignment of arms which was transported in a Zairean aircraft to Goma.[2] The report adds that the Zairean government provided the end-user certificate for the arms to be flown out from the Seychelles to Zaire.

The Genocide Conference

After a year and a half in Rwanda, I developed a theory to explain the undulating waves of xenophobia and 'UNAMIR bashing' that seemed to occur every six months. Tension would be orchestrated through speeches, radio broadcasts, demonstrations and government-sponsored policies that would, equally quickly, give way to co-operation, smiles and warmth at all levels. My theory was that every time an important event connected with the 1994 genocide approached, such as the 7 April anniversary or the renewal of

---

[1] The ICI's interim report contained in the Secretary General's letter to the Security Council, Document no. S/1996/67, dated 29 January 1996. The final report confirmed the interim.
[2] Colonel Bagasora has since been arrested and is to be tried at the International Criminal Tribunal for Rwanda.

UNAMIR's mandate, the government would orchestrate a rising tide of tension. Once the event passed, normal relations would be restored. For instance, we saw the gradual heightening of tension during the negotiations for the new mandates, before June and December 1995, tension that subsided immediately after agreement was reached.

A new tension high-point approached in November in the form of the much-heralded Conference on Genocide. Specifically, the conference was entitled 'Genocide, Impunity and Accountability, Dialogue for a National and International Response'. It was held from 1 to 5 November in Kigali. At this conference the Rwandan government aimed to discuss a number of issues relating to genocide, including the vital issue of justice. A build-up to the conference was visible several weeks earlier, with reminders on Radio Rwanda of the international community's 'reprehensible role' in not preventing genocide in Rwanda.

The conference was held at the National Assembly and was attended by representatives from the highest level of the Rwandan government. It began with a harrowing account of the genocide given by a woman whose face had been gashed by a machete but who had somehow survived. There were over 200 non-Rwandans attending, including approximately 50 experts on genocide history, journalism, law, psychology and therapy. These experts came from countries that had passed through a similar experience such as South Africa, Israel, Latin America and Germany. A number of legal experts gave advice in providing a framework that would cater for the punishment of those who were responsible for the genocide.

At the conference, two broad strains were visible: the rhetorical and the pragmatic. At the rhetorical level, there was a renewal of accusations against the UN and the international community for not 'saving' Rwandan people from genocide. Specifically France, Belgium and the UN were targeted as the main offenders while Zaire, Togo and Kenya were severely criticized for 'harbouring' the genociders and not arresting them despite being informed of the UN Security Council resolutions.

The accusations were again picked up by the European press, especially in Belgium where the brutal killing of ten Belgian soldiers still touched a raw nerve, and reference was made to the now famous Dallaire telegram of 11 January 1994, which had passed on to the UN an informant's warnings of impending genocide. The accusation was repeated in a paper compiled by Collette Braeckman, a distinguished Belgian journalist. As a result of this criticism, I set up a committee to examine all available telegrams in UNAMIR that could shed some light on this issue. The committee consisted of Colonel Tikoca who had been the Chief Military Observer throughout this period, Isel Rivero who had been the desk officer for Rwanda in the DPKO at the time and was now my Chef de Cabinet and Colonel

Fletcher, the Chief of Staff at UNAMIR's military headquarters. Their conclusions were as follows:

> As requested, Mr Tikoca, Colonel Fletcher and I [Isel Rivero] met on Saturday 18 November to exchange views on whether the former SRSG or Gen. Dallaire had warned UN/HQ that imminent genocide would occur in Rwanda.
>
> Based on the research carried out by Colonel Fletcher (his note to you dated 9 November 1995 attached), Mr Tikoca's notes and mine, we have found no such evidence.
>
> However, all of us have agreed that there was ample evidence of the escalation of violence substantiated by political assassination, arms shipments for the RGF, activities inciting to ethnic violence by Radio Mille Collines, and past history of ethnic violence in both Burundi and Rwanda including the murder of the democratically elected president of Burundi (Hutu), which should have sounded the alarm at HQ.

Apart from an element of catharsis, the most important substantive gain of the Genocide Conference was the collection of advice by a number of influential experts on addressing the judicial aspects of genocide. These experts discussed such issues as degrees of culpability, truth commissions, special laws and courts to punish genocide, tribal justice and plea bargaining. The conference tasked a special implementation committee to give concrete shape to these ideas with a view to providing a legal base to deal with the aftermath of the genocide. Overall, the conference had served the purpose of charting a future course for dealing with this aftermath.

The UN Secretary-General's Special Envoy's mission for a regional conference

In October 1995, Ambassador José Luis Jesus of Cape Verde was sent as the Secretary-General's Special Envoy on a mission to the countries of the Great Lakes to solicit their support for a UN-sponsored regional conference. Generally, during his visit to the regional capitals, there was support for the initiative, except in Kampala where the response was lukewarm and in Rwanda where it was negative.

The Rwandan leaders felt that the conference would open the door for the Rwandan opposition to be represented. Rwanda was totally opposed to any such attempt at a 'back door' entry for the opposition. Secondly, they felt that the conference would put Rwanda on the defensive as the issues to be discussed focused exclusively on Rwanda's role. They felt that the problems of the region sprung from diverse sources, not least the militarization of the refugee camps and therefore the asylum countries should be placed as much in the dock as Rwanda. Thirdly, the Rwandan leadership argued that the issues were already well known and had been thoroughly analysed with an appropriate action plan that had been meticulously worked out and agreed at the Bujumbura Conference. Rwanda felt that the need was therefore to implement the decisions already agreed and not to hold yet another conference to identify the issues. Accordingly, Rwanda opposed the regional conference concept. Another, unstated reason for Rwanda's opposition was that they saw the proposal essentially as a French/Belgian initiative. Rwanda continued to oppose this initiative though it participated in two subsequent rounds of regional summits initiated by former President Carter.

The Carter initiative

While Special Envoy Jesus's efforts were meeting with a negative response from Rwanda and, to a lesser degree, from Uganda, former President Carter announced one of his peace initiatives for the Great Lakes region and received a more positive signal from the countries involved. President Carter also allied the efforts of three distinguished African statesmen, former President Julius Nyerere, Bishop Desmond Tutu and also a francophone personality, former President Amadou Toure of Mali, to assist him in seeking a solution to the problems of the region. President Carter began his efforts with a careful, behind-the-scenes effort in which the centrepiece was a rapprochement between President Mobutu and President Museveni, long considered to be antagonistic to each other. The two presidents met three times over a short period of time and pronounced themselves in favour of the Carter initiative for a regional conference at Head of State level.

The scene was therefore set for the Carter visit to the region and especially to Rwanda which had, so far, been lukewarm to the idea of a regional conference. President Carter arrived in Kigali on 19 November, accompanied by Mrs Carter. They met the President and Vice-President and visited a mass grave, a sight so harrowing that Mrs Carter fell out half-way through. After his successful talks with the leadership, President Carter announced that the regional conference would be held in Cairo from 27 to 29 November. In his press conference, President Carter stressed the following points which were obviously aimed at reassuring Rwanda:

a) No opposition representation would be allowed.

b) The issue of the militarization of refugees would be discussed.

c) Implementation of the Bujumbura Action Plan would be given priority.

Except for Bishop Tutu, and the Tanzanian President, who was involved in his national elections, all the leading figures participated in the first Carter-sponsored conference. The atmosphere was cordial, an achievement in itself, given the tensions between several member states. Except for minor differences of approach, the Carter Declaration which ensued reaffirmed the decisions of the Nairobi and Bujumbura Conferences held earlier in the year.

Cairo's crucial test lay in the implementation of the agreements. This, in turn, was dependent on the financing of such projects as the separation and relocation of the refugee camps. Clearly, the Cairo Conference expected the UN – or more specifically the donor states – to pick up the bill for this expenditure. Personally, I was sceptical at the prospect because, exactly a year earlier, we had produced a comprehensive plan for the separation and relocation of camps in Zaire and Tanzania with an estimated cost of US$50 million per country over a six-month period. We were told that neither the finance nor the personnel was available. Now, a year later, with the donor community having spent hundreds of millions of dollars on humanitarian aid to the camps, we were back to square one in suggesting relocation and separation!

A second Carter-sponsored conference was held in Tunis on 14–16 March as a follow-up to Cairo. The Tunis Conference was held against a background of greater tension between the Great Lakes states and was therefore less cordial in its ambience. Rwanda's relations with Zaire and Kenya were at rock bottom while Uganda–Kenya relations had also nose-dived. Nevertheless, thanks to President Carter's determined efforts, the Tunis Conference produced a detailed consensus declaration on regional issues. Once again, the devil lay in the implementation which, as before, seemed a bridge too far!

Disbursement of aid to Rwanda

The issue of international aid to Rwanda had simmered since the Geneva Round Table Conference in January 1995. It would become critical in early 1996 when the Rwandan government would threaten to cancel the next Geneva Round Table Conference. In February 1996, the government would also close down a number of NGOs, a decision that was indirectly related to the problems of aid disbursement.

It will be recalled from Chapter 3 that the first Geneva Round Table had been a success, with donor countries pledging over US$587 million aid to Rwanda. Six months later, the Geneva Review Conference in Kigali saw the pledges more than doubled and raised to US$1.2 billion, a significant figure for a small country like Rwanda.

By autumn 1995, however, there were rumblings of discontent from the Rwandans who claimed that, out of the US$1.2 billion sanctioned by donors, only a trickle had reached Rwanda. They calculated this figure at 14 per cent. Privately, the Rwandans felt deeply aggrieved that while the donor community was cascading humanitarian aid into the refugee camps (US$2 million a day at its height), precious little aid was coming through to help the victims of genocide in Rwanda. The JEEAR commented on this issue as follows:

> The international community took steps to investigate the genocide and punish the culprits by establishing an International Tribunal; however, it has largely failed to incorporate the implications of genocide in the design and implementation of assistance programmes in Rwanda. It has treated and continues to treat the present crisis like other civil wars in which the international community intervened and assisted the suffering population. Such an approach has distorted assistance priorities, undermined the effectiveness of assistance programmes and alienated the present government. For example, the international community has tended to overlook the plight of the survivors of the genocide; by and large, they have not been treated any differently than other segments of the population. On the other hand, the international community has spent immense resources on the refugees. It is not that the refugees do not deserve assistance but such assistance should be balanced with assistance to survivors.

By October 1995, the UNDP and the donor countries had reviewed their data and came forward with the contention that 69 per cent of the committed aid had been disbursed. There was thus a wide gap, almost a chasm, between the figures put forward by Rwanda and the percentages claimed by the UNDP and the donor countries.

There is, of course, an element of semantics in calculating these percentages. To start with, donor countries announce the aid that has been 'pledged' to an aid recipient country. These pledges are then converted into 'commitments', a stage when actual contracts are signed between donor and recipient. The third stage is 'disbursement' when the sum contracted is actually conveyed to a bank in the recipient state. The Rwandans wanted to add a critical, fourth stage of 'mobilization' when the disbursed funds are actually spent on national projects.

I was disappointed that what seemed a generous commitment by donor countries should be viewed in such niggardly terms by the government of Rwanda. Part of the problem lay in the slow process of disbursing committed pledges. State bureaucracies have to pass through numerous stages before pledges convert to cashflow. Moreover, Rwanda admitted that its own planning for aid projects was faulty and led to inevitable delays. Despite these problems, the gap between donors and recipient was unwarranted and as the two sides moved towards a stand-off, I urged both donors and the Rwandan government to sit down together and rationalize the figures that they were working with.

In December 1995, the government decided to close down 38 of the approximately 90 NGOs operating in Rwanda. Three days' notice was given for them to clear out and a number of their vehicles and equipment were confiscated. Some NGOs had their bank accounts frozen. The sudden closing down of some NGOs' offices was part of the frustration felt in Rwanda over aid disbursement. Naturally, this arbitrary act on the part of the Rwandan government sent waves of concern across to the donor countries. Several NGOs requested me to intercede with the government, pleading that the action was not only unfair but counter-productive for them.

The government's action, though scarcely excusable, needs to be seen in perspective. During and immediately after the civil war, over 190 NGOs were operating in Rwanda. At the time, they had an open field as there was no central or local authority which could guide or control their activities. The NGOs brought in their vehicles duty-free, set up their communications networks, operated wherever they liked, came and went without visas, paid no taxes and generally carried out their programmes as they thought fit. Most of these NGOs were incredibly dedicated and lived through appalling psychological conditions and physical hardships in treating the traumatized people of Rwanda. They cared for the sick and wounded, found parents for separated children, opened orphanages and widows' homes, brought drinking-water to communes and distributed seeds and agricultural tools. They provided succour to raped women and traumatized children, vaccinated humans and cattle, dug pit latrines at refugee camps, provided kits to school-going children and food packs to returning refugees. They even cared for the rare silver-back gorillas that inhabit the border region of Rwanda and Uganda. In the most difficult scenario imaginable, the NGO performance in Rwanda was stupendous. Inevitably, there were a few NGOs who were in Rwanda simply to wave the flag and possibly get noticed by their governments. Fewer still were clearly out to make lucrative profits, often represented by insensitive buccaneers who hung around the local bars looking for instant gratification, easily discernible by their hyped-up cars, cowboy boots, dark glasses and pony-tails. As always, the misdeeds of a few tended to tarnish the extraordinary commitment of the majority of the NGOs.

With the passage of time and as the Rwandan government began to assume sovereign control over the country, there was a need for the NGOs – as indeed for all international organizations – to adjust to the new reality. Customs duties had to be paid, visas obtained, permission sought for communication networks, vehicles registered and government policy guidelines generally accepted. On several occasions, I called on NGO representatives gathered at UNREO meetings to be specially sensitive to the Rwandan government's legitimate expectations. Compliance was, however, desultory. This was due partly to a sense of indignity at being reined in by a seemingly puny government when the NGOs were performing their duties in such arduous conditions and partly to the inability of the government to deliver, in detail, on the conditions that it sought to impose. The result was that friction began to develop between the government and the NGOs. The government was determined to exercise control and direction over the NGOs while they, having earlier operated in an open field, now resisted attempts to circumscribe their activities. The NGOs felt that instead of appreciating their selfless, sacrificing contribution, the government was placing petty restrictions on them through a bureaucracy that hardly knew what it was doing. JEEAR comments on this issue in the following terms:

> While accountability to donors is important, it should not be forgotten that relief agencies should also be accountable to the populations they are seeking to assist. The team was struck by the very limited attempts by agencies to obtain the views of beneficiaries on the assistance they were provided with.

These tensions eventually escalated into a blow-out in December 1995. In my view, several of the complaints by the Rwandan government such as non-registration of vehicles, refusal to obtain permission for radio frequencies, non-payment of customs duties, were legitimate. They did not, however, justify the arbitrary manner in which the axe was wielded. Perhaps the object was to give shock treatment to a community that had been slow to respond to the government's demands. There was also a feeling that Rwanda wanted to weed out the French and Belgian NGOs whom the RPF continued to regard with acute suspicion.

9. December 1995 – April 1996

The equipment issue as UNAMIR prepares to leave

The second round of negotiations

By October 1995, there were two months to go before our six-month mandate ended on 9 December. This time I wanted that negotiations should not be conducted, as in July, at the eleventh hour, with haggling and horse-trading on UNAMIR's force strength carried out to the wire. I therefore urged UN HQ to begin discussions in good time. I also kept the major embassies and the OAU informed of the state of play.

The issues to be negotiated seemed fairly clear cut. Given existing targets, we could not reduce the force strength below the present number. Both General Tousignant and I were clear in our minds that retaining unarmed Milobs while phasing out the formed troops would not be acceptable. Therefore, if we were going to stay on with the present mandate, 1800 would be the formed troop contingent that we needed to retain. The hand-over of equipment was also a major factor to be considered which I have dealt with separately, later in this chapter.

The government – or to be more precise the RPF High Command – continued to take the stand that UNAMIR should phase out altogether as it was not actually assisting Rwanda in the revival of its economy and the repair of its infrastructure. The Rwandan leaders maintained that UNAMIR gave a false impression that it was providing security and the old argument of derogation of sovereignty was underlined. As regards responsibility for the safety of the diplomatic missions, UN agencies and NGOs, the Rwandan government stated that this was the government's responsibility and it was now fully prepared to assume it. The ICTR's office in Kigali which had, so far, been protected by UNAMIR, would now need to have its own protection units.

The choice, therefore, seemed fairly stark: either we continue for a further period with essentially the same formed troop strength, or we phase out altogether from 9 December. Some Rwandans informally suggested a half-way house solution in which UNAMIR retained Milobs in the prefectures, but no formed troops, except a battalion in Kigali. I considered this proposal to be the worst of both worlds and made my analysis and recommendations to headquarters accordingly.

This time, the Rwandan government nominated Claude Dusaidy, who was now Political Adviser to the Vice-President, for negotiations on the mandate. Dusaidy had the reputation of being a hard-liner. He was assisted by a team from the Ministries of Foreign Affairs, Communications and Defence and the Prime Minister's Office.[1]

Unlike the negotiations on the mandate in June, the present round of negotiations saw the United Nations taking a relatively neutral view regarding the continuation of UNAMIR in Rwanda. Our advice, which the Secretary-General accepted and presented in his report,[2] was that the UN should either stay in its present strength or fold up its tent and leave after 9 December, with a preference for the former. The issue was thus engaged not so much across the table at UNAMIR headquarters in Kigali where Claude Dusaidy and I would meet with our delegations every Tuesday morning, but directly between interested members of the international community, the regional countries and the UN agencies on the one hand, and the Rwandan leadership, the former interceding in favour of UNAMIR staying on.

The view of the international community was that at this critical make-or-break time for the voluntary return of refugees, UNAMIR's continued presence in Rwanda was important. The neighbouring countries, Zaire and Tanzania, were particularly insistent that UNAMIR should stay on, arguing that its departure would send the wrong signals to the refugee camps. All donor country ambassadors in Kigali interceded on similar lines with the President and Vice-President while senior Africa experts like Dr Ganns of Germany, Minister Jan Pronk of the Netherlands, George Moose of the USA and Bernie Dussault of Canada either visited Kigali or spoke to Rwandan leaders on the telephone, pressing for a continuation of the existing mandate. International figures like former President Carter and Dr Salim A. Salim, the OAU Secretary-General, also lent their support to the view that UNAMIR should continue in its present strength for a further period of six months, as did the heads of the UN agencies.

Despite this pressure, the Rwandan leaders did not commit themselves either way. At the weekly discussions on the mandate, the Rwandan delegation would raise the equipment issue and other issues of detail such as compensation, taxation and privileges. Then suddenly on 29 November came the news from Cairo, where the

---

[1] Claude Dusaidy died of an illness in 1997.
[2] Secretary-General's report to the Security Council on options for UN role in Rwanda after completion of withdrawal, Document no. S/1996/149, dated 29 February 1996.

Carter-sponsored conference was under way, that President Bizimungu had announced that UNAMIR's mandate would be renewed for a further six months. This announcement was obviously made under pressure from the gathered heads of state and in the presence of former Presidents Carter and Nyerere. However, by the time the President reached Kigali, the statement had first been garbled on Radio Rwanda and then turned around completely. It was evident, nevertheless, that the President was articulating the feelings of Rwanda's friends and neighbours, but not the view of the hard-line RPF. The President's statement and subsequent contradiction of it did, however, make Rwanda come out of the closet to announce that it wanted UNAMIR to phase out completely after 9 December.

This statement was ill received in the Security Council and among donor countries. While Rwanda's sovereign right regarding the stationing of UN troops was acknowledged, it was widely believed that a phase-out would be damaging for Rwanda's prestige and would put the brakes on efforts to induce the refugees to return home voluntarily. In the Security Council's informal meetings, the Rwandan Permanent Representative, Ambassador Manzi Bakuramutsa, was beleaguered from all sides and pressure was brought to bear on the Rwandan leadership to review and change its decision. During this melee, the UN itself stood back, allowing the international community and Rwanda to decide on the mandate. Eventually, no decision had been taken by 8 December and the Security Council had to postpone a decision by a further three days before a compromise was reached. Finally, the mandate was extended for a further three months on existing terms with a six-week winding-up period starting from 9 March.[1] The Rwandan government insisted on terminating our Civpol who were training the gendermerie and the civilian police and also pruning the strength of our Milobs and formed troops so that the total was reduced from 2140 (1800 formed troops and 340 Milobs) to 1400 (1200 formed troops and 200 Milobs). This decision was evidently taken by the Vice-President himself because, while his Permanent Representative was agreeing in the Security Council to a military strength of 1400, Claude Dusaidy was announcing on Radio Rwanda that the government would not accept a UNAMIR force strength beyond 800!

The figure of 1400 was regarded by General Tousignant, who was leaving on 11 December, as unacceptable. However, UN headquarters, General Tousignant's successor Brigadier-General Sivakumar and I felt that 1400 was manageable in terms of a phase-out period of three months. Canada was so incensed by the Security Council's acceptance of a reduced force that it decided to withdraw its logistic unit and also its headquarters staff immediately. I felt this decision, though understandable on a matter of principle, was regrettable in

---

[1] Security Council Resolution no. 1029, dated 12 December 1995.

the overall context as Canada had been a pillar of UNAMIR since its inception, having stood firm during the horrendous massacres and having given UNAMIR two outstanding officers as its force commanders.

On 31 December, a fortnight after the Security Council decision on the mandate, I received a telephone call from President Nyerere, who was visiting Kigali as a follow-up to the Cairo Summit. He asked to see me so I went immediately to the Hotel Mille Collines. I knew that the RPF had been particularly appreciative of President Nyerere's statements during the genocide as he had publicly criticized his own government for not taking a more forthright stand against it. Since then, President Nyerere had been invited to special occasions such as the 7 April commemoration and the Conference on Genocide. I was therefore eager to meet this famous and luminous international figure.

President Nyerere greeted me with typical graciousness and after a quick review of the regional situation, Mwalimu[1] came straight to the point. He said that he had been deeply distressed by events in Rwanda and Burundi and had decided to give his time and energy to seeking a healing process in these two countries. He had made himself available to President Carter and to the OAU and wanted to inform 'his good friend Boutros' about his initiative.

He then told me that during his two-day discussions with President Bizimungu and Vice-President Kagame, he had tried to persuade them to accept UNAMIR's presence for a further six months. President Nyerere believed that this would be beneficial for Rwanda, particularly because UNAMIR's presence would be viewed as a vital certificate of good conduct for the Rwandan government. He stated that he had held long discussions on this issue with the Rwandan leaders. He then pointed to the telephone and added, 'An hour ago I received a call from Vice-President Kagame who told me that although he still had some reservations in his mind, it was agreed that the Rwandan government would accept my advice and extend the mandate'. President Nyerere said that he had wanted to inform me immediately of the decision so that appropriate steps could be taken.

I thanked President Nyerere and told him that I was pleasantly surprised that the Rwandan leadership had indicated a change of course. I duly conveyed my conversation to headquarters and Mwalimu's request to meet the Secretary-General on his visit to New York.

On 16 January, President Nyerere briefed the Secretary-General on his discussions in Rwanda. Predictably, the Secretary-General was sceptical of Rwanda's intentions as, since Nyerere's visit, there

---

[1] Swahili for 'respected teacher'. Nyerere was affectionately known as this by Africans because of his venerable stature.

had been no change of tack in Rwanda's policies. In fact, they were continuing on the path of a final UNAMIR phase-out in March.

The Nyerere discussion had, however, percolated through to the main donor countries who now found renewed hope in the possibility of the extension for UNAMIR that they had unsuccessfully sought during the discussions on the mandate in December. The USA, Belgium, Germany, the Netherlands, Britain and the OAU were particularly interested in exploring the possibility of UNAMIR II extending beyond 9 March. The United States even circulated an informal paper proposing a mandate that would enable UNAMIR's engineering, logistic and communications contingents to perform a peace-building role. Other constructive suggestions were made, aimed at providing a face-saving way out for Rwanda to accept UNAMIR's extension in accordance with the Nyerere formula.

All these diplomatic efforts came to nothing as the Rwandan leadership and Dusaidy gave no hint of a change of course, even though a number of senior Rwandan figures indicated that an extension was on the cards 'provided the UN gives us something'. That something I took to mean a liberal hand-over of equipment and a capability to provide direct aid through the SRSG to assist Rwanda economically. By now UN headquarters, which was undergoing a financial crisis, was in no mood to play for an extension and, as no carrots were available, UNAMIR phased out on schedule. The mandate was completed on 9 March, and the remaining six weeks were spent packing up and leaving. A final passing-out parade was held which was attended by Foreign Minister Gasana. I felt it was a pity that none of the top three leaders came to attend the closure ceremony.

There was an interesting postscript to the Nyerere intercession which had given rise to so much speculation. On 28 February, I boarded an Ethiopian Airline plane for Addis Ababa, where the OAU and UNHCR had called a post-Bujumbura conference. As soon as I took my seat, I noticed President Nyerere sitting up front. I asked to see him and he immediately called me and gave me the following account of developments since his last meeting with me at the Hotel Mille Collines.

Mwalimu said that, after the Secretary-General had indicated his doubts that Rwanda would change course and accept an extension for UNAMIR, he returned to Rwanda for a one-day visit. He met the Vice-President and told him that he had learnt from the UN Secretary-General and from other sources that there was no change in Rwanda's policies. He inquired if there had been a turning back from the commitment given to him earlier. President Nyerere added that Vice-President Kagame told him that the issue had been discussed in great depth in the RPF High Command which had finally given its authority for the mandate to be extended. The Vice-President added that he himself might not be convinced, but since the advice came from President Nyerere, whom the government greatly respected, the government's decision was to extend the mandate. Kagame therefore confirmed the earlier decision indicated to President Nyerere which he had passed on to me.

I told President Nyerere that, despite several attempts to ease the Rwandan government's path into accepting UNAMIR's extension, the government had steadfastly maintained its initial stance. It was now certain that UNAMIR would phase out on 19 April, and would be replaced by a small purely civilian unit whose shape and size would be decided later. Mwalimu, shaking his head in disbelief, was clearly non-plussed and added that he would concentrate his energies on finding a solution for Burundi![1]

The equipment issue

Ever since the negotiations for a fresh mandate were engaged, in May 1995, I was clear in my own mind that the equipment issue would be critical at the time of UNAMIR's eventual departure. By mid-1995, it was apparent that UNAMIR had neither the funds nor the mandate to help repair Rwanda's infrastructure and revive its economy. There was no Trust Fund to oil the wheels of state. Nor had the mandate been adjusted to enable peace-keepers to play a peace-building role. Therefore the only way UNAMIR could directly help Rwanda was to leave behind, at the time of departure, as much equipment as possible for use in Rwanda. Politically, it was the only carrot, the only trump card UNAMIR possessed.

I was sure that if the UN were generous in leaving behind equipment, Rwanda would overlook the low points of our relations and would portray UNAMIR II and its stay in Rwanda as a success. On the other hand, if the bulk of the equipment were taken away, Rwanda would ensure that our departure would be difficult, acrimonious and contentious. Therefore, compared to the other issues related to UNAMIR's phase-out, I considered the equipment issue by far the most crucial and influential. It was no surprise, therefore, that throughout the negotiations on the post-9 December 1995 mandate, the equipment issue remained the critical factor under discussion.

The equipment that UNAMIR had brought into Rwanda consisted broadly of vehicles, communication items, computers, prefabrication units, air transport equipment, generators, furniture and office equipment. These items fell under the category of non-lethal equipment which was eligible for disposal. Obviously lethal items, like armoured personnel carriers, ammunition, etc could not be left behind. Moreover, equipment that was owned by the contingents themselves was also not available for disposal by the UN. In fact, some countries (like the Netherlands and India) decided bilaterally

---

[1] President Julius Nyerere died on 18 October 1999.

with Rwanda to leave behind some of their equipment while others, like Chad, insisted that even their worn-out vehicles be transported back at UN cost!

According to UN guidelines, UN-owned non-lethal disposable equipment was divided into three categories:

— *Category I*: equipment that was in good condition and usable in other peace-keeping operations. This equipment would either be transported direct to other peace-keeping operations or stored at the UN storage centre at Brindisi. This equipment would remain the property of UN headquarters.

— *Category II*: equipment that could usefully be transferred to other UN agencies (e.g. UNHCR, UNICEF, the UNDP) who continued to operate in the country. This equipment would be book-transferred to the agencies concerned, indicating a sale at depreciated cost.

— *Category III*: the remainder of the used, low-value equipment, which would either be sold to NGOs or handed over to the receiving state.

This categorization was based on UN General Assembly resolutions and applied across the board to all peace-keeping operations. Initially, I assumed that a fairly large amount of equipment would fall under Category III because much of the equipment UNAMIR had received was not second but third or fourth hand and since Rwanda was a landlocked country, transportation costs were prohibitively high for UNAMIR stock to be 'usable' in other peace-keeping operations or 'storable' in Brindisi which was already bursting at the seams.

From the outset, I put my weight strongly behind leaving as much equipment as was reasonably possible within the rules. I felt the rules provided some flexibility and that this latitude should be used to the maximum in pursuit of the overall objective of a positive, co-operative handshake at the conclusion of UNAMIR's mandate. Looking at the equipment available with UNAMIR, I had estimated that about 20 per cent would be transported out under Category I and that the remainder would either be left behind for use in Rwanda by the specialized agencies or gifted directly to the Rwandan government. I was surprised, therefore, to find that the UN Administration (FALD) was applying the letter of the law and insisting on a more complete transfer of the equipment out of Rwanda.

As expected, at the first meeting of the joint commission on the new mandate in October 1995, Claude Dusaidy formally requested a list of equipment that had been brought into Rwanda, expressing the hope that most of it could be left behind as a gesture of goodwill to Rwanda. In response, I quoted the broad parameters of General Assembly regulations on the disposal of equipment and added that, within these limitations, we would aim to leave behind as much equipment as possible. Dusaidy's intercession was followed by a letter to the Secretary-General from Foreign Minister Gasana indicating the items that Rwanda wished to keep.

My recommendations on the equipment issue were already known to headquarters. I was therefore surprised to receive telephone calls from the Department of Political Affairs insisting on as much equipment as possible being taken out of Rwanda. The messages added that, if the equipment was too expensive to transport to Brindisi, it should be sent to Nairobi for storage. Only absolutely redundant items were to be left behind. FALD tasked its Chief Administrative Officer, Ms Susan Mathew, and her team to assess each item of equipment with regard to its categorization. This process was time-consuming as each item had to be checked and assessed for depreciation. Surprisingly, these instructions were sent direct by FALD to the CAO in Kigali, even though they affected an issue of vital political importance.

Eventually in December 1995, the first list prepared by the Administration was sent to me. I was shocked to note that 93 per cent of our equipment was shown in Category I, i.e. to be transported out for use in other peace-keeping operations or for storage. Only 3.3 per cent was to be placed in Category II – UN agencies – and 3.7 per cent in Category III – gift for Rwanda. I felt that this division was unfair and, if it were carried out, it would create immense ill-will and resentment at the time of UNAMIR's departure.

On receiving the list, I questioned the rationale behind the usability of items shown in Category I. While some of the older items may have been 'usable', it made no economic sense to transport them out of Rwanda at great expense when there was no storage space available in Brindisi or Nairobi, particularly if the items were not actually required in other peace-keeping theatres such as Angola, Haiti (which was itself scaling down) or Liberia.

Meanwhile, members of the Security Council and the countries that had donated funds for the equipment, like Germany and the Netherlands, were aware of the importance of the equipment issue in UNAMIR's phase-out. They began to lobby the Security Council (of which Germany was a recent member) to adopt a more flexible approach. Accordingly, when UNAMIR's new mandate was agreed, paragraph 7 of Security Council Resolution no. 1029, dated 12 December 1995, required the Secretary-General to 'examine in the context of existing UN regulations the feasibility of transferring UNAMIR non-lethal equipment, as elements of UNAMIR withdrew, for use in Rwanda'. The term 'for use in Rwanda' suggested a liberal transfer of items from Category I to Categories II and III. Subsequently, on 13 February 1996, the President of the Security Council, Ambassador Madeleine Albright, addressed a letter to the Secretary-General in which the Security Council urged him 'in the light of unique circumstances and recent history of Rwanda to employ flexibility, while staying within the bounds of regulations established by UNGA in resolving the question of the disposition of UNAMIR's equipment'.

As a result of these pressures by donor countries and by myself, FALD agreed to review its initial recommendations. As before, corre-spondence took place directly between FALD and the CAO. I kept myself informed by constantly asking for CAO team assessments, finding two senior officials, Bill Clive and Mark Heyman, highly professional and fully comprehending the political implications of the equipment issue. By now, five months had elapsed since the Rwan-dan Foreign Minister's letter on the equipment issue was received by the UN Secretary-General without even the courtesy of an acknow-ledgement!

As time passed and no list was made available to the Rwandan side, Dusaidy and his colleagues became restive and suspicious that UNAMIR was pre-empting the issue by depleting equipment from the overall pool. The Rwandans suspected that when sending out items that were lethal or owned by the individual contingents, UNAMIR was surreptitiously transporting out non-lethal equipment. Accordingly, every outgoing consignment was meticulously and laboriously checked by the Rwandan authorities before it was allowed to pro-ceed. This caused frustration, delay and excessive transportation costs that led to tension rising between UNAMIR and the Rwandan government. The Rwandan government also turned the screw on a number of other issues, making life difficult for the departing civilian and military personnel.

For instance, they first questioned the applicability of the Stan-dard Operations Mission Agreement (SOMA) for Rwanda and asked for the payment of taxes by our civilian contractors, notably Brown and Root and the helicopter company used by the Canadians, on the grounds that they were not exempted by SOMA.[1] They also claimed large sums of money for damages to houses and properties, like the stadium, that had been occupied by UNAMIR. Departing personnel were minutely checked by Customs at the airports and generally a deliberate atmosphere of niggling rancour crept into institutional and individual relationships on both sides. UNAMIR personnel were particularly irked that sudden and seemingly gratuitous difficulties were placed in their way at the time of departure. I was convinced that by headquarters taking a restrictive approach to the equipment issue, UNAMIR's departure was being invested with tension and acrimony.

I cite an example of the heartache that our contingents suffered. Towards the end of their stay, as a parting gesture to their hosts in Rwanda, the Indian engineer contingent rebuilt a bridge that had

---

[1] SOMA is the agreement on the basis of which the UN operates administratively in a country. It details such matters as privileges, immunities, tax exemptions, radio wave-lengths and pay-scales for local personnel and contractors.

been blown up by the RGF. This bridge had been rebuilt by the Indian engineers with their own resources, and a small handing-over ceremony was arranged to which the Rwandan Minister for Public Works was invited. The Indians were under no obligation to rebuild the bridge but had done so voluntarily and as a gesture of goodwill. The Force Commander made his welcome address, followed by Major Panday the Chief Indian Engineer, after which I said a few words. The Rwandan minister then took the floor and, speaking into a Radio Rwanda microphone, engaged in a ten-minute diatribe against UNAMIR's perfidy and failure to prevent genocide! He rationalized Rwanda's desire to see the end of UNAMIR and only at the end did he manage a few words of appreciation. It was a most ungracious speech and since it came from a minister whom I had previously respected, I was appalled. The really sad part of the speech was that the minister was a Hutu whose speech would be relayed on Radio Rwanda. Perhaps, he felt obliged to toe the party line.

At the end, there was an embarrassing silence before we moved on to inspect the excellent bridge. I felt deeply for the Indian engineers who had given their sweat and blood to build the bridge, only to be rebuked in such offensive terms. Two days later, I met Major Panday at a reception. He had not forgotten the incident and remarked to me in Hindustani, 'I have never heard such a humiliating speech. Are they all so ungrateful?'

By February, there was still no final disposal list and understandably Rwandan doubts on our bona fides had risen to breaking-point. Dusaidy was now convinced that UNAMIR would transport out most of the usable items and leave behind only 'unwanted junk' for Rwanda. With this in mind, he offered that the Rwandan government should pay for the items that it sought, thereby satisfying UN Administration's insistence on equipment accountability.

During a visit to New York in February, I discussed the political implications of Rwanda's feeling aggrieved on this issue and worked out with the head of FALD, Hocine Medili, a formula that could help assuage Rwandan feelings. I recommended that, after a final disposal list had been decided, I should be allowed to utilize some funds from the UNDP Trust Fund that had already been set aside for the adjustment of 'loaned' equipment. Medili agreed and authorized me to loan Category I equipment to the Rwandans which could subsequently be adjusted through the Trust Fund. On return to Kigali, I arranged with my UNDP colleague Suki Hasegawa to earmark funds from the UNDP Trust Fund to pay for equipment that the Rwandans sought from Category I. I therefore felt I had about US$1.5 million-worth of good Category I equipment in hand to pass on to Rwanda at the time of departure. Regrettably, this arrangement fell through because FALD subsequently decided that no equipment of 'a sensitive nature' – i.e. the items sought by Rwanda – was to be handed over, even against purchase through the Trust Fund or by direct payment, thereby undermining the understanding reached with me in New York. This 'misunderstanding' would never have occurred if FALD had dealt with me as head of mission instead of directly with its CAO.

Eventually, the final disposal list was handed over to the Rwandan government on 6 March – three days before the conclusion of our mandate! It had taken six months to deliver our response to the Rwandan government's initial request on a vital issue on which the Security Council had also pronounced, asking the Secretariat to be as flexible as possible! The final list was an improvement on the initial 93 per cent in Category I and 7 per cent in Categories II and III. The ratio was now 62:38, but, in my view, it was still less than generous to Rwanda. In any case, the damage to Rwanda–UNAMIR relations had already been done.

Regrettably, the delay had led to deep suspicions being generated in the minds of the Rwandan government and, predictably, Dusaidy dismissed the offer as junk and told us to keep it all!

When I met Vice-President Kagame for my farewell call, I informed him that the final list conformed to General Assembly regulations and, within these constraints, it was the best we could offer. He ordered an inspection of the items and on my penultimate day in Rwanda, I walked Dusaidy through the compound where the items earmarked for Rwanda had been stored. Dusaidy was adamant that it was junk, but I managed to speak to Patrick Mazimpaka who had come to see me off at the airport, explaining to him that the items being left behind were not rubbish but in use by UNAMIR. I urged him to accept. It appears that my last-minute plea led to the Vice-President personally inspecting the equipment in the compound and deciding to accept it the day after we left.

I am convinced that a more sensitive handling of the equipment issue at the political level with a clear comprehension of the political implications could have led to an improved offer. The UNDP Trust Fund device would have sugar-coated the pill and instead of rancour and acrimony, UNAMIR could have ended its stay in Rwanda on a more positive note.

Ironically, when the Rwandan government tightened its screws on departing members of UNAMIR administration by threatening to arrest persons staying on beyond 19 April, FALD inquired from its CAO if the final list could not be adjusted to provide Rwanda with some additional items that it wanted, such as forklifts and hospital units! A classic case of offering too little too late to save the situation.

As we neared the end of our stay in Rwanda, this single issue exacerbated relations, with the RPA adopting a snarling, uncooperative attitude towards UNAMIR personnel who remained in Kigali.

One final incident will illustrate the frustration and acrimony that was created during the closing weeks of UNAMIR's stay in Rwanda.

On 12 December, in Gisenyi, the Zaireans handed back some of the equipment that the former government had carried across to Eastern Zaire. The Zairean government informed the Rwandans that a Rwandan helicopter was lying at a village about 50 kilometres from the border. It could not be lifted by the Zaireans who asked the Rwandans to make arrangements for the takeover themselves. The Rwandans were keen to take the helicopter back, not least because they feared that the Zaireans might change their minds! So the RPA asked for my help.

We first sent out our own helicopter pilots for a reconnaissance visit to Zaire. They reported that the only way that the Rwandan helicopter could be brought back was for a complicated operation to be carried out, involving our helicopter crew first dismantling the Rwandan helicopter, then forklifting it on to our cargo aircraft which would land at a nearby disused air strip. In short, two UNAMIR aircraft, a helicopter and a cargo plane, would have to co-ordinate the operation, taking a forklift, engineers and other experts to perform the operation. We needed also to obtain clearances from the Zairean government which always took time. By the time all these loose ends had been tied up, our mandate would have ended and the operation would have to be performed on the last day of the helicopter units' contract. There was also the problem of justifying the cost of the operation.

Force Commander Sivakumar and I agreed that, as a parting gesture of goodwill, we should mount the operation, even though it was our helicopter pilots' last day and the cost of the operation would, strictly speaking, be difficult to justify. Therefore, on 16 March, the complex manoeuvre was set in motion and executed flawlessly by our logistic experts and double air crews. Basically, our approach was that even if the RPA was being deliberately cussed with UNAMIR, we would continue to be helpful. The same afternoon the helicopter was handed back to the Rwandan government.

That night the helicopter crew gave a farewell barbecue at the airport hangar. I made a special point of attending because I wanted to show my appreciation for their performance which had been far beyond the call of duty, as demonstrated on their last day by the complex and remarkable rescue of the Rwandan helicopter from Zaire. By this operation the Canadian pilots had vividly demonstrated a classic example of going the extra mile.

Half an hour into a most pleasant, relaxed barbecue, three RPA officials barged into the party and summarily ordered the barbecue to be closed as formal permission had not been sought to hold a party in a security zone! The helicopter pilots reasoned in vain with the RPA security officials who insisted on closure. I became incensed by the insensitive and ungrateful attitude of the airport security officials and for the first and only time in Rwanda, lost my temper and told them that these pilots had, at great sacrifice to themselves, brought back Rwanda's helicopter at their government's insistent request and in return they were being asked to close down a perfectly innocent farewell party. I stormed out of the barbecue and immediately telephoned the Vice-President and his staff at this extraordinary demonstration of ingratitude on the part of the RPA security. Next morning I received a verbal apology and the explanation that the reception had been stopped because the President's plane was due, but it left a bitter taste in the mouth. Incidentally, we never received a word of thanks for bringing the helicopter back from Zaire to Rwanda.

The scene in Rwanda at departure

On 9 March, UNAMIR's mandate ended and though we still had six weeks to pack up and leave, I insisted that Radio UNAMIR stop broadcasting that day. The six weeks were spent in bidding farewells and ensuring as smooth an exodus for UNAMIR personnel as possible. In fact, my departure was delayed two days because Marrack Goulding, head of DPA, was sent out by the Secretary-General to finalize the details for UNOR (United Nations Office in Rwanda), the UN civilian successor office to UNAMIR. The President and Vice-President agreed in principle to UNOR, but said that Rwanda's formal agreement would come only when UNOR's mandate was spelt out in writing and its head's name conveyed and cleared in advance. It was Rwanda's way of asking the UN not to take it for granted. It took six months for Rwanda to agree to UNOR and later still to agree to the official who would head it.

During those last few days, it was time to take stock. Despite the government's many achievements, I felt four inter-related issues needed to be addressed before Rwanda could exorcise the ghosts of the past. These were (a) the return of refugees, (b) justice, (c) national reconciliation and (d) a rationalization of aid disbursement.

The return of refugees

Unlike the resettlement of IDPs, the flow of returning refugees had, in the main, been desultory. There were short periods when they had returned in fair numbers, but events such as Kibeho and Kanama had put a break on this flow.

Basically, there were three reasons for refugee reluctance to return voluntarily. The first of these was the intimidation exercised by the extremist political leadership over the mass of Hutu refugees in the camps. The second was the fear of oppression and arbitrary arrest on return, and the third the realization that life in the refugee camps was better and more secure than what most of the refugees had known at home in Rwanda. Given a combination of these apprehensions, the refugees were disinclined to take the uncertain step back in the dark. In my opinion, the best way to achieve a substantive return of the refugees was to implement, in a synchronized manner, the decisions of the Nairobi, Bujumbura, Cairo and Tunis Conferences. The common denominator of all these conferences was the prevention of intimidation in the refugee camps through separating and relocating the political elements from the mass of refugees, launching a revived 'Operation Retour' campaign in Rwanda and making it clear that, after a given period, all camps in Zaire, Tanzania and Burundi would phase down.

To achieve these objectives, funds would be required and also a focused campaign in which Rwanda, the asylum states, the donor countries, the OAU and UN agencies acted jointly and in a synchronized manner. Of course, the hard-core extremists would not return and would probably resist losing their 'electorate'. This hard-core would have to be dealt with effectively by the asylum countries, but the effort would be rewarded by the lightening of the political, economic and ecological burden that these countries had carried for so long. All the parties were prepared to take action, but the missing factor was international financing for the operation.

Justice

At the time of UNAMIR's departure, neither the International Tribunal nor the national judicial system had begun their trials. This delay, for good reasons or bad, led to frustration and widespread media criticism, particularly in regard to suffering in the prisons and also the fact that few of the big fish had been netted. I was convinced that until the judicial process began, the psychological pass-key to forgiveness and reconciliation would not be available. Banishing the culture of impunity could only begin when the first international and national trials were seen to dispense transparent justice. The ICTR began its first trial in December 1996 and a national court in January 1997. Though long delayed, the beginning of the judicial process would serve as an assuaging factor, particularly for the victims of genocide.

The international community must continue to support these parallel judicial processes if the horrors of Rwanda's prison population are to be alleviated and innocent people assured of fair, transparent justice.[1] It must also put much greater pressure on countries to apprehend known criminals against whom formal charges have been made. In fact, the unwillingness or inability to apprehend persons accused of genocide by the countries in which they have sought refuge has been one of the glaring anomalies of international conduct and a possible flouting of international legal

---

[1] In 1998, the prison population had grown to 110,000. In 2000 it stands at around 80,000.

commitments. Countries that have signed the International Conventions on Genocide and on Humanitarian Law are legally bound to take action against persons accused of humanitarian crimes. I know that the Rwandan government officially circulated a list of 443 persons wanted for such crimes and despite the additional direction of the Security Council in its Resolution no. 987, there was scarcely any response from the countries of asylum. Seemingly, no one wanted to make a distinction between genocide and civil war.

National reconciliation

In my briefing to the Secretary-General before his visit to Rwanda in July 1995, I had conveyed my opinion that reconciliation between the traumatized communities would begin when justice was seen to be done and when the bulk of refugees trekked back home. To expect Rwanda's political leadership to bury the hatchet with the leaders of the former government before the maturing of these two essential pre-conditions seemed unrealistic. Instead, a gradual reconciliation from the grassroots level upward appeared to be a more viable option.

This process requires the fair treatment of returning refugees, the restoration of their properties abandoned during the civil war, the re-employment of prefects, diplomats, magistrates, civil servants, etc after due scrutiny, the continuation of the Gako process and even appointments to senior positions as in the case of the Ministers of Foreign Affairs and Finance.

Admittedly, there have been set-backs to this process of reconciliation such as Prime Minister Twagiramungu's resignation and the sudden departure in late 1995 of some Gako-trained officers and judges.[1] But, over the long run, this appears to be the best way forward until justice and the return of refugees have their decisive impact on reconciliation.

Rational disbursement of aid

Finally, the stand-off between the donor community and the Rwandan government on the disbursement of funds needs to be resolved. Both sides need to draw nearer on this issue and, as a first step, rationalize figures. The Rwandan government needs to appreciate that the amount of aid pledged is generous by any standards and, even though a large part of it is being spent in the refugee camps, a substantial proportion is earmarked for Rwanda. The government should also ensure that viable projects are prepared and pledged aid is converted into disbursement and mobilization within the country.

---

[1] President Pasteur Bizimungu resigned on 24 March 2000 and was replaced by Vice-President Paul Kagame.

Donor countries, for their part, need to appreciate that Rwanda has the right to set its own priorities with regard to the projects on which aid is to be spent. Rwanda also resents its aid being filtered through the NGOs rather than being provided directly to the Rwandan exchequer. The Rwandans feel that much of this aid is spent by the NGOs themselves on experts, hotel bills, conferences, travel and the provision of expensive facilities.

Endgame and farewell

After 9 March 1996, the Amahoro Hotel, UNAMIR's headquarters, gradually emptied until it wore a deserted, cavernous look – a far cry from July 1994 when hundreds of journalists and media representatives thronged the hall and the courtyard. Gone now was the bustle of the past two years, the Force Commander's 'morning prayers', the press briefings, replaced by the lonely remnants of the Gurkha and Malawi regiments. There were hardly any tennis players left at the Belgian Village. Like commanding officers of a sinking ship, Brigadier-General Sivakumar and I were the last to leave, except for a small group of administrative staff who stayed on to hand over the buildings and equipment. We both left our comfortable residences at the Village and moved into the Meridian Hotel for the last two days of our stay, during which I paid my farewell calls on Rwandan leaders and my colleagues in the diplomatic corps and the specialized agencies. I also said goodbye to Isel Rivero, my experienced, cheerful and committed Chef de Cabinet who had seen me through so many crises, and to Gill Igro, my highly efficient and silent personal security guard.

As 19 April approached, I sat on the balcony of my hotel overlooking the beautiful landscape of rolling hills and green valleys, the kites serenely circling below my hotel-top windows. A vivid kaleidoscope of images of the past 21 months passed through my mind. Everywhere I recalled graves. The shallow graves around the hospitals in Kigali, around the stadium in Kibuye, beside the church in Nyarbuye. The child in Goma trying to revive her dead mother lying by the wayside. The shallow graves of Kibeho, around the churches where so many massacres had taken place. I heard the voice of the survivor at Nyarbuye. The gentle, dulcet tones of the two nuns in Gitarama Prison: 'It is perhaps God's will that we serve people in these dreadful conditions!' Then the stories of extraordinary courage like that of Sainte Hélène. I asked myself why Hélène was not a public heroine. Perhaps the reason could be found in the sentiment that prevented, at the last minute, the grave of honour at the martyr's memorial being given to the massacred Hutu Prime Minister.

In this short period, Rwanda had seen humanity at its most depraved and occasionally at its most courageous. During our stay, while we had our noses to the grindstone, barely able to look up and take a deep breath, the horror of Rwanda's genocide was almost taken in our stride. Now, with time to reflect, to look across the rolling hills towards a distant horizon, the impact was beginning to seep in. I began to have nightmares of shallow graves, of skeletons, of carcasses and of those fat dogs.

At the formal lowering of the UNAMIR flag, I looked back on my 21 months and said it all in my farewell speech, which I wrote with much thought and emotion. At the simple ceremony, I addressed the Rwandan Foreign Minister and senior RPA officers, ambassadors, heads of agencies and above all, UNAMIR colleagues, both military and civilian, who had gathered at the farewell parade. I would not alter a word of that speech, extracts of which I reproduce as my swan-song.

> I look back to the 4 July 1994 when I arrived in this very compound in the midst of horror and genocide that enveloped this beautiful land. I look back on a country devastated, pillaged and numbed by one of the most shocking and horrendous tragedies in human history. I look back on savaged families, shattered lives, on the macabre scene at Nyarbuye where dogs fattened themselves on the flesh of massacred children. I look back with pride at the brave UNAMIR soldiers who – severely depleted though they were – risked their own lives to save the defenceless and the innocent from the marauding killers. I look back on the deafening silence in the towns and cities that greeted me when I first arrived.

> And yet, today, 20 months later, we see around us thriving markets, bustling commerce, stability and security, children skipping to school in neat uniforms. The communes have come alive – agriculture, power water, healthcare is almost back to pre-war levels. Today, child immunization has exceeded pre-war standards. There are flowers in the circle at Kiyovu roundabout where once hundreds of displaced persons lived in the open. There are no curfews and few road blocks. The Amahoro Stadium where 10,000 frightened people were protected by a company of Ghanaian soldiers, is now the playground of youthful footballers and athletes. There is, all around us, normalcy, stability and peace.

> There can be no doubt that this remarkable transformation has been due to the efforts, the resilience and the spirit of the Rwandan people and the direction that its Government has provided. UNAMIR's effort has been to assist the people and the Government of Rwanda in achieving this transformation. Our resources were limited, our means scarce but within these constraints, UNAMIR has strained every sinew, called on all its resources of energy and more, to help the people of Rwanda in turning away from horror and despair towards dignity and progress.

> Here I must associate with a profound sense of gratitude, the support and co-operation that we have received from the UN family, the specialized agencies, NGOs and the common people of Rwanda. I am indebted, also, to the members of the diplomatic corps for their significant contribution in the uplift of the country. As the military leave and a civilian office carries forward the UN's banner, we shall join the Government and people of Rwanda in attempting to resolve the outstanding issues that face the

country. Over a million and half refugees must be encouraged to return home and to settle in an ambience of security and fair play. The Justice system must be revived so that each and every citizen is assured of transparent justice and that the climate of impunity is banished forever. The long road towards ethnic tolerance and national reconciliation has begun and must be encouraged. The suffering in prisons must be alleviated. These are some of the tasks that we shall address, jointly, with the Government of Rwanda. It is a difficult road ahead but I am encouraged by the example of the recent past.

I am deeply proud of the contribution that our formed troops, our technical cadres, our Milobs, our civilian personnel have made towards achieving this extraordinary recovery that we see around us. We have trained Rwanda's first gendarmes and communal policemen, we have provided medical support to over a million Rwandans, our engineers have dug canals, built bridges and repaired roads. We have revived water and power supplies across the country's communes, we have helped to expand detention centres, we have transported prisoners, refugees, food and agricultural seeds, we have helped to open schools for orphans and demobilized children, we have cleared land mines and have levelled sites for refugee resettlements. We have placed our helicopters and aeroplanes to meet the essential needs of the Government. In the communes, and prefectures, our soldiers have provided every conceivable assistance ranging from supporting an orphanage to reviving power supply, from transporting essential supplies to preparing transit camps. In the fields, our troops have helped to sow the seeds and reap the harvests with refugee farmers beginning their lives anew. And, as we depart, I can assure the Government of Rwanda that a significant proportion of our equipment will be left behind for use in Rwanda by the UN agencies and by the Government of Rwanda.

For this supreme effort, I am deeply indebted to the extraordinary zeal, discipline and commitment that UNAMIR's contingent, both military and civil have demonstrated. In addressing every member of UNAMIR's family, I want to state that I feel deeply honoured to have been associated with a group of such dedicated men and women who gave of their everything and more, who walked the extra mile and who risked their lives for the cause of humanity. Here, in Rwanda, African and European, Asian and American, Australian and Middle Eastern made deep personal sacrifices to help a people who had been traumatized by tragedy. We all served, not to seek appreciation, jobs or gratitude, but for the cause of human dignity and common fellowship in this global village that we share.

There are many lessons to be learnt by the international community from its experience in Rwanda. Many shortcomings to be corrected, many potential dangers to be pre-empted. Nothing, however, can take away the extraordinary heroism and commitment of those who served with UNAMIR during the traumatic period of genocide and who have, since then, helped the Rwandan people in their quest for recovery and stability.

As the bugles sound UNAMIR's last retreat, each one of you that has served in UNAMIR can hold your head high at the success of your mission. You only have to look around to see how far we have come – from devastation to revival: from degradation to dignity: from terror to security. Today, the military completes its task with distinction. Your achievements will form a roll of honour in the annals of the UN's peacekeeping history.

Your courage in the months of genocide, your discipline at Kibeho, your commitment throughout the traumatic period of 1994. Your dignified forbearance in the face of unfair criticism and calumnies levelled against you. Your assistance in the revival of Rwanda will form a golden chapter of the UN's peace-keeping. The names of General Dallaire, General Tousignant, Brigadier-General Anyidoho and Brigadier-General Sivakumar are now part of the UN's glorious history. We owe you – the military component of UNAMIR – a profound debt of gratitude.

In conclusion, I want to thank you, Your Excellency, Mr Foreign Minister and through you the Government and people of Rwanda for the support you have given UNAMIR. As we lower the UNAMIR flag for the last time, we depart with a deep sense of achievement and success. We have shared with you a part of your history – of your tragedy and of your revival – and though Government and politics have their own way of looking at issues we – the United Nations – will never forsake the cry of the innocent child for help, anywhere in the world.

10

The UN and Rwanda
What went wrong?

Could genocide have been predicted?

The crucial question in regard to Rwanda is why early warnings of impending genocide were not heeded by the international community with the result that nearly a million people were brutally slaughtered in the space of three months – a killing rate five times more intensive than in Nazi Germany. Could the genocide have been foreseen and could the worst of the massacres have been prevented? With the benefit of hindsight, blurred answers to these questions emerge from the shipwreck of international efforts at peace-keeping in Rwanda.

The critical issue relating to Rwanda was the international community's failure to make a distinction between a civil war and genocide. In recent years, murderous civil wars have taken place regularly across the globe. In Africa alone, civil wars have raged in Somalia, Mozambique, Liberia, Sierra Leone and Angola. Similar outbreaks have occurred in Cambodia, Afghanistan, Tajikistan, Georgia, Haiti, Sri Lanka and the former Yugoslavia. Genocide, on the other hand, was scarcely part of human experience. Alain Destexhe, the distinguished author, considers that Rwanda was only the third experience of genocide in this century.[1] Thus, after the breakdown of the Arusha Accords and against the backdrop of continuous ethnic strife, frequent violence and mounting tension, it was apparent that Rwanda was heading for a civil war. What the international community failed to discern was that, in addition to a civil war, Rwanda was entering the far more abhorrent syndrome of genocide. In fact, unlike Nazi Germany, in Rwanda genocide and civil war occurred simultaneously.

The international community's basic diagnosis was faulty and the prescription that the Security Council provided was the traditional one for civil wars, as in Somalia, Mozambique or Liberia. For in-

---

[1] Alain Destexhe, *Rwanda: Essai sur le genocide* (Brussels: Complex, 1994).

stance, there was a Chapter VI mandate that called for a ceasefire, reconciliation and a return to the Arusha Accords, when in fact the imminence of genocide demanded a heavily armed, peace-enforcing, Chapter VII presence to prevent civilian massacres. Eventually, in July 1994, the Security Council did approve a Chapter VII presence for Operation Turquoise but, by then, nearly a million people had been massacred.

The fact that genocide took place is no longer in doubt. The International Commission of Experts, the Special Rapporteur on Human Rights, and the Secretary-General himself, have all recognized that genocide was committed in Rwanda. The Joint Evaluation of Emergency Assistance for Rwanda (JEEAR) refers to the events in the following terms:

> The planned, deliberate effort to eliminate the Tutsi population of Rwanda that culminated in the massive slaughter of April – July 1994 fully meets the definition of genocide articulated in the 'Convention on the Prevention and Punishment of the Crime of Genocide', adopted by the UN General Assembly in 1948.

The crucial point is whether its planning was discernible. The RPF has consistently maintained that, between August 1993 and April 1994, it had repeatedly informed the SRSG, the Force Commander and important ambassadors in Kigali that genocide was being planned. The RPF leadership claimed that houses of Tutsis and Hutu moderates had been marked, personalities identified and armed militia trained to start executions at the appointed hour. They state that these warnings were not heeded.

Undoubtedly the most serious warning of impending genocide came in January 1994, from insider information conveyed to General Dallaire by a senior government (RGF) informant, 'Jean Pierre'. Significantly, this indication came not from the likely victims, who were prone to exaggerate, but from within the circle of genocide planners. The implications of the telegram Dallaire then sent on 11 January are discussed later in this chapter, but, it apart, a meticulous research of all cables and reports sent from UNAMIR to UN headquarters between October 1993 and 6 April 1994 found no reference to the kind of messages that the RPA claimed they had conveyed to responsible officers of UNAMIR. In UNAMIR reports and assessments, there is frequent mention of re-arming, of military confrontation, of high ethnic tension, of likely assassinations and of a descent towards civil war, but no reference to a planned and systematic killing of the civilian population.

The analyst J. Walter Dorn has drawn up a strong indictment of the UN bureaucracy as well as the Security Council for not reacting effectively to the clear signals of genocide that were discernible in Rwanda – Dorn points to the insider information given to Dallaire by 'Jean Pierre', RTLM's broadcasts that incited Hutus to kill innocent

Tutsis and to NGO warnings of planned massacres that went un-heeded. Dorn considers that UNAMIR's lack of ground intelligence and proper political analysis at headquarters led to the commission of monumental errors of judgement, as for instance the instructions to General Dallaire to contact Colonel Theoneste Bagasora – the high priest of the genocide group within the government – to seek stability and calm and UN headquarters' advice to convey Jean Pierre's insider information to President Habyarimana. In retrospect both these decisions were like asking the wolf to guard the chicken coop.

Dorn concludes his severe indictment of the UN Secretariat and the Security Council in the following words:

> The Rwandan genocide could definitely have been foreseen and could possibly have been prevented. At the very least, it could have been greatly mitigated by the UN. This conclusion takes into account the information and resources which were available to the UN, its mandate and its poten-tial and erstwhile demonstrated ability to adapt to difficult conflict situations. The UN peace-keeping mission could undoubtedly have ex-panded its activities and efforts (diplomatic, humanitarian and military) at an early stage, given the clear warnings available to it. What was absent was the political will, in the Secretariat and in the Security Council, to make daring decisions and to develop the means to create new informa-tion and prevention measures. The lesson of Rwanda is clear: we must build the international political will, as well as an enhanced UN capabil-ity, for prevention. The UN should develop its ability for gathering and analysing information, for making early warnings and for rapid reaction though deployment of troops as well as diplomatic creative initiatives. The world community owes it to the hundreds of thousands of human beings who were slaughtered during the Rwandan genocide, to try to predict and prevent future genocides. The redemption of the UN from its failures in Rwanda can occur only when the organization and its member states strive anew to achieve the goals set out in the opening words of the Charter: 'to save succeeding generations from the scourge of war ... to reaffirm faith in fundamental human rights ... to ensure, by the accep-tance of principles and the institution of methods, that armed force shall not be used, save in the common interest.[1]

Why, then, were these warnings not heeded by the international community and within the UN Secretariat?

There can be several explanations for this gap. The first is that the RPA leadership did not convey, as emphatically as it subsequently claimed, the indication that there was likely to be mass killings of innocent civilians. Secondly, that UNAMIR leadership either consid-ered the RPA's messages to be exaggerated expressions of fear, or they deliberately played down the accusations against the govern-ment of the time, preferring to project a picture of an even-handed descent towards civil war but not of a one-sided genocide of an ethnic minority. A third explanation is that the concept of genocide is so alien to human experience and so outrageous an image to con-

---

[1] J. Walter Dorn, Jonathan Matloff and Jennifer Mathews, *Preventing the Bloodbath*. Paper at Peace Studies Programme, Cornell University, 14 January 1999.

template that its signs were simply not absorbed by the ambassadors, senior UN representatives and members of the Security Council
who continued to prescribe antidotes for a civil war.

A fourth, more damaging explanation, is that the international
community deliberately disregarded the warning signals of genocide
for political considerations and preferred to treat the carnage as a
civil war until the evidence became so overwhelming that genocide
had, belatedly, to be recognized. The fact that it was not recognized
earlier may have been a result of the fall-out from the killing of
American troops in Somalia. At the time, strong opinion had built up
in the USA and Europe that their soldiers were not to be risked in
containing 'endless African civil wars'. Except that Rwanda was not
'just another' civil war!

Fifthly, it is possible that the coincidence of Rwanda being a
member of the Security Council at the time of the crisis led to an
inaccurate evaluation of the ground situation. At Security Council
meetings – formal and informal – the Rwandan Ambassador regularly
injected a strongly pro-government view into the proceedings, one
that conveyed a descent towards civil war, but naturally not planned
extermination.

Nevertheless, apart from specific warnings by the RPA, should it
not have been possible to gauge from the prevailing mood that a
massacre of innocent civilians was being planned? The signs that
were given were not the conspiratorial whisperings of scheming
villains, but public pronouncements by government leaders, broadcasts by the official Radio Mille Collines and the open training and
arming of the militia and Interahamwe, all of which were portents of
an impending calamity. These clear signals were being transmitted
by a number of the NGOs operating in Rwanda. The Joint Evaluation
of Emergency Assistance for Rwanda (JEEAR) has sharply criticized
the UN and the Security Council for not heeding the early warnings
of disaster, basing its main indictment on the fact that the Dallaire
telegram was ignored. The report states:

> Why were the signals that were sent ignored? Why were they not trans-
> lated into effective conflict management? Failures of early warning are
> attributable to many factors. The UN was poorly organized to collect and
> flag information about human rights violations and certainly genocide.
> There was a failure in both the UN system and the NGO community to
> link human rights reports to dynamic analyses of social conflict so as to
> provide strategic policy choices. There existed an internal predisposition
> on the part of a number of the key actors to deny the possibility of geno-
> cide because facing the consequences might have required them to alter
> their course of action. The mesmerization with the success of Arusha and
> failure of Somalia together cast long shadows and distorted an objective
> analysis of Rwanda. The vast quantity of noise from other crises preoccu-
> pied world leaders. The confusion between genocide as a legal term,
> referring primarily to an intent, and popular association of genocide with
> massive murder in the order of hundreds of thousands, created confu-

sion. Finally, a general desensitization developed with respect to mass slaughters, and the possibility of a massive genocide actually occurring seemed beyond belief.

The meticulously planned genocide started on 6 April. On 11 April the Security Council, acting against the advice of the Secretary-General, decided to reduce its peace-keeping representation in Rwanda from 2548 to 250. It was not until 21 April, almost three weeks later, that the Security Council, recognizing the unmistakable spectre of genocide, revised its earlier decision and decided to build up the peace-keeping force strength to 5500, although still with a Chapter VI mandate. Already, hundreds of thousands of Rwandans had been brutally massacred. It was a classic case of shutting the gate after the horse had bolted. It took a further three months for UNAMIR troop strength to build up. By then the civil war and genocide were over.

The international community's failure to respond to the threat of planned massacres has deservedly drawn fierce criticism in the media and by inquiry commissions in Belgium, France, Canada, the US Congress and the Scandinavian countries. In my opinion, a combination of the factors outlined above led to the Security Council turning away from adopting pro-active measures. I believe that if General Dallaire had been given a fully equipped force (2548 peace-keepers) as sanctioned in his October 1993 mandate, let alone the 5500-strong force approved in May 1994 for UNAMIR II, he would have been able to contain the massacre that followed the 6 April plane crash.

The Dallaire telegram of 11 January 1994

The telegram sent by General Dallaire on 11 January 1994 to the head of the DPKO's Military Division, General Baril, has led to the severest indictment of UN bureaucracy, notably of the DPKO's senior personnel. The telegram needs to be placed in perspective. In it General Dallaire reported that an informant ('Jean Pierre') belonging to the inner circle of President Habyarimana's government had conveyed information of plans to massacre Tutsis on receipt of a green signal. Tutsi homes had been earmarked, killer squads trained and arms procured so that '1000 Tutsis could be killed in 20 minutes'. The informer also described that part of the plan was to give the appearance of a civil war and to kill Belgian soldiers so that foreign troops would be evacuated and the field left open for the massacre of the Tutsis. Dallaire sought permission to act in order to neutralize the arms caches and to protect the informant. UN headquarters did not give the permission on the grounds that UNAMIR's mandate did not allow the pro-active action proposed by Dallaire.

Instead, UN headquarters proposed that President Habyarimana be made aware of the information without revealing the source.

With chilling accuracy, like a well-rehearsed play, the informer's scenario was gruesomely played out three months later. Even the brutal murder of ten Belgian soldiers was carried out, leading to the withdrawal of Belgian and Bangladeshi peace-keepers. For the next seven weeks, the Security Council dithered, eventually deciding, bizarrely, to withdraw from the scene, producing precisely the reaction that the genociders had sought to evoke. During this period, UNAMIR, reduced to 444 peace-keepers, played a heroic role, saving lives and protecting harassed Tutsis and moderate Hutus, but they had neither the mandate nor the personnel to control the genocide.

The JEEAR's severe criticism of the UN and specifically of the Secretary-General has been stated in the following terms:

> Those charged with leadership had a distorted view of events: both the Secretariat and the Security Council drew a picture of Rwanda as a failed state in which rogue troops and spontaneous mobs were killing Tutsi. The concept of a failed state, of course, suggested the analogy with Somalia, then uppermost in the consciousness of UN officials. Bureaucratic caution reinforced the conclusion drawn from that experience: the UN could not afford another peace-keeping failure, with failure defined as loss of UN peace-keepers in the field. Finally, the striking aspect of the first week of crisis was the physical absence from New York of Boutros-Ghali, who was travelling at a brisk pace in Europe and the former Soviet Union. During the fast-moving and critical first days of crisis, the Secretary-General was unavailable to provide leadership for action.

While I share the criticism that early warnings of genocide should have been picked up by the international community and pre-emptive action taken, the suggestion by some commentators of a hard-broiled, inured UN bureaucracy being insensitive to the fate of Rwanda is not justified.[1]

First, Dallaire's telegram did evoke an immediate reaction from the DPKO in that its contents were shared with key members of the Security Council. Their response was defensive, almost like a cold shower. Secondly, Dallaire's telegram sought permission to act at a military level, namely to neutralize the arms caches and to protect the informant. The proposal was duly studied but turned down on legalistic grounds. The political content of the telegram was acknowledged, acted upon and presumably awaited confirmation from the Secretary-General's Special Representative in Rwanda, Dr Booh-Booh, who was known to take a different view of the situation in Rwanda to General Dallaire. No such confirmation of impending genocide subsequently came from UN sources in Rwanda, especially from those responsible for political analysis. While there can be little doubt that a heavily understaffed, severely overburdened UN bureaucracy should have reacted with greater alacrity to the Dallaire

---

[1] Article by Philip Gourevitch in *The New Yorker*, 11 May 1998.

telegram, the responsibility for consistent inaction, including with
regard to the Dallaire telegram, lies squarely with the international
community and with UNAMIR's political wing that did not convey in
a single report after Dallaire's telegram the possibility of civilian
massacres instigated by government elements.

UNAMIR's failure to peace-build

The events described above took place before I arrived in Rwanda. My
analysis of the crisis is therefore based on a study of UNAMIR's
reports to UN headquarters and also discussions with people who
had lived through the nightmare of Rwanda's genocide. I was,
however, a first-hand witness of UNAMIR's next failure – its inability
to perform a post-conflict revival and peace-building role, an inability
that set the seal on the Rwandan government's initial stand-off and
eventual hostility towards UNAMIR.

The issue was simple. Rwanda and its people had been totally
devastated by the genocide. The country and its population cried out
desperately to be revived, like a critically wounded patient needing a
blood transfusion to survive and to enable its basic organs to start
functioning again. UNAMIR II had been mandated to keep the peace,
but by the time it arrived in strength, the crisis was over. The RPA
had won the war and formed a broad-based government. UN peace-
keepers could, of course, help keep the peace and prevent revenge-
killings, but in addition to this limited peace-keeping role, UNAMIR II
was the only entity with the capacity and the wherewithal to help
revive the people and repair the devastated infrastructure of the
country. Regrettably, UNAMIR II was given neither the mandate nor
the minimal finance to perform this essential post-conflict, peace-
building role.

UNAMIR had a fully equipped, disciplined force of 5500 peace-
keepers deployed throughout the country to 'protect civilians at risk',
but, agonizingly, not to help the people of Rwanda revive their
shattered country. UNAMIR had engineers to repair the water and
power connections, it had communications technicians to repair
telephone and telegraph lines, it had doctors and nurses to treat and
immunize the sick and injured, it had the equipment to secure areas,
it had carpenters, masons and electricians to revive destroyed
houses and office buildings, it had vehicles to help sanitation and
municipal services, it could repair roads and bridges, it could carry
medicines, food and agricultural tools to help people start earning
their livelihood again, it had the engineering and construction
capability to enlarge existing prisons and to convert go-downs and
bus depots into temporary detention centres, it could help build new
barracks, it could repair houses to be converted into orphanages and
widows' homes, it had graders and levellers that could prepare the

ground for returning refugees, it had aircraft and helicopters to meet emergency situations. Unbelievably, the UN was spending US$15 million a month to maintain these assets and equipment, but could not employ them for the revival of a devastated country and people!

With the best will in the world, these tasks could not have been carried out by any of the NGOs or UN specialized agencies in the twilight period of about six months after the end of the civil war. Only UNAMIR was equipped and capable of performing this essential peace-building role in the twilight zone. And yet UNAMIR did not have the mandate to perform this post-conflict repair role. Even more frustrating and incongruous was UN headquarters' direction that UNAMIR could not be given such a role as this task was the exclusive domain of the humanitarian agencies. It was maintained that peace-keeping was funded by assessed contributions which could not be spent on peace-building. Only voluntary contributions could be used to fund such post-conflict revival projects.

Of course, wherever possible, the Force Commander and I stretched the rules and employed our peace-keepers towards the revival and restructuring of the country. However, we lacked minimal funds to sustain such operations. My efforts to launch the Rwanda Emergency Normalization Plan fell on deaf ears with both the UN and donor countries (except the Netherlands and Britain). In the end, UNAMIR's inability to mobilize its force and equipment for Rwanda's revival was, in my view, the primary reason for its departure in an atmosphere of rancour and spite.

While performing our primary function of peace-keeping, UNAMIR could easily have been given the additional task of post-conflict peace-building by the Security Council adopting the following simple enabling clause in UNAMIR's peace-keeping mandate:

> In addition to its peace-keeping responsibilities, UNAMIR would assist, where possible, in the repair and rehabilitation of Rwanda's infrastructure.

Moreover, donor countries who were, at the time, spending US$2 million a day in the refugee camps and US$15 million a month in maintaining UNAMIR peace-keepers could surely have set aside US$10–20 million towards a UN Secretary-General's Trust Fund for Rwanda which would have acted as the essential fuel for the peace-building effort in the twilight zone. No turf wars would have been engaged because none of the agencies were operative during this twilight period. In fact, many of their subsequent emergency programmes would have been jump-started by UNAMIR peace-builders and handed over to them to conclude.

It is not easy to explain the reasons why a peace-building role was denied to UNAMIR. Part of the explanation lies in a lack of sharp focus by UN headquarters and by the Security Council on the detailed needs of the situation on the ground. In Cambodia, peace-keepers performed a post-conflict, infrastructure repair role 'to facilitate the elections'. In Somalia, UN peace-keepers dug tube wells for fresh water and opened hospitals for the local population. Surely an appropriate clause would have enabled UNAMIR to perform a similar dual role in Rwanda.

The other reason lies in the deep-rooted, rigid compartmentalization that exists within the four walls of the United Nations whereby assessed funds for peace-keeping can only be used to sustain military peace-keepers while civilian development and humanitarian aid are funded by voluntary contributions. There is also an element of turf preservation between the military culture on the one hand and the humanitarian and development agencies on the other. In Rwanda, these constraints on assessed and voluntary contributions were played out to an absurd extent.

The militarization of the refugee camps and the disbursement of aid for survivors

A third cause of the Rwandan government's resentment towards the United Nations was its perception that while the international community was freely cascading relief into the refugee camps located across Rwanda's borders, there was barely a trickle of support available for the survivors of genocide. Ironically, the camps, particularly in Zaire and Tanzania, were controlled by the same prefects, *burgomestres* and mid-level political leaders that had spearheaded the genocide in Rwanda. No one questioned their administrative and political control of the camps, as the humanitarian agencies claimed it was not their business to engage in political analyses but to provide humanitarian relief to the needy. The issue was faced only when it became apparent that a fair proportion of the humanitarian aid that had so generously been poured into the refugee camps at the cost of donor country tax-payers was being converted into military training, the purchase of military equipment and preparation for another round of violence through armed guerrilla raids into Rwanda. The hiatus led to the appointment of the International Commission of Inquiry which, not surprisingly, confirmed that humanitarian aid had, in fact, been diverted for military purposes in the refugee camps.

Meanwhile, at a conference in Geneva aimed at reviving Rwanda's economy and infrastructure, the international community pledged a vast funding campaign. For a small country like Rwanda, the international pledging of US$1.2 billion was overwhelming, but with the passage of time, it became apparent that none of these funds could be made available immediately to the Rwandan government which desperately needed liquid, up-front cash to revive its infrastructure. The pledged funding was intended to filter down gradually through government agencies, NGOs and international organizations. Eventually, the contrast sharpened between the immediate, up-front relief available in the refugee camps and the slow conditional trickle-down of aid promised to Rwanda.

This feeling of frustration by the Rwandan government and its people towards the international community and the UN was bred from a lack of overall focus and co-ordination in the funnelling of humanitarian and economic aid towards Rwanda. Each specialized agency, each country, almost each NGO followed its own charter and special priorities in its channelling of funds and relief. Yet the need of the hour was a balanced outlay of humanitarian aid to the refugees on the one hand and to the survivors on the other.

Co-ordination, command and control

The problems of inter-agency co-ordination and command and control in a major UN peace-keeping operation have been discussed in Chapter 4. Suffice it to note at this point that the United Nations needs to have its field operations structured with a clear-cut command and control organigram. At present, the UN agencies operate virtually independently, paying only lip service to the need for an overall co-ordinated approach. These turf wars are not limited to the UN agencies but extend in-house, even to various departments within UN headquarters, so that unnecessary tension develops between civilian and military, peace-keeping and humanitarian, political and administration. The prime example of this failure of establishing a proper command and control structure was the disaster of Kibeho which, in my opinion, would have been averted if agencies had fallen in line with the SRSG's political directions.

The absence of clear-cut authority for the most senior UN representative over the entire spectrum of UN activity in a region is a source of confusion for the receiving government and generally undermines the effective implementation of the UN's overall objectives. In Rwanda, this absence led to the gradual erosion of respect for UNAMIR peace-keepers performing their role under the authority of the SRSG. The fact that no funding whatsoever was channelled through the SRSG while agencies were freely dispensing largesse according to their own mandates added to the confusion and overall lack of effectiveness of the United Nations in Rwanda.

Reconciliation, justice and the return of refugees

Reconciliation, justice and the return of refugees were issues that were closely inter-linked. Transparent justice and fair play were essential for refugees to even begin thinking of returning home to resume a vengeance-free existence. In fact, neither internationally through the ICTR, nor internally in Rwanda, was the process of justice able to take off. The ICTR seemed to take an age to establish itself in Arusha, while in Rwanda, the delay in setting up a judicial process led to overcrowding in prisons that was so horrific that prisoners' limbs began to decay through gangrene. These conditions discouraged the return of refugees who, naturally, preferred to stay on in their camps. Without justice, therefore, the refugees would not return and if the bulk of refugees stayed away, it was apparent that reconciliation could not even begin to take root.

From the first day, UNAMIR attempted to seek forward movement on each of these three vital elements. It was our considered view that reconciliation could best be achieved from the grassroots upwards rather than through the Secretary-General's formula of a catalytic meeting of the top leadership from both sides. I felt the best opening was to attempt the return of a significant number of the RGF (who were mainly encamped in Bukavu) to rejoin the national army. From the first day of my arrival in Kigali my senior military colleagues, General Dallaire and Brigadier-General Anyidoho, had conveyed their assessment that the RPF considered the RGF as the 'least guilty' of the opponents ranged against them. Subsequently, I twice tested this contention with Vice-President Kagame and found him amenable to taking back duly screened members of the RGF who wished to return and rejoin the national army. From the Bukavu camps, we received reports from the UNHCR representative that a fair proportion of the RGF were prepared to return provided they were given guarantees of fair treatment. We began working on both sides and a number of RGF soldiers began trickling back and were billeted and re-educated at Gako. Then came the critical request from the Rwandan Chief of Staff for additional barrack space. Of course, UNAMIR had no funds to construct these barracks, though UNAMIR's engineers and logisticians would have put them up in no time and at little cost but we required basic financing. Regrettably, there were no takers from the agencies, the donor government or from the UN. The plan lapsed, the reconciliation stalled.

On the issue of justice, the UN system took a long time to establish and activate the ICTR. Judges had to be selected, money found for the tribunal, prisons built, accommodation found in Arusha, a set of procedures that could not be short circuited. Internally, the entire judicial system had to be rebuilt since everyone from the *greffiers* up to the senior judges had fled the country or been murdered. Public pressure for immediate justice for the genociders was intense, but with no judicial system in place, the agony of inevitable delay was overwhelming, both for the prisoners packed in prisons like sardines and for the survivors who clamoured outside for justice and retribution. In this tense atmosphere, an unseemly tug-of-war developed between the UNDP and the Human Rights Commission over the training of the newly recruited magistrates and judges. Again, rather than find a decision locally, the issue was referred back to New York and Geneva, which increased the frustration and delay for all sides.

As regards the refugees returning home, there were two basic inhibiting factors – their likely treatment on their return and the menacing hold of the political extremists in the camps. On the occasions when the government's hand was forced, as when Zaire forcibly closed some camps, the returning refugees were always well treated and efficiently dispersed to their communes, and generally seemed relieved to be back home. I consider it a great pity that greater efforts were not made to control the political elements in the camps; this would have released a much larger number of refugees to return home and begin living normal lives again. This issue, the lack of focus and the failure of the international community and the international agencies to act in unison led to the bulk of refugees staying in the camps and eventually becoming embroiled in the murderous events in the Democratic Republic of Congo.

Exit strategy and the equipment issue

By the time UNAMIR began its phase-out from Rwanda, one final opportunity offered itself to salvage some goodwill at the time of parting. This opportunity related to Rwanda's request that as many of UNAMIR's assets and equipment as was reasonably possible be left behind. I recognized that Rwanda's railing against the injustices and treatment by the UN and the international community was aimed, essentially, at the top, policy level. Occasionally, their anger was targetted also towards UNAMIR, but I felt that, deep down, Rwanda's leadership recognized that UNAMIR had gone the extra mile to help Rwanda revive itself despite UNAMIR's inadequate mandate and financing. For instance, the top leadership were aware that UNAMIR had provided them with an aircraft every time they requested, we had rebuilt roads and bridges, helped them settle refugees and IDPs, supported a revival of their agriculture, immunized thousands of children, treated all and sundry in our hospitals, co-operated closely in transporting Zairean refugees forced to return, launched new currencies and education curricula, recovered their helicopters, and so on. One last positive gesture by UNAMIR would, I believe, have led to a relatively friendly parting of ways. The fact that this opportunity was missed through avoidable bureaucratic manoeuvring has been described in some detail in Chapter 9.

It is my considered view that the United Nations should have allowed a larger proportion of assets and equipment to be left behind for use in Rwanda. Category I items (i.e. those required to be transferred out of Rwanda for storage or use in other peace-keeping operations) could have been reduced from 62 per cent to around 20 per cent and the remaining two Categories (II and III) increased to 80 per cent. In addition, a US$4 million Trust Fund that was already available with the UNDP for the specific purpose of purchasing equipment for the Rwandan government should have been used to 'buy' items from Category I for use in Rwanda. Finally, the Rwandan government's offer to purchase these assets and equipment from its own resources should have been taken up; this would have satisfied the requirement of 'usable assets' being 'accounted for' when left behind.

I appreciate that UN officials applied the rules honourably and with integrity in deciding on the issue of assets to be left behind in Rwanda. There was, nevertheless, a need for a more flexible interpretation of the rules on the grounds of political expediency, especially as the Security Council had clearly requested such flexibility in the disposal of the assets. Sadly, the opportunity was missed and UNAMIR exited from Rwanda in a spate of rancour and with its tail between its legs!

In describing Rwandan resentment at some of the main failures of the international community and the United Nations in Rwanda, I do not wish to convey an impression of a litany of failures. The fact is that UNAMIR's successes far outweighed its failures. Examples of these successes were UNAMIR's role in the peaceful takeover of the HPZ after the conclusion of Operation Turquoise; the remarkable success of Operation Retour which saw 500,000 IDPs return safely home; UNAMIR's building of bridges and roads; its efficient settling of refugees forcibly returned from Zaire; its inoculation of over 47,000 children; its reassurance of security and calm across the country through the presence of its peace-keepers; its transportation of Rwandan leaders in its aircraft, and refugees and IDPs in its vehicles; its support in restructuring and reviving the economy, in building refugee camps, in distributing seeds and agricultural implements, in opening schools and starting a new currency, in training Rwanda's police and gendarmerie, in rebuilding schools and Parliament buildings so that these essential institutions could begin functioning again, in restarting the airport through the supply of a generator, and in extending prison space. All these actions were taken out of the deep sympathy and goodwill that UNAMIR personnel felt for the traumatized people of Rwanda which, despite a limiting mandate and no funds, made them go the extra mile.

Lessons drawn from peace-keeping in Rwanda

Definition and objectives of multi-functional peace-keeping

The lessons to be drawn from peace-keeping in Rwanda need to be assessed, evaluated and framed in the broader context of the future role of peace-keeping. Until recently, the role of peace-keepers was conceived in the rather narrow military terms of restraining belligerents, engaging in peace negotiations and maintaining sufficient order to enable humanitarian relief to reach the beleaguered population. The lessons of Rwanda – and indeed of other peace-keeping operations – indicate that peace-keeping needs to be redefined and conceived as a much broader, multi-functional role.

For a start, peace-keeping must be taken out of the strait-jacket of performing a basically militaristic role. This strait-jacket severely inhibited the UN from playing an effective preventive and peace-building role in Rwanda. The mandates did not keep pace with events on the ground and were therefore neither precise nor relevant. Moreover, the peace-keepers were not equipped with adequate personnel or assets to deal with the crisis. Similar constraints have operated on UN operations in other theatres of peace-keeping. In future, peace-keeping needs to be framed in a multi-functional role, ranging between the following broad objectives.

Peaceful settlement of disputes

This initial stage of peace-keeping would aim at the pre-emption of emergent crises through the peaceful settlement of disputes and would include conciliation, arbitration, mediation, good offices and in the event of their failure, recourse to sanctions. These efforts would essentially involve civilian action conducted at the instance of the UN and regional organizations and would be implemented through experienced, professional and transparently neutral peace-keepers.

Conflict prevention

This second stage of peace-keeping would encompass diplomatic efforts and troop deployment aimed at preventing the escalation of disputes into armed conflicts. These efforts would include consultation, warnings, fact-finding missions, monitoring and the deployment of troops to avert violence. A military presence in conjunction with civilian leadership would be necessary in such initiatives.

Peace-keeping

The traditional role of peace-keeping would encompass an armed force deployed, usually in tandem with a political process, for conflict resolution and the restoration of peace. The presence of an armed force, acting under a Chapter VI mandate, would be mandated to preserve peace and to provide security to humanitarian relief operations and to civilian operators such as civilian police and human rights observers.

Peace enforcement

In cases of extreme violence, a peace-keeping force acting under Chapter VII could be deployed to restore peace in a crisis area, enabling humanitarian relief and civilian personnel to operate in territory where institutions have collapsed.

Peace-building

This stage of peace-keeping would encompass action to strengthen structures aimed at achieving durable peace in a conflict region, mainly in order to prevent a slide-back into conflict and anarchy. Post-conflict peace-building would include revival of infrastructure, reconciliation, refugee rehabilitation and support for institutions such as civilian police, judiciary, the civil services, etc.

Peace-keeping parameters

It needs to be emphasized, of course, that there can be no single, perfect, antidote for all the crises of peace-keeping and that each crisis needs to be dealt with on its merits. Nevertheless, broad parameters for peace-keeping operations need to be set and peace-keeping mechanisms developed to the highest possible levels of readiness and efficiency. These parameters may be summarized as follows.

UN Security Council's approval

Article 24 of the UN Charter gives the Security Council the primary responsibility for the maintenance of international peace and security. Article 33 in Chapter VI, however, provides that parties to any dispute 'shall resort to any regional organization for the settlement of disputes'. Article 53 of Chapter VIII goes on to state that the Security Council 'shall where appropriate utilize such regional arrangements and agencies for enforcement action under its authority'. But that 'no enforcement action shall be taken without the authorization of the Security Council'.

Accordingly, all peace-keeping operations – whether international or regional – must have the sanction and approval of the UN Security Council. Even if the peace-keeping operation is primarily handed over to a regional group (e.g. NATO in Kosovo or ECOWAS in Liberia or the CIS in Georgia), the overall authority of the Security Council needs to be obtained before peace-keeping action is undertaken. The degree of responsibility between the UN and the regional groups would depend on each situation but a basic minimum sanctioning approval of the UN Security Council is essential.

Consultation between relevant institutions

In order to achieve political consensus and operational capability for a peace-keeping operation, it is essential that close and regular consultation should take place between the following important institutions that play a leading role in international peace-keeping efforts:

— the Security Council

— the UN Secretariat

— the UN specialized agencies

— the donor states (who provide the finance, training and equipment but normally not the troops)

— the troop-contributing nations (TCNs) (who mostly provide the troops but do not normally have financing and equipment)

— the regional groups.

It would be possible through these consultations to assess, for instance, the degree of complementarity between the UN and a regional group, the financing and troop contribution for each peace-

keeping operation and the speed with which equipment and financing would become available to the peace-keepers. These
consultations would help provide political focus for multilateral
operations, thus preventing agencies from acting independently, as
happened in Rwanda when vast financial aid was given that was
converted into an arms build-up and neglect of the survivors.

Preparing the peace-keeping 'fire engine'

Peace-keeping efforts have suffered because all the essential components such as trained troops, equipment, transport and financing,
have not been readily available. The peace-keeping fire engine,
therefore, needs to be in a state of readiness to enable it to meet
crises at short notice. This fire engine requires the immediate availability of a trained standby peace-keeping force, equipment,
transport, communications, financing, medical and engineering
capability and a corps of well-trained military and civilian officials.
The non-availability of such a fire engine was a critical factor in the
failure of UN peace-keeping operations in Rwanda. For UNAMIR I
General Dallaire had neither the equipment nor the troops promised
to him several months after they had been approved, so that when
the crunch came on 6 April, UNAMIR was helpless in attempting to
control the violence. I am convinced that if General Dallaire had been
given the full complement of peace-keeping troops to which he was
entitled he would have prevented the worst of the massacres.[1] For
UNAMIR II, it took six months (December 1994) for the full component of troops to reach Rwanda and longer still (March 1995) for
equipment such as armoured personnel carriers to be matched with
peace-keeping troops on the ground.

Clearly financial and national constraints prevent a permanent,
fully equipped standby peace-keeping force from being kept in
readiness to meet crises across the globe. Nevertheless, short of such
a permanent force, the international community should be able to
achieve the next best option of quickly marshalling trained peace-
keeping units with access to equipment and basic financing as a
standby force that can become operational in the shortest possible
time. This readiness can be achieved through consultation between
donor states and troop-contributing nations, the availability of
minimal financing in a UN Secretary-General's Peace-Keeping Trust
Fund, a well-trained standby force of peace-keepers at the regional
and national level and the availability of equipment, transport, etc for
immediate use in a crisis. These are the essential components of a

---

[1] Scott R. Feil, *Preventing Genocide. How the Early Use of Force Might Have Succeeded in Rwanda.* A report to the Carnegie Commission on Preventing Deadly Conflict (New York: Carnegie Commission, 1998).

fire engine that can be quickly assembled for as early a response as is reasonably possible to a peace-keeping crisis.

Recent developments in this direction, especially those initiated by the government of France in co-operation with African countries, are particularly welcome. The concept of RECAMP (Renforcement des Capacités Africaines de Maintient de la Paix) is based on a partnership between donor states and troop-contributing nations that would ensure financial, equipment and logistic support to essentially African peace-keeping troops. RECAMP has already been launched and peace-keeping exercises have taken place in full consultation with the UN and OAU.

A clear and precise mandate

It is also essential for the peace-keepers to operate under a clear and precise mandate. Peace-keeping operations have been severely inhibited by mandates that are not focused on the real needs of the situation, are out of date and are unsupported by financial and logistic back-up. In Rwanda, these shortcomings were particularly glaring, inhibiting UNAMIR in preventing the massacres and later in playing a post-conflict, peace-building role.

Of course, part of this lack of focus stems from the inevitable political compromise prevailing in the Security Council where states tend to view crises from differing political standpoints. When the crises broke in Rwanda on 6 April 1994, the Secretary-General recommended a doubling of the peace-keeping force. Instead, the Security Council voted to reduce the peace-keeping force to 10 per cent of its existing strength! Sometimes, the blurred focus is due to a lack of information and ground intelligence that tends to give a distorted image of a crisis. Another reason for unfocused mandates is the inflexible line drawn between peace-keeping operations, which are funded by assessed funds, and post-conflict revival, which is financed by the UN specialized agencies through voluntary funding. These distinctions lead to peace-keeping operations being conducted in compartmentalized strait-jackets, with each player charting its independent course of action as ordained from its respective headquarters.

In order to make an accurate assessment of the ground situation that would help in devising a clear and precise mandate, there is a need for the UN, and especially the Security Council, to have a more extensive and in-depth knowledge base. An information and intelligence data unit that would service the Security Council could, for instance, seek assessments from academia, journalists, the NGOs operating in the region, military experts and satellite information. The Rwanda crisis demonstrated that with the withdrawal of most diplomatic missions, the Security Council knowledge base was too

narrow and too reliant on media imagery to form an accurate assessment of the crisis. Nor were the UN political cadres operating on
the ground sufficiently trained and equipped to gather such information for headquarters to analyse objectively.

The regional context

At the time when UN peace-keepers were sent to Rwanda, international commitment to the United Nations playing a peace-keeping
role across the globe was already on its post-Somalia decline. Since
then, UN peace-keeping disengagement has been precipitated so
that, from a highwater mark in 1993 of 79,000 peace-keepers
participating in 19 UN peace-keeping operations, in 1999 UN peace-
keeping operations were reduced to 14,500 peace-keepers operating
in nine countries.

New concepts of peace-keeping incline towards regional organizations playing a more prominent role in association with the United
Nations. Recently, the OAU has performed peace-keeping operations
in Liberia, the Democratic Republic of Congo and Sierra Leone, as
have the OAS in Haiti, the CIS in Georgia and ASEAN in East Timor,
while NATO has taken on similar tasks in former Yugoslavia.

The emergence of regional organizations playing a prominent role
in peace-keeping needs to be analysed in the context of global
security. Clearly, regional organizations have an advantage in playing
such a role since they have a better feel for the issues involved in the
conflict and their leaders are usually personally acquainted with the
main players. Regional peace-keepers are also familiar with the
customs and traditions of the local population so that they are better
able to adjust to the local environment.

Moreover, intra-state violence is on the increase, as is apparent
from recent crises across the globe. These crises lead to the mass
movement of refugees and the breakdown of law and order, civil
society and state infrastructure, and lend themselves more easily to
regional peace-keeping influences, provided due authorization is
given by the Security Council. As of March 2000, 16 regional or sub-
regional organizations are co-operating with the UN in peace-keeping
initiatives, having responded to the call of the Secretary-General for
partnership and burden-sharing. About a third of these organizations are well equipped to engage in multi-functional peace-keeping
operations. NATO, for instance, is not only far advanced in playing a
peace-keeping role, but is resource-rich in terms of financial back-up
and equipment availability. Other regional organizations are in
varying degrees of preparation for playing a peace-keeping role, with
the OAU having recently arranged a meeting of the African Chiefs of
Staff in Harare. Regrettably, Asian regional organizations have fallen

way behind other continents in their sensitivity towards the needs of peace-keeping.

Of course, sometimes these very advantages act as negative factors, militating against a regional involvement in a particular peace-keeping operation. For instance, in Rwanda the battalion from francophone African countries like Senegal, Mali, Chad and Guinea was accepted with reluctance by the RPF government which insisted that, in UNAMIR's phase-out, they should be the first to leave. Similar reservations were expressed against the Zambian battalion, probably on ethnic grounds. Of the regional personalities, President Museveni was highly respected by the Rwandan government while there was a cold reserve towards other neighbouring leaders. OAU involvement in Rwanda therefore had its pitfalls and required a heavy injection of non-regional peace-keepers to maintain acceptability.

Sometimes, regional participation is unwelcome because of single-state domination in the peace-keeping effort. It is evident, therefore, that even when regional organizations are associated with the UN in a peace-keeping role, the consent of the parties concerned is essential. Furthermore, regional states and leaders usually have a political axe to grind which influences their intercession in one direction or the other. However, the co-operation of neighbouring states in assisting the peace-keeping effort is also an important consideration especially as airport, transit, logistic and communications facilities normally rely on this co-operation.

The main reason for the transference of peace-keeping to regional organizations is that donor states are no longer willing to commit their personnel to dangerous operations. This syndrome came to a head in Somalia with the killing of US peace-keepers. The savage murder of ten Belgian soldiers in Rwanda probably sealed the fate of any such commitment by donor countries to Third World countries. Coupled with this reluctance is the fact that the United Nations is heavily cash-strapped, limiting its capacity to engage in expensive peace-keeping operations.

It is evident that, given the parameters of a debt-ridden UN and donor states reluctant to commit their troops except in their own backyards, the future trend for peace-keeping is likely to be the greater involvement of regional groups. Accordingly, regional organizations need to prepare themselves to play an effective peace-keeping role through closer co-ordination, with the UN preparing member states towards playing a more effective peace-keeping role by training civilian and military personnel in peace-keeping and setting aside financing for such operations.

In anticipating this new trend the following elements need to given due importance in order that peace-keeping operations are made effective:

a) Troop-contributing nations need to be identified and peace-keeping training and preparedness imparted to them on a national or regional basis.

b) Adequate financing, assets and equipment should be ensured to these countries, with Third World TCNs being assisted with matching assets and equipment from those donor states that are disinclined to commit troops into dangerous Third World theatres.

c) An intelligence and information database should be available, especially in areas of potential conflict or violence, so that adequate contingency planning is achieved in anticipation of a crisis.

d) Leadership in the political, humanitarian and military fields needs to be prepared and trained for peace-keeping operations.

While a more assertive role in peace-keeping for regional groups is essential, care must be taken that the operation does not become part of a single country's attempt to dominate the crisis zone. Regional intervention must therefore be transparently neutral and free from the personal or state ambitions of the more powerful states.

Mechanisms for successful peace-keeping

The micro-management of a peace-keeping operation that involves the political, military, humanitarian and logistic dimensions needs to be streamlined under the following headings.

Clear-cut command and control structure

Co-ordination, command and control in peace-keeping need to be defined, as the various actors in the field tend to follow their independent charters. At the top of the pyramid, an overall political focus must be prescribed; this was transparently lacking between UN headquarters and the humanitarian and development agencies in Rwanda with the appalling result that the genociders in the refugee camps defiantly converted humanitarian aid into arms and military training.

Secondly, in a crisis situation the principle and most senior UN representative in the theatre of operations – the SRSG – must be given the primary responsibility for co-ordinating UN peace-keeping and humanitarian and development actions on the ground. He or she must be seen as the head of the entire UN family and not just of the peace-keeping force. All major negotiations, instructions and financial outlays need to be channelled through the SRSG. Command and control need also to be tightened up at the grassroots level so that the civilian administration, military peace-keepers, political analysts and humanitarian agencies dispense action as a co-ordinated whole and not through instructions sent directly to their representatives in the field, which in Rwanda ended in the fiasco of the equipment issue.

Experienced and neutral peace-keepers

Secondly, the choice of SRSG and indeed of all senior peace-keeping officials needs to be made with care so as to ensure transparent impartiality and neutrality. Each crisis therefore demands a case-by-case study relating to the assignment of UN representatives and peace-keeping contingents to the region. It is important, however, that the UN and regional organizations should have a list of competent and experienced peace-keepers, both civilian and military, from which to draw on at times of crisis.

Training, contingency planning and preparedness for peace-keeping operations

Military peace-keepers need to be trained and prepared for the multi-functional duties that they are increasingly expected to perform. As this training cannot, mainly for financial reasons, be imparted in a single, UN-operated centre, it falls on troop-contributing nations and regional organizations to train and prepare peace-keeping units. Urgency and sensitivity need to be shown by TCNs in raising units, both military and civilians, towards peace-keeping preparedness so that they are able to operate in a cohesive and professional manner with other units in the same theatre of operations. Preferably, every TCN should have trained units that can be quickly inducted into a peace-keeping operation with equipment, transport and financing that would sustain them for at least the first 90 days.

In Rwanda, it was evident that the Ghanaian contingent came highly trained in the task of peace-keeping. In fact, the Ghanaian armed forces specially train units for peace-keeping tasks. Other units operating in Rwanda – Australian, Indian, Ethiopian, Canadian, Nigerian and Zambian – were given peace-keeping induction courses before coming. Some units arrived without any such preparation and learned their specialized trade on the job.

Multi-functional peace-keeping is a highly specialized operation for which training needs to be given in a variety of skills, for instance gaining the goodwill and co-operation of the local population, the legal constraints of peace-keeping, the specific requirements of a mandate, ensuring a safe and secure ambience, reconciliation, sensitivity towards human rights, revival and reconstruction of institutions, buildings, etc, demilitarization, demobilization and the collection of small arms, assisting in law and order, de-mining, organizing elections, refugee rehabilitation, attending to medical, engineering and humanitarian needs, respect for property rights and sensitivity to local customs and traditions. Normally, national military units are not trained to deal with these challenges. It therefore requires a special effort at the national and regional level to train such a standby force that would effectively combine with other units to form an efficient, multi-functional peace-keeping force.

A peace-keeping force should also be equipped to address the gender issue as the female population of the affected country normally requires special consideration. In Rwanda this need was critical as the genocide survivors were mainly women. They had been raped, sexually violated and widowed, had fathers, sons and brothers killed and were often the only bread-winners. It was imperative that peace-keeping units should be capable of extending a helping hand towards the female population of Rwanda. Yet, except for the Ghanaian unit which had a significant number of women peace-keepers from majors down to the common soldier, none of the other peace-keepers in Rwanda had women components who could interact easily with the women population. For instance, the Indian Gurkhas and the Tunisians were highly efficient and motivated but, except for the occasional female nurse or doctor, were exclusively male. While training their peace-keeping units, troop-contributing countries need to bear in mind that the gender gap must be addressed.

At present, civilian contingents assigned to peace-keeping operations in the field, especially those in the junior echelons, are drawn on an ad hoc basis from disparate, non-cohesive and untrained backgrounds. In the UNAMIR team of political analysts we had a young American political science graduate, a Yugoslav human rights worker, a Sierra Leonean junior diplomat, a Cuban-American UN official and an Iranian emigré. The diversity of nationalities was welcome, but creating a cohesive unit to serve as the UN's field corps from people with different languages and professional and cultural backgrounds was difficult. Ideally, the UN needs to create a permanent corps of political analysts, rather like career diplomats, who would be permanently available to the UN and would have learnt their trade through a unified training process.

Public relations and UN radio

It is important for a peace-keeping force to address the public relational aspect of its mandate in a professional manner. In crisis situations, a peace-keeping role can easily be distorted by vested interests, leading to gratuitous problems and opprobrium for the peace-keepers. Transparency of effort and professional public relations should therefore become an integral part of a peace-keeping effort. An independent UN radio station is an ideal vehicle for such an effort, as would also be the assignation to the peace-keeping units of a trained team of media specialists. Certainly the impact of UN Radio in Rwanda, once it was fully operational, led to significant positive returns.

Conclusion

As we look ahead to the twenty-first century, the continuance of peace-keeping operations by the UN can be regarded as a virtual certainty. The precise shape or form of these operations, however, is not so clear and will be dependent on global power play, the availability of funds and the credibility of the UN itself. Refining and improving peace-keeping operations must therefore remain a concern for the international community. From the earliest days of UN peace-keeping in Korea and the Congo to the recent operations in Rwanda and Sierra Leone, the world has gathered a vast experience. This experience needs to be translated into the formulation of procedures and into a capability that will enable the peace-keeping operations of the future to be effective. Clearly this need has started to be recognized as countries large and small engage in preparing their troops for peace-keeping operations, seminars and conferences are organized across the globe to learn from peace-keeping experience and steps are actively taken internationally for troops, equipment, transportation, logistics and inter-agency cohesion to prepare the peace-keeping fire engine for emergencies. The UN experience in Rwanda has provided a rare catalyst towards achieving the objective of better peace-keeping across the globe.

Bibliography

Bührer, Michel, *Rwanda: Mémoire d'un genocide* (Paris: Editions UNESCO, 1996)

des Forges, Alison, *Leave None To Tell the Story: Genocide in Rwanda* (New York: Human Rights Watch, 1999)

Destexhe, Alain, *Rwanda: Essai sur le genocide* (Brussels: Complex, 1994)

Dorn, J. Walter, Jonathan Matloff and Jenifer Mathews, *Preventing the Bloodbath.* Paper at Peace Studies Programme, Cornell University, 14 January 1999

Feil, Scott R., *Preventing Genocide.* A report to the Carnegie Commission on Preventing Deadly Conflict (New York: Carnegie Commission, 1998)

Gourevitch, Philip, 'The Genocide Fax', *The New Yorker*, 11 May 1998

Joint Evaluation of Emergency Assistance for Rwanda, *The Rwanda Experience: International Response to Conflict and Genocide* (Copenhagen, 1994)

Omar, Rakiya and Alex de Waal, *Rwanda: Death, Despair and Defiance* (London: Africa Rights Publications, 1994)

Prunier, Gerard, *Crisis in Rwanda. History of a Genocide* (Kampala, Uganda: Fountain Press, 1994)

United Nations, *The United Nations and Rwanda 1993–96.* UN report and documents (New York: UN Press, 1996)

Index